R. E. Ad

BOOK
PRODUCTION
WAR ECONOMY
STANDARD

PRINTED IN GREAT BRITAIN AT
THE UNIVERSITY PRESS
ABERDEEN

THE
SECOND SPRING
1818-1852

*A STUDY OF THE CATHOLIC REVIVAL IN
ENGLAND*

By DENIS GWYNN

THE CATHOLIC BOOK CLUB
121 CHARING CROSS ROAD
LONDON, W.C. 2
1944

PREFACE

THERE is scarcely any parallel in modern religious history for the sudden revival and expansion of the Catholic Church in England during the few decades between the Catholic Emancipation Act of 1829 and the meeting of the first Synod of the restored hierarchy in 1852. The story is of such interest and is so little known that an account of it within one volume for the general public has seemed well worth attempting. The contrast between the conditions of a hundred years ago and the present times of upheaval needs no emphasis. But the curious resemblance in other directions will surprise many readers.

The phenomenal expansion of the Catholic community in Great Britain in the years which followed the Catholic Emancipation Act was due much less to the accession of converts under the influence of the Oxford Movement than to the immigration of great numbers of Catholics from various countries, and particularly from Ireland, who found employment in the rapidly growing industrial and shipping centres during the most active years of the industrial revolution. A considerable stream of immigrants was already apparent in the first decades of the nineteenth century. It assumed immense proportions during and after the potato famine in Ireland, which began in 1845 and lasted through the two following years. The marked increase in the number of Catholics in England had led to preparation for restoring the hierarchy before Newman's conversion in 1845 brought about the collapse of the Oxford Movement and swept a large number of converts into the Catholic Church. Still more, the growth of important industrial towns in the north and elsewhere had created entirely new problems which the Vicars-Apostolic were unable to solve without obtaining much wider authority for the creation of new missions and parishes.

The Second Spring

The Catholic immigrants had congregated in great numbers in these new crowded districts, where no previous facilities for Catholic worship or direction had existed ; and in all the subsequent period up to the outbreak of war in 1939, the Catholic community has been concentrated overwhelmingly in these overcrowded areas, while the Catholic revival had made relatively little progress elsewhere.

The dispersal of population which began with organised evacuation of children from the principal cities in the autumn of 1939—and developed further with the destruction caused by air raids, the creation of many new centres of war industry and the general scattering of the people on many forms of war service— has produced once again a situation resembling that which preceded the restoration of the hierarchy in 1850. It was significant that the names taken for the new sees then created should have been those of modern cities, such as Liverpool, Birmingham, Portsmouth, Plymouth, Northampton, Middlesbrough, Newcastle, or of districts within the orbit of other similar cities such as Manchester or Bristol, or London itself. In all these principal areas the Catholic settlers have since multiplied, and gradually developed well-organised religious communities, equipped with many churches and schools upon which vast sums have been spent during the past hundred years. But the war has left many of the churches and schools in ruins, while the formerly large congregations have in many places been widely scattered. To repair the ruin and dislocation caused by the war will require an immense effort of reconstruction, and it is at least doubtful whether some of the affected cities will ever assume their former proportions and regain their full industrial and commercial activity. New centres have sprung up, and many smaller centres have increased in size, and are likely to increase further in the post-war years.

In the meantime the dispersal of Catholics much more widely over the country has created new and unexpected problems and opportunities of providing churches, schools and clergy, that suggest an analogy with the conditions of a century ago. As a statement of the altered conditions created by the war, the first pastoral letter of Mgr. Parker, after his nomination as Bishop of Northampton in the autumn of 1941, may become as notable a document in the story of the Catholic revival as many of the statements or documents which will be found quoted in this book. The diocese has been for years the largest in England, embracing the seven counties of Norfolk, Suffolk, Cambridgeshire, Huntingdonshire, Bedfordshire, Northamptonshire and Buckinghamshire. Yet its Catholic population was only 15,000 out of nearly two million people at the outbreak of the last war ; and although it had more than doubled by 1939, it was still only 33,000, and the smallest in any English diocese. The number of churches had increased in the same period from 77 to 105, and the priests from 88 to 202. Even so, its Catholic life was chiefly centred in the larger towns, especially on the coast, and these towns were among the first to experience the effects of the evacuation scheme, and later the more general exodus during the months of air attack. But inland it became one of the principal centres for the settlement of refugees and evacuated children, while military establishments multiplied in all its counties.

Describing the effects of these upheavals in his Advent pastoral for 1941, Mgr. Parker notes that "in one county alone we find 17 extra Masses in different places, arranged for the military, but to which the public in most cases have access. This entails a strain upon our clergy. Their activity is amazing and admirable. God give them health as well as devotion ! Very many of them have now to offer Mass three times on a Sunday, and generally in places widely apart. One priest has told me that he has now to travel more than 90 miles each Sunday ; another one that he motors in the black-out to supply Mass at seven for Irish workers making a factory in the country, before he offers the Divine Sacrifice twice again in his own church. We have also Italian prisoners to be served, and large new rural emergency hospitals. To this picture of an unusual Catholic population through war work, or military occupation there is a reverse side ; it is of the desolated and deserted eastern areas. The once active and hard-working clergy have now few of their parishioners to see. And there is no livelihood . . . their congregations have evaporated. We cannot allow these priests to desert the remnants of their flocks ; besides, their areas cover hundreds of square miles."

Encouragement in confronting those tasks may certainly be derived from a study of the little-known story of the revival in the eighteen-thirties and forties and the following decades. The story has never yet been told in a compact narrative. Many biographies of the principal figures in the period have appeared over a long period, and the volumes concerning Newman and Manning alone would fill many shelves in a library. The late Bishop Ward, in his two large volumes on the *Sequel to Catholic Emancipation*, assembled a great deal of important material from his personal researches in various archives. His work supplemented that of his brother, Wilfrid Ward, as the biographer of their father, W. G. Ward, of Newman, and of Wiseman. But the book was intended primarily for ecclesiastics, and it was occupied largely with matters unlikely to interest readers who were not themselves clerics ; and it has been unobtainable for years. Since his last volume appeared in 1915, however, other important biographies have added fresh records of a very interesting period. Abbot Butler's two-volume *Life of Bishop Ullathorne* was in fact intended to carry on the story beyond the period covered by Mgr. Ward, and it threw a different light on many well-known controversies and events. Still more revealing have been the volumes published by Father Urban Young, C.P., as the biographer of Father Dominic Barberi, and of his disciple, the convert Father Ignatius Spencer.

In compiling the present survey the writer has been deeply

impressed by the extremely vital contribution to the Catholic Revival which was made both by the Italian missionary, Father Barberi, and by the small group of " Cambridge converts " who encouraged his desire to undertake apostolic work in England. They, too, were largely instrumental in directing the attention of Wiseman, when he was absorbed in his brilliant career as a young Oriental scholar and Rector of the English College in Rome, to the prospects of promoting a religious movement in England. The " Cambridge converts " had become Catholics independently some ten years or more before the Oxford Movement had begun to exercise any effective influence upon religious life in England. They were already actively engaged, with the co-operation of Lord Shrewsbury and of the young convert architect, Augustus Welby Pugin, in creating new missions and building churches in the Midlands. Their zeal and enthusiasm, and their astonishing success in unlikely places, made a very deep impression upon Wiseman, and hastened his decision that he must abandon his congenial life in Rome and come to England.

Wiseman's return to England in 1840 was the beginning of that awakening which transformed the character of English Catholic life. He became an important factor in influencing the Tractarian leaders towards their final secession from the Church of England. And it was he, with Ambrose Phillipps, who enabled Father Dominic Barberi to undertake his self-imposed task as a foreign missionary among the English people, in such a spirit of sanctity and sacrifice that Newman eventually decided to be received by him into the Catholic Church. On the relations between the " Oxford men " and the Catholics who surrounded Wiseman, the life and letters of Father Barberi throw a fresh and brilliant light. His letters from England to his superiors in Rome contained in Father Young's *Dominic Barberi in England*, are still more illuminating for their many glimpses of the swarms of destitute and famine-stricken Irish immigrants among whom he worked so devotedly.

His life's work was indeed one of the chief factors in the whole Catholic revival of those years ; and it is strange that both his work and that of Cardinal Wiseman should have been so widely forgotten. In this brief sketch of the whole revival an attempt has been made to trace the various threads in a complicated story, which embraces a very varied range of outstanding personalities.

February, 1942.

CONTENTS

FIRST AWAKENINGS

" It was on December 18, 1818," wrote Cardinal Wiseman forty years later, in his *Recollections of the Last Four Popes*,[1] " that the writer of this volume arrived in Rome with five other youths, sent to colonise the English College in that city, after it had been desolate and uninhabited during almost the period of a generation." That occasion would have been an outstanding date in the revival of the Catholic Church in England even if the small party of students, who were to bring the English College back to life after its evacuation during the Napoleonic wars, had not included the chief organiser of the Catholic revival and future head of the restored hierarchy in England. That " period of a generation " had witnessed a remarkable transformation of Catholic life in England. Revolutions and wars in Europe had broken up the famous English colleges on the Continent to which Catholic families had sent their sons to be educated during the centuries of religious persecution and suppression. The colleges had been re-opened in England, where refugees in large numbers, both English and foreigners, had found shelter after their homes and property had been confiscated in France and elsewhere.

The era of active persecution had ceased after the reign of Queen Anne, during which the most crushing and vindictive of the penal laws against the Catholic religion had been enacted. Although the penal code was never enforced in England as rigorously as it was enforced in Ireland, yet the laws against the Catholics were very much the same in both countries, and the code fully justified the famous description [2] by Edmund Burke, when he wrote to one of the Irish members of Parliament who were attempting to secure its partial repeal : " You abhorred it, as I did, for its

---

[1] Abridged edition, 1935, p. 3.
[2] *Works of Edmund Burke,* Oxford Classics, Vol. V, p. 210.

vicious perfection. For I must do it justice : it was a complete system, full of coherence and consistency ; well digested and well composed in all its parts. It was a machine of wise and elaborate contrivance ; and as well fitted for the oppression, impoverishment and degradation of a people, and of the debasement in them of human nature itself, as ever proceeded from the perverted ingenuity of man. . . . My opinion ever was (in which I heartily agree with those that admired the old code) that it was so constructed that if there was once a breach in any essential part of it, the ruin of the whole, or nearly of the whole, was, at some time or other, a certainty." In England, where the small Catholic remnant could no longer be regarded as a menace to constituted authority, the more rigorous provisions of the code were soon allowed to fall into abeyance. No serious attempt was ever made to enforce the penalties which were constantly applied in Ireland against those who even dared send their children to foreign countries, to receive there the education of which they were otherwise deprived by the absolute prohibition of Catholic schools in their own country.

The English Catholic families were thus able to continue the Catholic education of their children by sending them to the schools which had been established for them in France, and in the Low Countries ; whereas the Irish Catholics were compelled to emigrate to the Continent if they wished to enjoy even the elementary rights of freemen. The future Cardinal Wiseman's family were typical victims of such conditions among the Irish gentry. Debarred from the ownership of land or from the exercise of any profession, or even from most forms of trade, the Irish Catholic gentry could find no occupation except as merchants, usually in the provision or clothing trades. James Wiseman, the Cardinal's grandfather, had thus become a merchant in his native Waterford, and had, like many others, established business relations with continental countries. He left Ireland in the middle of the eighteenth century to settle as a merchant in Spain ; his son became a merchant in Seville, and there married the daughter of a Spanish General. On her death he married again, his second wife being Miss Xaviera Strange of Aylwardstown Castle, County

Kilkenny. Their son, Nicholas Wiseman, was born in Seville in 1802, and on his father's death soon afterwards his mother brought him back to Waterford before sending him to school at Ushaw in County Durham.

The penal code had completely broken down during the lifetime of his father, although Catholics were still deprived of the franchise and unable to sit in Parliament unless they were willing to take an oath which repudiated their Catholic faith. A number of Catholic Relief Acts had been passed, both in England and Ireland, which had removed the menace of active persecution for their religion, opened to them the professions, and restored most of the civil rights which had been previously taken from them. The reliefs had been granted chiefly because there was need of military service from all classes, first during the American war and later during the revolutionary wars in France. In England the first Relief Act of 1778 repealed the clause passed under William II for the prosecution of " bishops, priests and Jesuits ; " it enabled Catholics to keep schools without incurring imprisonment for life, and it permitted them to inherit or acquire real property. But even these modest concessions resulted in the Lord George Gordon riots of 1780, in which Catholic churches and private houses were sacked and set on fire, and almost the whole of London was for some days at the mercy of the rioters until the King intervened to restore order. The English Catholics, however, were too small a minority to be regarded with fear or jealousy, and they included a number of influential landowners who had for one reason or another been allowed to preserve their estates. Some of them, like Lord Petre and Mr. Weld of Lulworth, were on terms of personal friendship with George III, who even stayed at their houses. And although the second Catholic Relief Act of 1791 did not concede so much as was won after a formidable agitation by the Irish Catholics from the Protestant Parliament in Dublin in 1793, their position grew steadily stronger after the revolution in France. The Government was committed to befriending refugees from the French revolution, and many priests and religious communities came to England during the period of upheaval.

Among the refugees who came to England during those years were the teachers and pupils from the old English College at Douai. It had been founded by Cardinal Allen in 1579, and had for generations been one of the chief places of education for the sons of the English and Irish gentry until it was seized and confiscated by the French revolutionary forces in 1793. At St. Omers the Jesuits had also established another English College in 1592, which served a similar purpose, and when the Jesuits became involved in conflict with the *Parlement* of Paris in 1776 they contrived to move the school to Bruges. The Jesuits had also established another flourishing college at Liège, and the college at Bruges was absorbed into it, under secular control, when the Jesuits were expelled from Belgium after the suppression of their order within the Austrian dominions in 1776. In the summer of 1793, when the French revolutionary armies were advancing into the neighbourhood, the college at Liège was obviously threatened, and the Jesuits decided to seek refuge in England, where the former prohibition against Catholic schools had now been removed.

So the year 1793, which saw the reign of terror in France, was to bring back to England the long-established Catholic schools on the Continent. The Jesuits obtained generous assistance from one of their former pupils, Mr. Thomas Weld of Lulworth Castle, who presented them with the magnificent Tudor mansion of Stonyhurst in Lancashire. The other colleges, of Douai and St. Omers, had to search more widely for support when they also decided to re-open in England. A number of Catholic schools on a more modest scale had already been opened in England since the repeal of the penal laws, and Bishop Douglass, the Vicar-Apostolic of the London District, saw opportunities of developing the small school which had been founded some years earlier, near Ware, in Hertfordshire. Most of the students who had not been previously withdrawn from Douai and St. Omers had been in the meantime imprisoned by the revolutionary government in France. But they were liberated early in 1795, and by that time arrangements had been made for their reception at two colleges in England. Some went to St. Edmund's College, near Ware, and others to St. Cuthbert's College which was opened for them at Ushaw in county Durham, with the assistance of a number of leading Catholic families.

Both colleges, St. Edmund's and Ushaw, were opened in 1795, and the number of their students grew rapidly. The continued wars in Europe gradually put an end to all thought of ever reconstituting the old colleges abroad, and in 1798 the continental tradition was further interrupted by the French invasion of Italy and the occupation of Rome. The English College in Rome could trace its origins back to a Saxon king, who established it as a guest-house for pilgrims, before it was converted into a college for seminarists by Gregory XIII in 1578. During the French occupation of the city in 1798 it was sacked and its inmates were dispersed. It was to remain unoccupied except by an aged caretaker for twenty years. But peace had returned at last after Napoleon's downfall ; and among the foreign statesmen who came to England for the meeting of the Allied Powers was Cardinal Consalvi, who had been the chief representative of the Vatican during the conflict between Napoleon and Pius VII when the Pope was kept a prisoner in France. Even a Roman Cardinal was by this time welcomed with real sympathy in England, and on his return to Rome he undertook the necessary preparations for a reopening of the English College after its long abeyance. Arrangements were made in due course with the Vicars-Apostolic in England for sending a picked number of their students to complete their ecclesiastical training in Rome. Twenty students in all were to form the nucleus of its resuscitation, and of these six were to come from St. Cuthbert's College at Ushaw, which shared with St. Edmund's at Old Hall the tradition of the old college of Douai.[1] Among the six students was young Nicholas Wiseman, who had been sent to Ushaw from Ireland at the age of eight in 1810. He was now sixteen, and had decided that his vocation lay in the priesthood. As a shy and studious boy he had made few friends at school, but among the professors at the College he had made one friend particularly, in Dr. Lingard the historian, who was Vice-President

[1] For the history of both colleges see *The Catholic Schools of England*, by Mgr. A. S. Barnes.

at Ushaw, and by far the most distinguished scholar among the English Catholics of his age. The first volume of his *History of England* appeared in the year that young Wiseman left for Rome.

The old era had gone with Waterloo, and in the north of England particularly the industrial revolution was transforming the whole appearance of the country, besides introducing immense social changes. But even in the autumn of 1818, when Wiseman and his young colleagues set out for Rome, it was still, as he wrote in his recollections,[1] " long before a single steamer had appeared in the Mediterranean, or even plied between the French and English coasts. The land journey across France, over the Alps, and down Italy, was then a formidable undertaking." They travelled by sea from Liverpool to Leghorn, and the journey took almost three months. There were numerous adventures even at sea, for the ship caught fire besides being obliged to run for shelter and to disembark its passengers during a sudden storm. Even the land journey across Italy was not without danger, and the boys were to see the bodies of executed highwaymen suspended from poles along the road when they went beyond Florence. And the English College itself, when they arrived there at the end of December, was not only empty but partly ruined since the wreckage of twenty years before. The roof of the chapel was still lacking, but the building still stood, " nave and aisles, separated by pillars connected with arches, all in their places, with the lofty walls above them. The altars had been, indeed, removed ; but we could trace their forms ; and the painted walls marked the frames of the altar pieces. . . . Around lay scattered memorials of the past. Shattered and defaced lay the richly effigied tombs of an Archbishop of York, and a Prior of Worcester, and of many other English worthies, while under wreckages of the recent storm was piled on one side—the skulls and bones of perhaps Cardinal Allen, F. Persons, and others whose coffins had been dragged up from the vaults and converted into munitions of war."

It was no longer a question of English Catholics seeking refuge in continental countries, where they could find the freedom denied

[1] *Recollections*, p. 3.

6

to them at home. Rather it was the awakening Church in England sending its slender reinforcement to assist in religious revival on the Continent, and in Rome itself. The reopening of the English College was regarded as being an event of sufficient importance for the Pope to receive in person the students who had newly arrived. Pius VII still reigned, an old and infirm Pope, unable to take part in the great ceremonies which normally added so much colour to the life of Rome. But the memory of his imprisonment by Napoleon, and of his stubborn resistance to military or political coercion, gave the glamour of martyrdom to his old age, and inspired a sense of high courage and apostolic zeal in the new generation who had to restore the wreckage of recent years. The city itself had shrunk seriously during the interval of foreign occupation. Its population had fallen from over 150,000 at the opening of the century, to less than 120,000. " Many of the best families had left it,[1] some indeed to occupy posts of trust in other portions of the Empire, others to escape the responsibilities and honours of a government towards which they felt no attraction. Money had become scarce ; the abundant sources of public and private charity had been dried up ; assignats had first been freely circulated, and then suddenly made valueless ; and many honest families had been driven to want. The sweeping away of the Court, with its many dependencies, the breaking up of the households of perhaps fifty cardinals, and of many prelates and ambassadors, had thrown thousands out of direct employment, and tens of thousands of workmen, artists and artisans, to whom such establishments gave occupation. At the same time were necessarily closed the various offices for the administration of ecclesiastical affairs, local and general, which give bread to more laymen than clerks." Looting and private dispersal of the great collections of art had also deprived the Eternal City of much of its former glory ; and even after the Pope's return to Rome amid scenes of extraordinary rejoicing, his infirmity had reduced the splendour of the usual celebrations in St. Peter's, where the high altar could be used only by the Pope himself.

[1] *Recollections,* p. 31.

But to Wiseman and his young contemporaries the atmosphere as well as the external magnificence of Rome were infinitely impressive and devotional. They had left England too young to be personally conscious of the restrictions of social tradition among the small Catholic minority ; and England grew increasingly remote during the six years while he completed his studies for the priesthood, until he obtained his doctorate of divinity with exceptional distinction. He was ordained a priest some months afterwards, early in 1825. He had attracted attention among many learned men, particularly by his study of Oriental languages, and he won the approval of Mgr. Mai, the prefect of the Vatican Library, to such an extent that he was allowed to work with him in the Library at times when no one else was admitted there. The chair of Oriental Languages in the university fell vacant soon after his ordination, and Mgr. Mai urged him to apply for it, although he was only twenty-three. The rule recently made, which required that all professorships should be open to competition, was being suspended in this case, as few qualified candidates were likely to present themselves. But Mgr. Mai urged Wiseman to appeal personally to the Pope against that decision, and he showed his courage by persisting in the attempt after it became known that the chair had already been filled. Pope Leo XII had been elected in succession to Pius VII two years before, and he allowed Wiseman's appeal, but told him that he must first submit published work for approval before he would be considered as a candidate. So his first book, *Horae Syriacae*, was put together and published, and it met with such cordial approval among experts in several countries that he was appointed to the professorship.

In the same year, 1825, he was appointed Vice-Rector of the English College, which was now firmly re-established under the presidency of Dr. Gradwell. Before long he was ordered personally by the Pope to inaugurate and undertake a series of public sermons each week for the benefit of the large number of English visitors and residents in Rome. Relations between England and the Holy See had been receiving much more attention since the College was restored, and Leo XII was already preparing to nominate an

English Cardinal for the first time since the Reformation. But Bishop Baines, the Vicar-Apostolic of the Western District, succeeded in avoiding the dignity, which would have resulted in his having to live permanently in Rome. Not until after the Catholic Emancipation Act had been passed in 1829 was the first English Cardinal actually appointed, and the choice then made was significant. Cardinal Weld was by training singularly unsuited for such a position. He was an elderly widower who became a priest late in life, but he was the brother of Thomas Weld, the benefactor of the Jesuits, who had presented them with their college at Stonyhurst, and who had years before entertained George III in his home at Lulworth Castle. A still stronger reason for his choice was the fact that Cardinal Weld's eldest brother had been the first husband of Mrs. Fitzherbert, whose secret marriage with George IV had been recognised in Rome as being valid.

By 1828 Wiseman had already become rector of the English College in Rome, when the rectorship was left vacant by the appointment of Dr. Gradwell as Vicar-Apostolic of the Northern District in England. Dr. Gradwell had been in Rome almost without interruption for eleven years, and he returned to conditions where Catholic life was still overshadowed by the traditions of persecution and social seclusion. The agitation for equality of political rights had been dormant for years. Even in Ireland the popular agitation led by Daniel O'Connell had fallen into complete abeyance after the failure of the Catholic Emancipation Bill in 1820, which O'Connell had rejected because it required that the Government should exercise a veto over the appointment of Catholic bishops. But it had come to life again suddenly in Ireland in 1826, when O'Connell had made one more attempt in founding the Catholic Association with an unlimited democratic membership. He embarked upon a whirlwind campaign throughout Ireland, and the agitation gained momentum with astonishing speed. In 1828, when a by-election arose in County Clare, he took the bold step of standing as a Catholic candidate for the parliamentary vacancy, with the declared intention of refusing to take his seat at Westminster until the oath against the Catholic religion was repealed. His election as member for Clare created a crisis so acute that the Duke of Wellington and Sir Robert Peel decided that continued refusal would lead to civil war in Ireland. They capitulated in February, 1829, and informed the King that if he persisted in refusal he must find other Ministers. So the Catholic Emancipation Bill became law, and the Catholic peers were able to take their seats as hereditary legislators, while in the General Election of the following year a small number of Catholic gentlemen in England were elected for territorial constituencies where they had wide local influence.

But although Catholic Emancipation removed practically all the legal disabilities under which the Catholics in both countries had suffered for generations, the English Catholics had played a very small part in the final victory. Their outlook and their social habits were very little affected by the new freedom for years afterwards. Centuries of seclusion, intermarriage and diffidence in the open practice of their religion had left them with no desire to assert themselves as Catholics more openly than in the past. But no different attitude could have been expected, when one recalls the severity of the restrictions that had compelled them to live in a condition of private obscurity. Their condition could not be better conveyed than in the reflections on his own life which were written [1] in his old age by one of the most important Catholic landowners of his day, Mr. Thomas Corby :

" We were all obliged before 1778 to seek for education abroad, and consequently seldom saw home or parents for six or eight years. The army being my choice, I did not see either for more than three days during ten years. I was sent to the Teresian Academy at Vienna ; but neither my father, his relatives, nor the kind endeavours of that excellent gentleman, Sir Robert Murray Keith, our ambassador, under whose eye I had been for four years, could obtain leave for me to serve in our army : I even in 1779 offered to serve as a volunteer in America, but did not receive any encouragement. . . . In 1723 the late Duke of Norfolk tried to obtain for me admission

[1] See *Catholic Magazine,* April, 1842.

into the German part of the military establishment of His Royal Highness the Duke of York. At last I had to give up my favourite object : thus the best part of my life had passed away in unavailing attempts ; and when later I endeavoured, through the kind offices of Sir George Howard, to procure a commission for a very fine young man, my brother, I found it still inadmissible. In the hope of more favourable times, he entered into the Sardinian service ; but there, in a small village in Piedmont, was carried off by a fever, without having a single Englishman near him. . . . A seat in Parliament in my neighbourhood was offered to me in a very flattering manner, with other advantages, which the law forced me reluctantly to decline. Like other Catholic gentlemen, when the laws respecting us began to be relaxed in their execution, I served in the militia, went to Ireland, and afterwards, by the friendship of many distinguished men in this country, who placed themselves under my command, I formed a volunteer corps (the Cumberland Rangers) and we served till peace broke us up. Such *par force* has been my inefficient life."

Such was a fair example of the life led by the English Catholic gentry even when they possessed important social position and influence. A picture of them, as they appeared to the world outside their circumscribed social circle, is to be found in the recollections of Cardinal Newman as he recalled them in one of his most famous sermons.[1] " You have seen it on one side, and some of us on another," said Newman in 1852, after the restoration of the hierarchy under Cardinal Wiseman ; " but one and all of us can bear witness to the fact of the utter contempt into which Catholicism had fallen by the time that we were born. You, alas, know it far better than I can know it ; but it may not be out of place if by one or two tokens, as by the strokes of a pencil, I bear witness to you from without, of what you can witness so much more truly from within. No longer the Catholic Church in the country nay, no longer, I may say, a Catholic community ;—but a few adherents of the Old Religion, moving silently and sorrowfully

[1] *The Second Spring.*

about, as memorials of what had been. 'The Roman Catholics' —not a sect, not even an interest, as men conceived it,—not a body, however small, representative of the Great Communion abroad,— but a mere handful of individuals, who might be counted, like the pebbles and detritus of the great deluge, and who, forsooth, merely happened to retain a creed which in its day, indeed, was the profession of a Church. Here a set of poor Irishmen, coming and going at harvest time, or a colony of them lodged in a miserable quarter of the vast metropolis. There, perhaps, an elderly person, seen walking in the streets, grave and solitary, and strange, though noble in bearing, and said to be of good family, and a 'Roman Catholic.' An old-fashioned house of gloomy appearance, closed in with high walls, with an iron gate, and yews, and the report attaching to it that 'Roman Catholics' lived there ; but who they were, or what they did, or what was meant by calling them Roman Catholics, no one could tell :—though it had an unpleasant sound, and told of form and superstition. And then, perhaps, as we went to and fro, looking with a boy's curious eyes through the great city, we might come to-day upon some Moravian chapel, or Quakers' meeting house, and to-morrow on a chapel of the 'Roman Catholics' : but nothing was to be gathered from it, except that there were lights burning there, and some boys in white, swinging censers ; and what it all meant could only be learned from books, from Protestant Histories and Sermons ; and they did not report well of 'Roman Catholics,' but, on the contrary, deposed that they had once had power and had abused it.

"And then, again, we might, on one occasion hear it pointedly put out by some literary man, as the result of his careful investigation, and as a recondite point of information, which few knew, that there was this difference between the Roman Catholics of England and the Roman Catholics of Ireland, that the latter had bishops, and the former were governed by four officials, called Vicars-Apostolic. Such was about the sort of knowledge possessed of Christianity by the heathen of old time, who persecuted its adherents from the face of the earth, and then called them a *gens lucifuga*, a people who shunned the light of day. Such were

Catholics in England, found in corners, and alleys, and cellars, and the housetops, or in the recesses of the country ; cut off from the populous world around them, and dimly seen, as if through a mist or in twilight, as ghosts flitting to and fro, by the high Protestants, the lords of the earth. At length so feeble did they become, so utterly contemptible, that contempt gave birth to pity ; and the more generous of their tyrants actually began to wish to bestow on them some favour, under the notion that their opinions were simply too absurd ever to spread again, and that they themselves, were they but raised in civil importance, would soon unlearn and be ashamed of them. And thus, out of more kindness to us, they began to vilify our doctrine to the Protestant world, that so our very idiocy or our secret unbelief might be our plea for mercy."

Little more than twenty years had elapsed since the passing of the Catholic Emancipation Act when Newman spoke those words as a Catholic priest, having been chosen as special preacher for the first synod of the restored hierarchy. Yet nothing could have been further from his thoughts at the time of the Catholic Emancipation Act than that he would ever become a member of the despised Catholic communion. He had become a tutor at Oriel College in 1826, being then twenty-five years of age, and he soon exercised a remarkable personal influence in the University. In 1828 he preached his first University sermon, and was appointed vicar of St. Mary's in Oxford. Keble's *Christian Year* had appeared in 1827, and Newman regarded Keble thenceforward as his master. But while his thoughts were thus directed towards the spiritual traditions of the past, he had as yet no sort of feeling that the revival of earlier traditions in the Church of England implied any approach whatever towards the Church of Rome. To Newman and his friends the Catholic Church still appeared rather as a political corporation which was allied to many forces which they deeply detested. The agitation for Catholic Emancipation had stirred up these deep-seated prejudices, and the Emancipation Bill was regarded by them rather as a manœuvre in party politics than as the concession of equal civil rights to the Catholic minority in

England. The matter became of direct concern to them when Sir Robert Peel felt it his duty to face his constituents in Oxford and seek re-election after he had concurred in Wellington's decision that resistance to Catholic Emancipation could no longer be maintained. He showed courage, if also a guilty conscience, in thus offering gratuitously to his constituents an opportunity to express their disapproval for his change of front. But the constituency was in no mood to admire his virtues. A determined opposition was quickly mobilised, with the result that he was ignominiously and decisively defeated. Among those who took an active part in securing his defeat was the young tutor at Oriel. " We have achieved a glorious victory," Newman wrote [1] to his mother in March, when the chief sponsor of the Catholic Emancipation Bill had been defeated ; " it is the first public event I have been concerned in, and I thank God from my heart both for my cause and its success. We have proved the independence of the Church and of Oxford. . . . We had the influence of government in unrelenting activity against us, and the talent so-called of the University."

[1] *Life of Newman*, I, p. 44.

CHAPTER II

THE CAMBRIDGE CONVERTS

EARLY on most Sunday mornings during the year 1827, two young gentlemen could be met riding together along the twenty-five miles of road from Cambridge on their way to St. Edmund's College at Old Hall, Ware. They rode not only in all weathers but fasting, so that they could receive Holy Communion as well as hearing Mass at what was then the nearest Catholic chapel to Cambridge. One was some ten years older than the other, and had graduated in 1819, but still resided as a private student in rooms belonging to Trinity College. The other was an undergraduate of seventeen whose delicate health was to prevent him from completing his course at the University. He was a precocious but greatly gifted young man, whose early enthusiasm for religious matters had led him to become a Catholic before he was yet sixteen, overcoming the most determined efforts of his family to divert him from a decision which caused them acute distress. Both converts, they were the only two Catholics in Cambridge, but their ardour in their new faith, and their unceasing industry in later years, were to have an extensive influence upon the whole religious life of England.

Kenelm Digby, the elder of the pair, was of Irish Protestant stock, and descended from a strongly clerical family. Both his great-grandfather and his great-great grandfather had been bishops in the Church of Ireland. His grandfather, John Digby of Landestown, had been M.P. for County Kildare ; his father became Dean of Clonfert and rector of Geashill in King's County. The Dean married three times and had children by each wife, and Kenelm Digby was the younger son of the third marriage. Owing to neglect of the parish registers, the date of his birth is uncertain, but he was probably born[1] in his father's parish at Geashill in 1797.

[1] *Memoir of Kenelm Digby*, by Bernard Holland, p. 6.

He was sent to school in England at Petersham, near Richmond, where he became an accomplished oarsman. At Cambridge he rowed for Trinity College in the year of Waterloo, and he was instrumental, with some of his friends, in introducing an improved type of boat. In one of his poetical reminiscences he could modestly claim long afterwards to have been the "founder of boating on the Cam." He appears to have never visited Ireland again, except for his mother's funeral, but he cherished romantic memories of Geashill Castle and of the lovely country around the Slieve Bloom mountains ; and it was in Ireland he had learned to ride with an enthusiasm that lasted through his long life. Much of his time at Cambridge was spent on the river, and he took an undistinguished degree in 1829. But he was a diligent student on the matters that interested him, and in the year after he took his degree he won the Norrisian prize with an essay on "Evidences of the Christian Religion."

His main interest, however, was in books of chivalry and medieval history, to which he had been attracted from boyhood by reading Sir Walter Scott. As an undergraduate he once solemnly kept vigil until dawn in King's College Chapel at nightfall. A young friend, George Darby, had shared these romantic tastes, and Digby's biographer records some of their early adventures.[1] They "held a solemn tournament at Marlyke in Sussex, with ponies for steeds and hop poles for spears. In imitation of the bold Doleraine they rode one night to Hurstmonceaux Castle and touched its walls with their lances. One day, when Kenelm was riding by himself, he had a knightly adventure. A pretty damsel of seventeen came down a side lane and said that she had been molested by a felon. Would he let her walk by his horse, and protect her, into Hastings ? In a vacation ramble in the Tyrol he swam by moonlight, in hope of adventure, across a lake to a huge old castle called Sigismundsberg, standing on an island, but found nought but ruins, and heard nothing but owls. On an earlier journey he first saw the Castle of Ehrenbreitstein, opposite Coblenz, on the Rhine, and conceived the title of his book, the

[1] *Kenelm Digby,* p. 10.

Broadstone of Honour." He was a born romantic, and looked the part, as his contemporary Edward Fitzgerald records—" a grand, swarthy fellow, who might have stept out of the canvas of some knightly portrait in his father's house—perhaps the living image of one sleeping under some cross-legg'd effigies in the church."

He had dedicated his Norrisian essay to " the Rev. Christopher Wordsworth, Master of Trinity," the rather formidable brother of the poet. Of the younger tutors during his student days the best remembered was Julius Hare. Among his immediate contemporaries were the historian Macaulay and the poet Mackworth Praed ; and he was still at Cambridge, and a conspicuous figure there, when more celebrated contemporaries came up—Edward Fitzgerald, Frederick Maurice, Richard Chevenix Trench (afterwards Archbishop of Dublin), Alfred Tennyson and Arthur Hallam. His private means left him free from any necessity to earn his living, and he spent his youth largely in travel both in England and on the Continent, walking or riding prodigious distances, and swimming in rapid rivers or wide lakes. He loved scenery and magnificent buildings, and he travelled much on the Continent in pursuit of them, making sketches as he went and keeping careful diaries. His travels had begun during his long vacations at Cambridge, and it was then that his romantic temper was inevitably attracted to Catholic churches. At Ostend, when he was about nineteen, he first entered a Catholic church, and recorded his impressions in his journal. " On entering this Church we had our first view of Popish superstition. There were persons at their devotions and a dead silence reigned around. The effect was imposing. The women, wearing black hoods, were kneeling before the altars. The men opened their arms and grasped their hands with fervour. One knelt by himself in a corner praying very earnestly to some thin wax candles on which his eyes were riveted."

At Ghent he was similarly struck by the " attention and propriety of the people present. Indeed I do not believe that there is a man in existence who would not be struck with reverence on entering these solemn places, where, if we except the service and operations of the priests, there is everything in character with the

17

awful purpose to which the place is dedicated. Undoubtedly the attention of the people is sometimes observed when an Englishman of the most sober disposition can hardly refrain from laughter. For instance, when the priests, like so many conjurors, are going through their incomprehensible operations before the altar. What can be more ridiculous than to see these grave persons turning themselves about like so many idiots ?" That paradox disturbed him, but his sense of belonging to a superior race comforted him for the time. " The simple honest Englishman," he wrote in his journal, " is told, and he believes, that the religion of his country is infinitely more pure and sublime, and yet he knows that the behaviour of the people in the English churches is as strongly characteristic of levity and inattention as that of these persons is of reverence and decorum. A little philosophy will remove this mystery by teaching him that there is a natural tendency in the human mind to love error rather than truth."

He had a gift for writing, and after he had graduated he set to work on a study of the traditions of chivalry which he called the *Broadstone of Honour*. It was published while he remained on at Cambridge, and it gained him some celebrity among the younger men. His personal friendship with Julius Hare, the chief teacher of religious philosophy at Trinity, led him to read widely the Fathers of the Church and histories of the Reformation—which left him with a disillusioned feeling that its leaders had been actuated by material motives—and various modern writers on the Continent who shared his own instinct towards religious revival. It was Julius Hare, though he still persisted always in referring to Luther as " that god-like man," who put Kenelm Digby in touch with the books of French Catholic writers such as de Bonald and de Maistre, and particularly the German Catholics Schlegel and Görres.

In his foreign travels he felt increasingly drawn towards the old Catholic churches, finding in them an atmosphere of living faith which he could not find at home, and by the autumn of 1825 he had decided to seek direct instruction from a Catholic priest.[1]

[1] *Kenelm Digby,* p. 42.

An old friend, M. Chevalier, recommended him to a learned ecclesiastic at the Sorbonne. But when he told the French priest that he wished to become a Catholic the suggestion was met with "blank dismay." He was already approaching thirty, but the French priest thought him too young to entertain such wild ideas. His family had not been consulted, and they might disapprove. Anyhow, the Sorbonne professor had no desire to become involved in such matters, and pointing to piles of proofs on his table, he advised him to go home and consult his family. If he should still desire to change his religion he could surely find in England someone better suited to deal with such cases. Here certainly he had found no desire to proselytise, and Digby met with a scarcely less discouraging reception when he renewed his attempt in England. Having heard of a priest who lived in Castle Street in London, he travelled up from Cambridge to find him. But once again he was handed on to another priest, living in the slums of Westminster. Several attempts to find him were unsuccessful, and Digby then turned to a Catholic layman, the veteran lawyer, Charles Butler, whom he had known years before when he was a small boy at Petersham. Butler had been an ardent controversialist all his life, besides taking a leading part in the agitation to repeal the anti-Catholic laws, and he was prepared to give real help. He recommended his young friend to a Jesuit, Father Scott, who undertook his instruction at last, and in due time received him into the Catholic Church.

As a convert he returned in 1826 to Cambridge, to continue his private reading in the library of Trinity. The college authorities allowed him to live in Bishop's Hostel, south of the Great Court. His book and his romantic reputation had made him many friends, and he was regarded as an amiable eccentric who was unhappy away from the University. Yet his change of faith had made him appear a dangerous influence, and not everyone was willing to forgive it. The Oxford Movement had not yet ruffled the placid waters of conventional orthodoxy, and his former professors regarded him with no active suspicion. One of the dons, Adam Sedgwick, even went out of his way one day to summon Digby to his rooms to convey a wholly unexpected tribute of sympathy. " You know that some people blame me—I need not say who they are," he told him, " because I like to greet anyone I meet without any regard to their creed. Well, I have been all this long vacation in Syria and Carinthia, where I have seen Catholic populations, and I swear I don't care what our Dons say, believe me that never did I see a people I liked better or whom I would rather remember as the best of mankind. Of course I know very well what you are now, and I thought you would like to hear me tell you this, as it was sure to please you. So come again, and soon."

Kenelm Digby's acceptance of the Catholic faith had caused some sensation during 1826, but he was joined at Trinity in the same year by another young gentleman whose change of religion had been much less easy to explain. Mr. Ambrose Phillipps was little more than seventeen when he arrived at Trinity College in the autumn of 1826, but it was nearly two years since he had caused consternation to his family in Leicestershire, by insisting upon being received into the Catholic Church. His father was an important landowner and Deputy-Lieutenant for the county, the owner of two famous mansions, Garendon Park and Grace Dieu Manor. Like Kenelm Digby, Ambrose Phillipps also had a background of clerical relationships. Two of his uncles, William and Edward March Phillipps, were clergymen, and zealous members respectively of the High and Low Church parties, and his aunt was married to the Bishop of Gloucester. He had received his first schooling from the Rev. Mr. Wilkinson at South Croxton, and at the age of eleven had been sent to a private school called Maizemore Court, near Gloucester. On the staff of the school was an elderly French priest, the Abbé Giraud, a refugee from the revolutionary days, who had settled in England, and gained his livelihood by teaching French. The boy's religious instruction was entrusted to his Low Church uncle, who had taught him a proper abhorrence of Roman superstitions and practices, but the personal piety and distinction of the old French abbé won his sympathies, and he insisted on being informed on religious questions which had perplexed him. He began reading religious literature when he was still little more than a child, and he had an absorbing interest in religious ritual. On a holiday in Paris with his parents he frequented Catholic churches with his sister's governess, and his father took him to see some of the impressive ceremonies at Notre Dame cathedral. Like Kenelm Digby, he had been moved to laughter by his first sight of Catholic ceremonial. His father's diary records [1] that "Ambrose laughed at the walking up and down of twelve priests in copes during the 'Magnificat,' for which his father chided him, saying that all R.C. ceremonies had deep religious meaning."

His father evidently made a habit of frequenting religious ceremonies during his continental tours, with the result that when they returned to Garendon young Ambrose "persuaded the Rev. W. Allsop, the Vicar of Shepshed, to adopt a cope, showing him it was ordered in some canons of the Church of England." [2] Moreover, "the ardent boy had an altar made for the Shepshed church like those he had seen in France, and as soon as the altar was erected, he carried round the church and amidst a very large concourse of people a black wooden cross, his brother Charles, who afterwards became the vicar, serving as his acolyte. This cross was placed by the old vicar with much ceremony, which budding Ritualists of a later date might have envied, on the holy table, where it remained for some time. It was the first cross planted on a communion table in the Established Church since the Reformation." But the cross was not allowed to remain in position for long. Protests against the restoration of "Popish symbols and idolatrous emblems" were urgently made to the Bishop of Peterborough, and he at once insisted upon its removal.

Ambrose's father had little idea of how far these early enthusiasms were to affect the future of his son. The boy was not only a born ritualist but a mystic. It was during the same year, as he recalled long afterwards in conversation with his biographer, that "As I was rambling along the foot of the hills in the neighbourhood of the school and meditating, as was my wont in those

[1] *Life of Ambrose Phillipps de Lisle,* by E. S. Purcell, I, p. 6.
[2] *Ibid.*

boyish days, over the strange Protestant theory that the Pope of Rome is the anti-Christ of Prophecy, all of a sudden I saw a bright light in the heavens and I heard a voice which said ' Mahomet is the Anti-Christ, for he denieth the Father and the Son.' On my return home in the next holidays I looked for a Koran, and there I found these remarkable words, ' God neither begetteth nor is begotten '." Years afterwards Ambrose Phillipps was to devote much industry and fervour to writing a work entitled *Mahometanism, in its Relation to Prophecy*, which contained the results of his protracted study on the same subject. But other religious doubts occupied his boyhood. He sought comfort in turning from the anti-Popish doctrines of his uncle Edward to the conviction of his uncle William that the Church of England was a living branch of the Catholic Church. In the following year his mother's brother, the Bishop of Gloucester, was translated to the see of Lichfield, and among his first acts was to promote the director of Ambrose's school to the archdeaconry of Stafford. The new archdeacon then transferred his school from Maizemore Court to Edgbaston, where Ambrose accordingly followed him.

Birmingham was to be the focus of many of Ambrose's plans and dreams in the subsequent years, when Wiseman lived at Oscott and Pugin was completing the Catholic cathedral of St. Chad. But in Birmingham at this time the Catholic Church was still confined to a few poor chapels. Nevertheless young Ambrose paid visits to them in his quest for ritual. He called one day at St. Peter's chapel and asked permission to see the religious vestments used in it. The priest, Mr. Macdonnell, showed him the few shabby vestments that the chapel possessed, and must have been surprised by so unusual a request. His surprise must have been greater when he received a letter from the boy, who had received another mystical communication during his dreams. He had in fact dreamed [1] that " our Lord seemed to reproach him with not having fully complied with the light he had received," and this impressed him so deeply that he wrote at once to Mr. Macdonnell asking him to meet him at a certain cottage belonging to an old

[1] *Life of Ambrose Phillipps*, I, p. 11.

Irish woman in Loughborough in order to "receive him into the communion of the Roman Catholic Church." Mr. Macdonnell was a man of exceptionally independent character, and spent much of his life in conflict with his religious superiors. But he was entirely devoted to the extension of the Catholic Church in England. On this remarkable occasion he appears to have had much less hesitation than had been encountered by Kenelm Digby in his similar requests when he was of much more mature age. He agreed to meet the schoolboy, but explained that he must first discover how far he was acquainted with Catholic doctrine. "To his great surprise," according to Mrs. Ambrose Phillipps, in recounting afterwards what she had been told by her husband, "the priest found the youth perfectly instructed on every point : so after recommending certain devotions as a preparation, he appointed an early day to baptise him conditionally and to receive him into the Church."

The old Abbé Giraud, his former French master, was by this time on his death-bed, but Ambrose wrote to inform him of what happened on the day in June that he decided to become a Catholic. The abbé burst into tears, and exclaimed *Nunc dimittis*. Very different were the feelings of his schoolmaster, Archdeacon Hodson, to whom Ambrose courageously reported his intentions without delay. He would have to account not only to Ambrose's father, but to the Bishop, for the disaster that had befallen his nephew while committed to the Archdeacon's care. He was in fact furious, and demanded that the boy should be immediately removed from the school. In an indignant letter to Mr. March Phillipps, he said that Ambrose "was already beginning to pervert some of his companions," although "in everything else he was perfectly satisfied with his moral conduct as well as with his application to his studies."

His schooldays were thus brought to an abrupt close, and his subsequent preparation for the University was conducted by private tutors. His father came to fetch him home from Edgbaston and to receive the mixed condolences and indignation of his schoolmaster. There was still hope of changing his mind. A few weeks later

2

when he found that Ambrose had in his room, " a gold-looking cross tied to a ribbon," for which the boy said that he had paid half a crown, Mr. Phillipps broke the cross to pieces, though he felt " very sorry afterwards " for what he had done. Meanwhile he engaged a clergyman as his mathematical tutor ; but late in October the tutor " informed him of the total apostasy of Ambrose from the Protestant to the Roman Catholic Faith." It was not, however, until December 21 that he was formally received into the Church by Mr. Macdonnell. His reception took place " in a poor Irish pavior's cottage outside Loughborough. The nearest Catholic chapel at that time was at Leicester, fifteen miles off, and he could not have absented himself for so long without incurring the displeasure of his tutor."

Whatever might be the attractions of Catholic ritual during his foreign travels, Ambrose Phillipps can have had no illusions concerning the prospect of finding it practised in noble churches in England. On the contrary he was now cut off from the services which had appealed to him so strongly in the beautiful pre-Reformation churches and cathedrals of the Established religion. He would be deprived of them even when he went up to the University. His father had first wished him to go to Oxford, and had applied to Oriel for his admission there, but found that there was no vacancy. Newman's name was still unknown outside Oxford, though he was already fellow of Oriel, and neither Ambrose nor his father can have known how much he would miss by going to Cambridge instead. He obtained an admission to Trinity College in the autumn of 1826. There he came in contact with Kenelm Digby, who had graduated five years earlier but was still resident in the precincts, as a young author who spent his days mostly in the college library, but continued his favourite relaxations of boating and riding. They became fast friends, and after his first Christmas vacation Ambrose wrote to Bishop Poynter at his modest residence in Holborn to inform him, as Vicar-Apostolic of the London District, that he and Kenelm Digby desired to attend Mass at St. Edmund's College at Ware on Sundays if that were feasible.

Digby had made himself known to the bishop some time before, and had just sent him a copy of the second edition of his *Broadstone of Honour*, which like all his many works was published at his own expense. The bishop replied at once with a most cordial letter, saying that " Mr. Griffiths," the president of St. Edmund's, " will be most happy to see you and Mr. Digby whenever you may go over. You will see duties well performed there on Sundays. When I go down I will let you know if it be for a Sunday." In a later letter he added, concerning Kenelm Digby, " you cannot cultivate a more valuable correspondence than that which you hold with him." Bishop Poynter at Castle Street, Holborn, lived in a style very different to that which Ambrose had known as a boy when he went to stay with his uncle as the Anglican bishop first of Gloucester and later of Lichfield. The London District was naturally a chief centre of Catholic ecclesiastical life, and Ambrose appears to have addressed him in their early correspondence with titles which he thought fitting to his responsibilities. But the bishop discouraged such compliments with gentle firmness : " When you write," he replied, " pray do not give me such high titles. I am not an Archbishop but I am sincerely your Friend and humble servant in I.C., William Poynter."

With Bishop Poynter's introduction the two young men accordingly presented themselves at St. Edmund's College, and soon made a practice of riding there each Sunday morning from Cambridge to attend Mass and receive Holy Communion. Although Digby with his powerful physique and athletic training was none the worse for the long ride of twenty-five miles each way, Ambrose Phillipps was attempting far more than his constitution could stand. Their weekly pilgrimages continued through 1827 until the following April, when Ambrose undertook the ride while he was suffering from a severe cold. He arrived ill at the College and ruptured a blood-vessel in his lungs. The doctor insisted that he must leave Cambridge at once and spend the following winter in a warmer climate. So his University career was cut short during his second year, and he spent the following two winters with his father in Italy. There he was to make the acquaintance of the young rector of the English College and of other ecclesiastics, to whom he communicated his ardent and astonishing belief in the imminence of a religious revival in England, which he believed would reach such dimensions that within a measurable time the communions of Rome and Canterbury would be united in a restoration of Catholic unity.

CHAPTER III

GEORGE SPENCER AND DOMINIC BARBERI

It was after his return from Italy in 1829 that Ambrose Phillipps first made the acquaintance of a young Anglican clergyman in the neighbourhood of Northampton who, like himself and Kenelm Digby, had been at Trinity, Cambridge. The Rev. George Spencer was the youngest of seven children of the second Earl Spencer, of Althorp, who had been First Lord of the Admiralty during the Napoleonic wars. The eldest son had been in the House of Commons for some years as Lord Althorp, and was to become Chancellor of the Exchequer in 1830 in Lord Grey's Reform Ministry. His youngest brother, George, was born in 1799, and spent some years as a boy at Eton. He had entered Trinity College, Cambridge, a year or so junior to Kenelm Digby. His parents had already destined him for the usual career of younger sons in taking Holy Orders, and at the age of twenty he obtained his Cambridge degree, having by a perfunctory attendance of the divinity classes easily gained the certificate which admitted him to ordination whenever he so felt inclined. " My mother has lately been planning a house," he wrote in a diary [1] in January, 1819, " for the parsonage at Brington, which they say is to be mine when I am old enough ! It might be made most comfortable and even a pretty place : and if I like to come to it, I can figure myself some happy years there, with a fond partner of my joys, if I can meet with a good one. Here then—and ' with thee, my Eleanor,' would have been my language two years ago. But how my opinion, even of such important things, changes with increasing years. This thought often occurs to me and will, I hope, prevent me ever making engagements which cannot be broken, in case my fancy should be altered during the time which must elapse before the completion of them."

[1] *Life of Father Ignatius Spencer,* by Urban Young, C.P., p. 12.

Like Digby and Ambrose Phillipps, George Spencer had spent long holidays abroad, and the inevitable contact with Catholic churches as a visitor had provoked him to the same feelings of ridicule and bewilderment. At Milan he met the great Cardinal Mai (who had not yet made the acquaintance of young Nicholas Wiseman at the English College in Rome), and was brought to see the ceremonies in the cathedral in October, 1819. " There was a processional round the buildings, with incense burning," he wrote in his diary,[1] " and with the priests singing anthems all the time and a quantity of their mummery, the sight of which might well have driven Calvin to the extremities he went in the contrary way. The whole service is always in Latin, so that the people may not reap even the smallest benefit from them." He spent the whole of 1820 travelling on the Continent, from Rome to Sicily and homewards through Austria and Germany. In retrospect long afterwards he wrote that his chief concern had been to " go on in the stream of the English society with which almost all the towns in Italy are filled." He came home for the usual family gathering at Althorp at Christmas, and the following year was spent mostly at home or in London, while he passed the time pleasantly until he should be old enough to enter the ministry. Towards the end of the year the Bishop of Peterborough suggested that he should be ordained before Christmas, and the opening of the year 1823 saw him installed as curate in charge of the parish of Great Brington, comprising a group of villages close to his father's place at Althorp. As curate he was in sole charge, for the rector had been obliged by his debts to reside on the Continent. George Spencer spent a good deal of his time in visiting poor families in his district, and found that many of his parishioners had become Methodists, so that he was soon inveighing vehemently against Dissent. At first he adopted the High Church attitude in attempting to convert them from schism, but he was soon reprimanded by a certain Dr. Elmsley, who came as a visitor to Althorp, who told him that " these would be very convenient doctrines if we could make use of them, but they are available only for Roman Catholics :

[1] *Life of Spencer*, p. 14.

they will not serve us." [1] He fell back disillusioned upon other lines of argument. In the mood of puritanical reaction which followed he cultivated a greater austerity of life, giving up theatre-going and shooting, but without any real conviction in his theological views.

In June, 1824, Spencer received " priest's orders " from the Bishop of Peterborough, and soon afterwards Lord Spencer persuaded the rector of Great Brington to resign his living and retire on a pension from his patron, who also paid off his debts. Spencer thus succeeded to the living, and began to take his duties very seriously. His brother-in-law, Lord Lyttleton, who had married his eldest sister, was already impressed so much by his increasing piety that he wrote to his wife at the end of that year : " He seems to have very vague ideas of the Scriptural meaning of the world, which we are enjoined not to form ourselves to, and I am convinced that he would be a monk if he could once persuade himself that it was lawful. I am not sure that he won't be the founder of some new Order. His look, too, in society is strangely dreamy and abstracted. He is, however, in general, a very happy creature, for there is almost always a smile on that musing face of his, and he told me that when he was alone at Althorp and had a clear day before him to lounge and look about the house, he was most happy. . . . But since he can't be a monk what is the solitude and musing to end in ? "

His religious opinions were still entirely vague, but he was absorbed in his ministry. His personal generosity to the poor in his neighbourhood was carried to extremes which his family found disconcerting. A lady who knew him from childhood writes [2] of him during these early years that " his great charity to the poor and wandering beggars was unbounded. At times he gave them all the money he had, and stripped himself of his clothes to give them to the distressed ; and when he had nothing to give, he would thank God he had only his holy truth to impart, and would speak of the love of God so fervently, that he would call forth tears from the poor objects of misery who came miles to beg

[1] *Life of Spencer*, p. 3.   [2] *Ibid.*, p. 29.

money or clothes of him. Many impostors presented themselves with the rest, but even these he thanked God for, and thought nothing of relieving them, as he said he lost nothing by them, but got a lesson of humility. Some poor afflicted mendicants would present themselves with loathsome sores, and these he would assist in dressing and trying to cure. His house was always open for the distressed, and he often longed to make a hospital of it for the poor. He was all for gaining souls to God ; he would often walk to Northampton to visit the lodging houses, and most infamous dens of the dissolute, to speak to them of God's holy law and mercy to sinners. He did not often allow himself the privilege of riding, but would walk to Northampton or further, carrying his clothes in a knapsack strapped over his shoulders, and would smile at the jeers and laughs against him, glorying in following out the practice of the apostle. He fasted as well as he knew how, much stricter than when he became a Catholic, and allowed himself nothing but plain living."

In the yard of the military barracks, on one of these pilgrimages to Northampton, he made his first acquaintance with a Catholic priest. Father Foley had been ordained some eight years before, and had stayed on the staff at Oscott until 1825, when he was sent to Northampton to open a small Catholic chapel there. He had found stray Catholics here and there in the town, and he had come to the military barracks in search of others, when he encountered Spencer who had come on a similar mission. As Lord Althorp's brother, Spencer could enter with much more confidence into such places, and he at once generously assisted the young priest by introducing him to the commanding officer. Soon afterwards they met again in the streets of Northampton, and Father Foley thanked him for the introduction, saying that Providence had sent him at the right moment. But it was not this shy young priest who was to bring Spencer into contact with Catholic society. Old Lady Throckmorton heard of his visits, invited him to dine at her house, and brought a learned ecclesiastic, Dr. Fletcher, to meet him. Their first theological discussions were continued, at Spencer's invitation, in the vicarage at Great Brington, and through these chance acquaintances in Northampton Spencer was told of a young landowner in Leicestershire named Ambrose Phillipps, who had not yet come of age, but had been received into the Catholic Church some years before going to Cambridge. Towards the end of 1829 Father Foley arranged that the young convert and George Spencer should meet at his house in Northampton ; and there their first acquaintance resulted in a discussion which lasted for some five hours.

Spencer was naturally attracted by the enthusiasm of Ambrose Phillipps. He scarcely expected that so young a man would be able to sustain a serious discussion, but he found that Phillipps had complete answers for all the questions that he put. Phillipps invited him to his father's house at Garendon, and made preparations for a much more ambitious exchange of views. He wrote to Spencer before long, announcing that his uncle, the Bishop of Lichfield, would be staying with them at the end of January, and hoping that Spencer would be their guest for a week. " I hope so the more," he wrote, " as I think your conversation might induce him (the bishop) as well as my father, to think more seriously on that awful subject on which we conversed when I had the great happiness of being introduced to you at Northampton. I assure you, a day has not passed without my offering up my unworthy prayers to Almighty God in your behalf ; and I cannot refrain from again saying, that I hope one day we shall be united in the same faith of the One Holy and Apostolic Church of Jesus Christ." Ambrose's father may well have regarded the prospect in a different light, with hopes that the united efforts of the bishop and of this earnest young clergyman might yet make him retrace his steps before he came of age. Spencer's reply was both edifying and encouraging to such hopes. He explained that in ordinary circumstances he would not leave home at such a time, as his mother and father would be still at Althorp. But he had told them that the invitation was most unusual and important, and he looked forward to coming to Garendon. He hoped very much that he would have the chance to renew his acquaintance with the Bishop of Lichfield, and he would write to him beforehand. " I hope nothing will prevent his coming," Spencer wrote.[1] "And if we are allowed to have freedom of conversation with him on these things, which I pray to God may be given us, I must particularly interest you to hear and consider what he says with meekness and humility, though you may have the clearest conviction that he is in error. Surely his age and rank, and the work to which he has sincerely devoted himself, and his relation to you, make this a double duty ; and by acting so you will not be hurt, for though you may be perplexed for awhile, God will not suffer you to lose one point of what is really good, but will finally establish you the more firmly for acting in this humble spirit."

Unsupported by any Catholic friend in this formidable conference, Ambrose Phillipps faced the bombardment which he had brought upon his own head, and spent many hours every day during the whole week in close discussion with Spencer. He held his ground so firmly that Spencer found [2] that "the advantage always appeared on his side in the arguments which took place between them, notwithstanding their superior age and experience ; and I saw how weak was the cause in behalf of which I had hitherto been engaged ; I felt ashamed of arguing any longer against what I began to see clearly could not be fairly disproved. I now openly declared myself completely shaken, and, though I determined to take no decided step until I was satisfied, I had little doubt now of what the result would be." He had arranged to be back in his church on Sunday morning. But on Friday Phillipps went part of the way with him as far as Leicester, so that they could call on the priest in charge of the Catholic mission there. Father Caestryck was a Belgian Dominican who had escaped to England when his community was dispersed during the revolution, and after some twenty years' residence and work in England he had managed to build the small church in Leicester.

The meeting with the Belgian Dominican was more decisive than any of them had imagined it might be. Spencer listened and argued, and was completely subjugated. Phillipps accompanied

[1] *Life of Ambrose Phillipps,* I, p. 46.
[2] *Life of Spencer,* p. 39.

him to his inn, from which he was to return to his parish early in the morning. "I am overcome," Spencer said without any further reserve between them. "There is no doubt of the truth. One more Sunday I will preach to my congregation and then put myself into Mr. Foley's hands, and conclude this business." Yet even before they parted he felt that this last appearance as an Anglican clergyman would compromise his conscience. Had he any right, he asked himself, to "stand in that pulpit, being once convinced that the Church is heretical to which it belongs?" After further reflection he told Phillipps of his final decision:[1] "If this step is right for me to take next week, it is my duty to take it now. My resolution is made; to-morrow I will be received into the Church." They sent a message that evening to Lord Spencer to tell him that he would give up the living of Great Brington. Spencer had felt deeply, but had overcome, the fear that the shock of such news might even endanger his father's life. "The words of our Lord rose before me," he wrote afterwards, "and answered all my doubts. 'He that hateth not father and mother, and brothers and sisters and houses and lands, and his own life too, cannot be my disciple.' To the Lord then I trusted for the support and comfort of my dear father under the trial which in obedience to His call I was about to inflict upon him. I had no further anxiety to disturb me. God alone knows the peace and joy with which I laid me down that night to rest." Next day they sought out Father Foley at Northampton, and on Sunday morning he received George Spencer into the Catholic Church.

George Spencer's austerities and his prodigal charity had prepared his family for some unusual decision, but the news of his becoming a Catholic was a sore and unexpected blow. His father had provided handsomely for him by making him vicar of Great Brington; but there could be no question of his retaining the income like his predecessor and appointing a curate. He consulted the Dominicans at Hinckley a few days after his conversion, as to whether he could continue to receive any part of the income which was his sole means of support. When they told

[1] *Life of Spencer*, p. 41.

him that no compromise was possible, Spencer wrote a formal letter at once to the bishop resigning his cure. He closed the envelope with a cheerful comment. " There goes £3000 a year." He was prepared to face complete destitution, but his father showed his forgiveness by making him a personal allowance. Nevertheless, his decision had cast a gloom over the whole family at Althorp. " My dear poor brother ! What shall I say of him," wrote [1] his sister, Lady Lyttleton, to a friend a few weeks later. " I mean George, who is become a Catholic—we fear, a Catholic priest. His motives have been pure, and such has been his state of uncertainty and doubt, and unfixedness upon all but practical piety in religious matters for years, that we have no reason to be surprised at this last fatal change. But it is so deep an affliction to my dear Father and Mother, so great a breaking up of our family, so painful a loss at Althorp, where his presence and ministry, though but imperfect pleasures were yet invaluable pleasures to us, that it weighs us all down. He took this step so suddenly, and with very insufficient forethought and knowledge. Altogether a bad business."

Convert parsons were a problem with which Bishop Walsh was during the following years to become very familiar, but George Spencer's sudden accession to his flock found him unprepared. Spencer himself wished to become a Catholic priest without delay, and to start work for the conversion of England, beginning in his former parish. For the moment he avoided Brington, and sent money to his housekeeper to pay all outstanding bills. He sent a letter at the same time, asking her to inform them that " I have acknowledged the Authority of the True Church and therefore resigned my ministry for the present. If they care for my advice, tell them to send for Mr. Foley, the priest at Northampton, and hear him as the minister of God." Bishop Walsh, who had his official residence at Wolverhampton, was in the meantime informed of his conversion, and replied most kindly, but urged that the convert should take time before deciding his next step. On reflection, he advised that Spencer should

[1] *Life of Spencer,* p. 45.

proceed to the English College in Rome to receive his theological training there. Lord Spencer agreed cordially, being anxious that his son should go abroad until the excitement had died down, and he arranged to give him a generous allowance. The decision that he should go to Rome was confirmed by an interview with Bishop Bramston in London, whom Spencer went to see in the hope of finding some alternative employment at home. Early in March, 1830, he arrived in Rome, and there found Kenelm Digby, whom he had not seen since they were undergraduates together at Cambridge. They had both passed their thirtieth year, while Ambrose Phillipps had only just come of age.

Spencer's arrival among the College students aroused intense interest in the mind of Dr. Wiseman, who had succeeded Dr. Gradwell as rector two years before, but was considerably younger than his new disciple. It was impossible to include Spencer in the usual classes with his juniors, and he was accordingly set to study privately under the direction of Dr. Wiseman and Dr. Errington. News of his arrival spread quickly among the English colony in Rome. One of the first to seek his acquaintance was Miss Trelawney, who was living there with her old father, the Cornish baronet, Sir Harry Trelawney. He had followed his daughter in becoming a Catholic some twenty years previously, and had now, at the age of seventy, by special permission been accepted for the Catholic priesthood. Cardinal Odescalchi was supervising the preparations for the old gentleman's ordination, and in view of his age special attention had to be given to instructing him in the detailed ceremonial of celebrating Mass. The Cardinal applied to the General of the Passionists in Rome to supply a priest for this purpose, and his choice fell upon the strangest figure among the unlikely group who had thus become connected with the English College.

Father Dominic Barberi, the Passionist priest to whom this task was allotted, was at this time in his early thirties. He had been admitted to the priesthood at a comparatively late age because he came of a humble peasant family, and had received very little education in his childhood. His persistent endeavours to enter the Passionist Order had at first succeeded only so far as to secure admission as a lay brother, to work in the kitchen and in the fields. But when his intense faith and his humility had impressed everyone, he was allowed to study for the priesthood. As a young lay brother he had visions and mystical communications which convinced him that his life was to be spent in apostolic missions far from Italy, and especially in England, although there appeared to be no likelihood of his learning any language but his own. Since 1824 he had been in Rome, teaching theology to the students at Vetralla. His uncontrollable attraction towards England had never diminished, and although he knew practically nothing of the country, and could not either speak or read English, he made a practice of making his students recite prayers for the conversion of England at the end of all his classes. His colleagues suggested to him, perhaps in irony, that he should apply direct to the Pope for leave to go to England, but he replied : [1] " I am the son of obedience, and obedience must order me. God will see to the manner of it."

No fulfilment of his desire had occurred in all these years until he was unexpectedly deputed to instruct the aged Sir Harry Trelawney in the ceremonies of saying Mass. It was a preposterous choice, for not only was Father Dominic unable to speak either English or French, but Trelawney could not speak Italian. An interpreter was required, and Trelawney's daughter supplied the need by introducing George Spencer, who thus became the first Englishman with whom the Passionist had any intimate conversation. Spencer soon introduced Phillipps to him as well, and the two young converts seemed to personify all that Dominic Barberi had dreamed of for years. Every day [2] they took walks together in the garden of SS. John and Paul overlooking the Coliseum, and Father Dominic was soon teaching the lay brother who admitted visitors to the gardens a series of catechism questions in broken English, which were crudely intended to enlighten them on the difference between Catholic and Protestant faiths. Spencer introduced him to an Anglican clergyman called Ford, who was travel-

[1] *Life of Dominic Barberi,* by Urban Young, C.P., p. 35.
[2] *Ibid.,* p. 46.

ling in Italy, and Barberi immediately attempted to convert him and persisted in his efforts, though without making any serious impression, for years afterwards. Barberi had become a prolific writer, and among his other works he composed a *Lamentation of England* based upon the prophet Jeremiah, which Phillipps translated into English and got published at Leicester after he went home at the end of the year. The enthusiasm of Spencer and Phillipps gave him a most exaggerated conception of the state of religious feeling in England, while his persevering efforts to make an impression upon Mr. Ford gave him a better notion of the difficulties to be encountered among the Anglican clergy.

Phillipps went back to England in the autumn of 1830, but kept up a correspondence with Dominic Barberi which inspired him greatly. Writing in November,[1] he thanked him for sending his "very beautiful prayer for England," and pointed out that whereas "only fifty years ago, to offer to God the most Holy Sacrifice in England was judged a crime deserving the severest chastisement of the law," yet when religion was persecuted in France the British Parliament "with the consent of its august and clement king" had repealed this infamous law and the priests of France had fled to England. "I owe my conversion to a French priest," he wrote, "and how many others can say the same! At this moment the Catholic Faith is daily increasing in England, and I have reason to believe that within fifty or eighty years this my dear but unhappy native land will be entirely Catholic."

In the summer of 1831, Father Dominic's contact with Spencer in Rome was abruptly terminated by his appointment as head of the new Passionist foundation at Lucca. But he continued to receive letters from both Spencer and Phillipps, and Sir Harry Trelawney had come to see him at Lucca after his ordination. "How much I have at heart the return of that island to the Catholic Faith," he wrote. "If with my death I could procure such a grace, how willingly would I die. Well, I hope against hope." Meanwhile he confessed that his occupation left him no time even to continue his efforts to learn English. But Phillipps kept up his

[1] *Life of Barberi,* p. 52.

spirits by reporting definite signs of a religious revival in England, as well as making predictions which grew always more sanguine. In October, 1831, he wrote [1] that " This year we have made great progress. Seven or eight new missions have been founded, from which we have received great good. All these missions have been established in the district of our Bishop, i.e. in the Midland District of England. There have been many conversions of Protestants. In the town of Leicester, the capital of our county, more than a hundred persons have embraced the faith this year. Last Sunday the Bishop administered Confirmation to them."

Father Dominic replied in January with his usual fervour. " I shall never die content until I see England again returned to that Mother from whom she was torn three centuries ago." Spencer had just been ordained, and on the day he wrote, was to " begin in Rome his apostolic ministry, and preaches his first sermon to the Roman people in the Church of the English." Spencer had received the priesthood on May 26, and was ordered by Bishop Walsh to return at once to England. On his journey home he was able to visit Father Dominic in person. After he had gone, Father Dominic wrote to the irresponsive Mr. Ford : " He is leaving for England, whither he will bear with him the half of my heart, if not indeed the whole ; since if the heart is more where it loves than where it lives, I may venture to say that, loving England as tenderly as I do, my heart is more there than in Italy or Lucca."

Outside that little circle of devoted friends there was indeed not much sign to encourage the hopes that they had fostered. Phillipps reported [1] during the summer that Spencer had arrived safely, and that " he is with his father, Lord Spencer, for the first time since his happy conversion to the faith." They had derived more encouragement from Dominic Barberi than from any other source, and Phillipps now wrote [2] solemnly that " the day will come, I have no doubt, wherein you, my dear Father, will come here to England, to found the order of Passionists, and I hope to assist you in this holy enterprise, if my sins do not render me unworthy." Spencer wrote [3] also, saying that his father had

[1] *Life of Barberi,* p. 65. [2] *Ibid.,* p. 80. [3] *Ibid.,* p. 83.

received him " with the greatest affection," and that his brother Lord Althorp, his former bishop in the Church of England, and all his other relations and friends, were " disposed to treat him in the same way." " None of them as yet has shown any disposition towards the Catholic religion ; but all are contented that I should continue to exercise my ministry with diligence as long as I do not interfere with them." Meanwhile Dominic Barberi continued his passionate but quite unavailing attempts to convert Mr. Ford. In April, 1833, he found a chance at last to promote his larger desires by formally appealing to his Order that they should open a house in England. He had been appointed a Consultor, and as such was able to raise the matter directly at the General Chapter when it met. The suggestion was rejected, but it had at least been put upon record in the official proceedings. Soon afterwards he was made Provincial, in charge of a large section of the Passionists in Italy, and his dream seemed more remote than ever.

CHAPTER IV

DR. WISEMAN IN ROME

BOTH Spencer and Sir Harry Trelawney had returned to England as Catholic priests, to undertake whatever duties might be found for them by Vicars-Apostolic who were rather embarrassed by the accession of such unusual recruits to the small number of clergy in England. Ambrose Phillipps had gone home to Leicestershire and Dominic Barberi had left Rome to become provincial of the Passionists in northern Italy. They had shared great dreams together while they were all in Rome, and the English College had been a focus for their meetings while George Spencer was studying there. But they had left little impression at the College, apart from a pleasant memory. Dr. Wiseman had been too much absorbed in other activities to take much notice of these enthusiastic but rather eccentric visitors. He was in the early stages of a career of swift distinction and achievement in many fields, which occupied all his time and attention. He had become Rector of the College when he was only twenty-five. When he gained his doctorate of divinity at the age of twenty-two, he had acquitted himself with exceptional distinction at a public disputation, which was attended by many of the most learned men in Rome, curious to see whether the revived English College was living up to expectations. Among them had been the Benedictine theologian Capellari, who was before long to become Pope as Gregory XVI, and the Abbé Felicité de Lamennais, whose brilliant gifts and capacity for leadership had won him a great following among the new generation in France, and whose reputation at Rome was so high that he was already expected to become a cardinal. Before such an audience Wiseman had proved himself before he was yet ordained, and his reputation grew rapidly. He had become absorbed in the immensely varied and highly coloured life of Rome, with its gorgeous churches and their brilliant ceremonies, the teeming activity of its cosmopolitan life, its endlessly new social contacts, and its unrivalled scope for the pursuit of scholarship. He was so versatile and so full of eager enthusiasm that he enjoyed every aspect of it.

Since his appointment to the chair of Oriental Languages in 1825, his ambition had been to follow in Mgr. Mai's footsteps as an oriental scholar. But the Pope, soon after appointing him as Vice-Rector of the English College, had become aware that there was no church in Rome where English visitors could hear a sermon in their own language. He had summoned Dr. Gradwell, as Rector of the College, to instruct him to make the necessary arrangements, and Wiseman's name was mentioned again as a suitable preacher. He had never previously preached anywhere, and was now most reluctantly compelled to undertake a course of public sermons in Rome as part of his duties. The Pope not only ordered that the sermons should be preached, but chose where they were to be delivered, provided the expenses of special decoration of the church and of advertising the sermons, and sent part of his choir to assist their success. Wiseman undertook the task with diffidence, but acquitted himself most successfully. He had discovered himself to be a preacher with unusual powers of attracting audiences. Soon afterwards Dr. Gradwell was appointed one of the Vicars-Apostolic in England, and Wiseman had to act as rector during the brief interval, before the Pope sent for him again and told him that he was to be Rector of the College.

A new phase in his career opened early in 1829, when he had been rector for only a few months. Leo XII died, and Rome became more active and exciting than ever during the election and coronation of a new Pope. Wiseman had witnessed the similar ceremonies and excitements as a student when Pius VII had died and Cardinal Della Genga had become Pope Leo XII. This time Cardinal Castiglioni was elected, and chose the name Pius VIII. As Rector of the College, Wiseman had occupied a privileged position at all the ceremonies, and had been closely involved in all the excitement behind the scenes. In that capacity also it fell to him to bring a deputation to the new Pope, soon after his election, to announce the good news that the Catholic Emancipation Act had at last been passed by Parliament and received the royal assent. It was so long since he had seen England that even the Catholic Emancipation Act seemed a remote matter, scarcely affecting the busy life of the English College in the cosmopolitan atmosphere of Rome. Wiseman had been little more than a schoolboy when he left Ushaw, and he had known very little of English life outside its walls. " We had left our country when young," he wrote afterwards, in his reminiscences,[1] " and hardly conscious of the wrongs that galled our elders ; we should return to it in possession of our rights ; and thus have hardly experienced more sense of injury than they who have been born since that happy era." George Spencer, whose father had voted for Catholic Emancipation during those bitter years, was more directly affected by the news while he was still an Anglican clergyman at Brington. In retrospect Wiseman felt afterwards that he had gained rather than lost by being so far removed from the strife that raged at home. " No ' winged words ' of anger or scorn, however powerfully fledged for flight, could well surmount the Alps ; and if they did, the venom must have dropped from their tip, as this must have lost its pungency, in so long a course. Scarcely any amount of roaring on platforms could have sent even a softened whisper across the sea ; and the continuous attacks of a hostile Press could only reach in the broken fragments that occasionally tessellated a foreign paper. Thus, one hardly knew of the bitter things said against what was dearest to us."

In that serene atmosphere of scholarship, of diplomacy, and college administration in Rome he had become so fully immersed that he was scarcely conscious of events at home. His prestige and importance had grown rapidly, and as Rector of the English College he acted as agent for all the English bishops, and also for the Primate of the American hierarchy, the Archbishop of Baltimore. And by the year 1830, when George Spencer arrived unexpectedly as a student who could not easily be fitted into the ordinary routine of the College, Wiseman had become more than ever absorbed in

[1] *Recollections*, p. 143.

42

the ecclesiastical life of Rome. Pius VIII died after a pontificate of barely nine months, and he was succeeded by one of Wiseman's closest friends in the Sacred College, Cardinal Capellari, who took the name of Gregory XVI. The new Pope had taken a close interest in Wiseman's studies as well as his work at the English College. He had urged him to expand one of his recent essays, and have it translated into Italian for publication. He had promised to correct the proofs himself, and when the young rector went to present his respects formally to the new Pope after his election, Gregory XVI greeted him with the usual warmth, and told him that he would now have to correct his proofs himself, because the Pope would have no time to spare. The young rector had become one of the most notable personalities in Rome, and his reputation and the range of his friendship were extended by his unusual gifts as a linguist. He was reputed to speak seven languages fluently, and when that encylopædic linguist Cardinal Mezzofanti arrived to take up residence in Rome about this time, Wiseman gained further celebrity by being able to greet and address him in Persian or Arabic when they met at public gatherings.

George Spencer had been astonished to find so distinguished and so versatile a scholar among the younger English Catholic clergy. But he soon came to feel that Wiseman's great talents might be more directly employed in working for the conversion of England. With his natural honesty and courage he told Wiseman frankly [1] " that he should apply his mind to something more practical than Syrian MSS. or treatises on geology, and that he would rather see him take up what suited a priest on the English mission as it then was." The rebuke even took some effect. Wiseman sent two of his recent sermons to England to be published there, expressing the hope that they might further the " great cause," and that he might thus do " some little good from this inactive retreat—inactive at least as far as it concerns the public cause." He wrote to Dr. Husenbeth to tell him of his conversations with an English visitor, which had resulted in his becoming a Catholic. And when the *Catholic Magazine* was founded in

[1] *Life of Cardinal Wiseman,* by Wilfrid Ward, I, p. 101.

London that year, Wiseman promised to contribute to it, and that
he would apply his studies more directly to the furtherance of the
Catholic revival. But his other interests and activities distracted
him from such concerns. He was still the young Roman prelate,
increasingly conscious of his great gifts, and enjoying their exercise
and the prestige which they brought to him. Even Newman was
to be so much impressed by his versatility in later years that he
wrote of him,[1] " he can speak with readiness and point in half a
dozen languages, without being detected for a foreigner in any
of them, and at ten minutes' notice can address a congregation
from a French pulpit or the select audience of an Italian academy."
His biographer, Wilfrid Ward, writes [2] of him at this period that
" his reading had given him a real acquaintance with the literatures
of France, Germany and Italy. He was, as we have seen, a musical
critic as well as an art critic, and a practical musician into the
bargain. He possessed minute knowledge on points of ceremonial
and liturgy ; he was a collector of old china, and knew something
of the history of stained glass. If to older men such variety of
acquirement carried the inevitable suggestion of superficiality, to
those who followed his researches as a specialist, in these early
years of his career, his laborious work in one department prevented
this suggestion from being a reproach."

Neither Spencer nor Ambrose Phillipps, and still less Father
Dominic Barberi, could be regarded at that time as anything more
than enthusiastic dreamers, who knew very little of actual conditions or prospects in England. Wiseman regarded them rather
with kindly sympathy than with any sense of obligation to throw
his energies into the work that they saw before them. But while
Spencer was at the English College in 1831, Wiseman's ambitions
and hopes were aroused in new directions by the arrival in Rome
of a group of men who had devoted themselves to organising a
great religious revival on the Continent. In December of that
year there came to Rome on an urgent mission Lamennais,
Lacordaire and Montalembert. They had been provoking acute

---

[1] *Life of Cardinal Newman,* by Wilfrid Ward, I, p. 89.
[2] *Life of Wiseman,* I, p. 89.

controversy in France by advocating in the *Avenir* a reconciliation between the Catholic Church and the new ideas of democracy, with such slogans as " a free Church in a free State " or " freedom of the press " and " freedom of association." They had aroused fierce opposition among the older clergy in France, and Lamennais had come to Rome with his friends to try and obtain support and approval for his campaign. Gregory XVI had received many earnest complaints of the unsettling influence of these young propagandists, and he delayed for months before granting the audience for which Lamennais had asked. During the interval the three men saw much of Wiseman at the English College, and his personal friendship with the Pope encouraged them in their hopes. Their conversation impressed him deeply, and it opened up prospects of a religious revival in France which coincided with what he already knew by personal correspondence with Görres and Döllinger and other German Catholics whose work he had studied closely.

George Spencer's earnest appeals to Wiseman to prepare for a Catholic revival in England were being made at the time when the new impulse was given to his ambitions by contact with the young leaders of the religious movement in France. He was still preaching his weekly sermons to English audiences in Rome, and there was a continual, if not a large, number of private conversions to the Catholic faith among the many English visitors and residents in Italy. Gradually the vision of a wider movement of conversion formed in his mind. He was already under its influence when, in March, 1833, nearly a year after Spencer's departure, he received a visit from two Englishmen who came from Oxford to consult him directly concerning the possibilities of reconciliation between the Church of England and Rome. John Henry Newman had been Vicar of St. Mary's in Oxford for some five years, and as a tutor at Oriel he had acquired a most unusual influence throughout the University. He had just completed his history of the Arians and was in need of rest during the winter, when he agreed to accompany his friend, Hurrell Froude, on a tour in southern Europe. He went in no such spirit of eager curiosity and sympathy as had

45

attracted the young Cambridge men to frequent Catholic places of worship before they had made any acquaintance with Catholic life on the Continent. Writing of his tour afterwards in the *Apologia*,[1] he says : " The strangeness of foreign life threw me back into myself ; I found pleasure in historical sites and beautiful scenes, not in men and manners. We kept clear of Catholics throughout the tour. I had a conversation with the Dean of Malta, a most pleasant man, lately dead ; but it was about the Fathers, and the Library of the great Church. I knew the Abbate Santini in Rome, who did no more than copy for me the Gregorian tones. Froude and I made two calls upon Monsignor (now Cardinal) Wiseman at the Collegio Inglese, shortly before we left Rome. Once we heard him preach at a church in the Corso. . . . As to church Services we attended the Tenebrae, at the Sestine, for the sake of the Miserere ; and that was all. My general feeling was ' all save the spirit of man, is divine.' I saw nothing but what was external ; of the hidden life of Catholics I knew nothing. I was still more driven back into myself, and felt my isolation."

By Newman's account, his meeting with Wiseman made very little impression on him, and there appears to have been no important intention in their interview. It may be indeed that Newman's friend Blanco White in Oxford had urged him to visit Wiseman, whom he had known intimately as a child, when both Wiseman's father and White's father had been engaged in commerce in Seville. Blanco White had been a young priest in those years, and even spiritual director to Wiseman's family. He had subsequently abandoned the priesthood and left the Catholic Church. He went afterwards to Oxford, and there became an intimate associate of Newman and his group. But, if Newman was little impressed, the interview with Wiseman left a deep impression on Hurrell Froude. A recent writer [2] even declares that " it is impossible not to think that the two friends went to the interview, unofficial as it was, in something of the spirit in which

[1] *Apologia pro Vita Sua*, Popular Edition, pp. 20-21.
[2] *Oxford Apostles*, by Geoffrey Faber, p. 302.

46

Lord Halifax met Cardinal Mercier nearly a hundred years later at Malines." The only ground for that remarkable surmise is the record [1] of his visit contained in Hurrell Froude's Remains. " It is really melancholy to think how little one has got for one's time and money. The only thing I can put my hand on as an acquisition is having formed an acquaintance with a man of some influence in Rome, Monsignor Wiseman, the head of the English College, who has enlightened Newman and me on the subject of our relations to the Church of Rome. We got introduced to him to find out whether they would take us in on any terms to which we could twist our consciences, and we found, to our dismay, that not one step could be gained without swallowing the Council of Trent as a whole. We made our approaches to the subject as delicately as we could. Our first notion was that terms of communion were within certain limits under the control of the Pope, or that in case he could not dispense solely, yet at any rate the acts of one council might be rescinded by another—indeed, that in Charles I's time it had been intended to negotiate a reconciliation on the terms on which things stood before the Council of Trent. But we found, to our horror, that the doctrine of the infallibility of the Church made the Acts of each successive Council obligatory forever, that what had been once decided could never be meddled with again —in fact that they were committed finally and irrevocably, and could not advance one step to meet us, even though the Church of England should again become what it was in Laud's time, or indeed what it may have been up to the atrocious council, for Monsignor Wiseman admitted that many things (e.g. the doctrine of the Mass) which were final then, had been indeterminate before. . . . We mean to make as much as we can out of our acquaintance with Monsignor Wiseman, who is really too nice a person to talk nonsense about. He desired me to apply to him if on any future occasion I had to consult the Vatican Library."

Extraordinary conclusions were to be based afterwards upon this interview in Rome. In a *History of the Romeward Movement in the Church of England*, which was published long after Newman's

[1] *Life of Wiseman*, I, pp. 117-118.

death, Mr. Walter Walsh solemnly implied that "Dr. Newman was at this interview with Dr. Wiseman in company with Froude, formally ordained a priest of the Roman Church, being then in fact a member of that communion," and that he "was actually a priest while officiating in the Anglican Church." In fact the Oxford Movement in its full sense had not yet begun, but it was to be born a few months later. "The fatigue of travelling was too much for me," wrote Newman in the *Apologia*,[1] "and I was laid up for several days at Lyons. At last I got off again, and did not stop night or day (except a compulsory delay at Paris) till I reached England and my mother's house. My brother had arrived from Persia only a few hours before. This was on the Tuesday. The following Sunday, July 14th, Mr. Keble preached the Assize Sermon in the University Pulpit. It was published under the title of ' National Apostasy.' I have ever considered and kept the day, as the start of the religious movement of 1833." Wiseman can have had no conception of the imminence of those events when the two Oxford men called upon him in the spring of that year. But he had been deeply moved by the earnestness of his visitors, and surprised by their apparent desire for unity with Rome. In the preface to his essays he wrote afterwards that it was their visit which had turned his attention to "the wonderful movement then commenced in England. From that moment it took the uppermost place in my thoughts and became the object of their intensest interest." In the same volume he recurs to it, and says that "For many years it had been a promise of my affection to St. Philip that I would endeavour, should opportunity be afforded to me, to introduce his beautiful Institute into England. But little could I foresee, that when I received that most welcome visit, I was in company with its future founder. From that hour, however, I watched with intense interest and love the Movement of which I then caught the first glimpse. My studies changed their course, the bent of my mind was altered, in the strong desire to co-operate with the new mercies of Providence."

A serious illness caused by protracted overwork compelled

[1] *Apologia*, p. 22.

Wiseman to reduce his activities during the remainder of the year, and he had to give up his weekly sermons to English audiences. Meanwhile he continued to receive from George Spencer and from Ambrose Phillipps news of the new religious movement which was developing in Oxford and elsewhere. The immediate occasion of Keble's sermon had been the Irish Church Temporalities Bill, by which the Whigs of the Reform Ministry sought to abolish ten Irish bishoprics. Keble and his followers, among whom Newman was one of the most devoted, believed that this was but the prelude to a general attempt at spoliation of the Established Church. The broadening of the franchise had created fears of more revolutionary changes, at a time when Catholic Emancipation had at last been granted and the Test and Corporation Acts had been repealed. There was a widespread feeling, not only among Church circles, that the old prerogatives of the Established Church were directly endangered. Keble's sermon had been a cry of alarm against what he described as a national apostasy. His followers felt acutely that a concerted movement must be organised to defend the position of the Church if it was to resist the dangers which threatened it. Urgent discussions followed after Newman's return to Oxford, to find some means of awakening the Church to its dangers, and Newman himself conceived the idea of publishing a series of " Tracts for the Times," of which he undertook the editorship. The first Tract was written by him, though he declined to put his name to it. He wrote as only one member of the clergy, whom he addressed in it as " my brethren in the sacred ministry, the presbyters and deacons of the Church of Christ in England, ordained thereunto by the Holy Ghost and the Imposition of Hands." " Fellow labourers," he wrote, " I am but one of yourselves—a Presbyter ; and therefore I conceal my name lest I should take too much on myself by speaking in my own person. Yet speak I must ; for the times are very evil, yet no one speaks against them. Is not this so ? Do we not look one upon another yet perform nothing ? Do we not all confess the peril into which the Church is come, yet sit still, each in his own retirement, as if mountains and seas cut off brother from brother ? " In these first Tracts Newman set

49

himself, as he explained later,[1] to "bring out with precision the relation in which we stood to the Church of Rome. We could not move a step in comfort till this was done. It was of absolute necessity, and a plain duty from the first, to provide as soon as possible a large statement, which would encourage and reassure our friends, and repel the attacks of our opponents."

The first Tract appeared on September 9, 1833; and although the effect of their publication was immediate it may be doubted whether the earlier Tracts received any serious attention among Catholics for some time afterwards. In January, however, some four months after the first issue, Ambrose Phillipps discovered them for the first time, when the fourth Tract of the series was shown to him by his cousin, the Bishop of Lichfield's son. It dealt with the doctrine of the Blessed Eucharist, and he read it with the keenest emotion. "Mark my words," he wrote in returning it, "these tracts are the beginning of a Catholic Movement which will one day end in the return of her Church to Catholic unity and the See of Peter." Nothing in fact could have been further from Newman's intention in what he wrote. The whole purpose of the Tracts was to define the position of the Established Church as a communion which was not in schism, and which had never departed from the Catholic unity which Phillipps desired it to attain by acceptance of the Roman claims. But he and Phillipps were at least at one in their fervent desire for a revival of religious faith and practice among the English people.

In that same year Henry Edward Manning had arrived at Lavington in Sussex, as its young curate, and in later years he described to his biographer the very typical conditions which had prevailed there at the time.[2] "When first I went to work in Sussex in 1833 the churches were open only once a week on Sundays, and on Christmas Day. There were no Saints days observed; Ascension Day even not kept. Communion was given only once a year, at least in the country; in London and other cities not oftener than four times a year. Spirituality had died

---

[1] *Apologia*, p. 40.

[2] *Life of Cardinal Manning*, by E. S. Purcell, I, p. 498.

out of the church." The Oxford Movement was to arouse an astonishing spiritual revival all over the country. "Now," said Manning in the same retrospect, "there are daily services almost everywhere, and frequent communions; in the cities the communions are weekly; Saints days are kept; special devotional services and spiritual exercises are common. Churches have been multiplied all over the land and Christian schools founded and endowed. The Church of England has made a marvellous progress. The wave of agnosticism, which has passed over the land and affected the intellectual classes, has not retarded its advance. It is going steadily towards some great end—who shall doubt it?—in the designs of Providence."

CHAPTER V

WISEMAN'S TOUR IN ENGLAND

THE example of Lamennais and Lacordaire, and the frequent correspondence which he was conducting with Döllinger in Germany, had convinced Wiseman that a similar effort for religious revival must be undertaken in England, and that he personally should take an active part in it. He had lived entirely in an intellectual atmosphere in Rome, and his thoughts were at first concerned chiefly with making the English Catholics acquainted with the leaders of the intellectual revival on the Continent. He had already put Döllinger in touch with Dr. Lingard, his former teacher at Ushaw ; but Lingard could not read German, and Döllinger expressed to Wiseman his regrets that he was " consequently incapable to profit of the historical works lately written in that language." [1] " Are there no persons of literary pursuits among your clergy," he wrote, " who are capable and inclined to study our theological literature of the last years ? , There seems now to be a sort of literary apathy and inactivity on the side of English Catholics, and yet you are continually attacked, and if I mistake not, your numerous adversaries take too much advantage of your silence. Your Milners, Butlers, and others are gone, without having left successors, and meanwhile the attacks of heresy are becoming daily more various and virulent. . . . Upon your arrival here you will, I trust, rectify my ideas, for I must tell you, you are expected to give us a full and circumstantial account of the state of the Catholic religion in your country, a subject which is of paramount interest for every one of us (meaning me and the rest of your friends here)."

His ill-health and enforced inactivity during 1834 had left more time to consider his future. " I am living a hermit's life this winter," he wrote to a friend,[2] " going out nowhere, and making

[1] *Life of Wiseman,* I, p. 140.   [2] *Ibid.,* p. 121.

no new acquaintances. Though Rome was never so full as this year since I came, I never knew so few people." His thoughts were now definitely turned towards England. He had been corresponding particularly with Bishop Baines, the Vicar-Apostolic of the Western District, who had bought the palatial Georgian mansion of Prior Park on the hill overlooking Bath, with the object of founding a school and also a seminary there. The Bishop had now conceived the ambitious plan of developing it into a Catholic University with Wiseman as its first president. Wiseman regarded the plans as being almost complete. In a letter [1] to Archbishop Whitfield of Baltimore, for whom he acted as agent in Rome, he wrote in August, 1834, that it might be necessary for him to appoint another agent. " At present the business stands as follows : I go to England in Spring to undertake the establishment of a new Catholic University under sanction of His Holiness, who has been pleased to express his approbation with a kind reserve that I give up none of my situations in Rome till I see, after a year or two, whether I shall continue them. In the meantime a Pro-Rector will fill my situation, one every way qualified for the office, formerly Vice-Rector. Should the establishment flourish, and my presence be of service to it, it is the declared intention of the bishop, Dr. Baines, to propose me for his coadjutor. Indeed he has done so already, but a delay has been proposed till some other affairs of his diocese are satisfactorily arranged. The probabilities are strong that I shall return no more to Rome to reside. At any rate, my absence will be prolonged."

Meanwhile it was decided that he should pay a prolonged visit to England to explore the ground. Believing that he was soon to leave Rome for ever, he put together for publication the substance of some of his more recent studies. He used them for a series of lectures *On the Connexion between Science and Revealed Religion*, which were delivered in Cardinal Weld's rooms in the Lent of 1835. It was seven years since he had made a decisive reputation by the publication of his *Horae Syriacae*. His new lectures enhanced that reputation greatly in a different direction, and they attracted wide-

[1] *Dublin Review,* October, 1918, p. 160.

spread attention in Rome at the time. They ranged over a wide field of scholarship and science, facing with a modern outlook the challenge that was being delivered against the traditional acceptance of the Scriptures. In a letter [1] to a friend he described them as " long lectures upon the increase of evidence to Christianity resulting from the progress of the sciences. I have delivered two on the comparative study of languages to very crowded audiences, in which were many literary men of great reputation, and have had the good fortune to engage their attention and interest beyond expectation." The experiment gave him a new courage before his departure to England, where he was later to be invited to deliver other courses of lectures, to audiences of a kind which had never before come together to hear a Catholic priest. In the same weeks while he was delivering his lectures in Rome, Lacordaire was preaching the first of his famous series of Lenten sermons in Notre Dame Cathedral in Paris ; and when Wiseman learned later of Lacordaire's extraordinary success, he could feel that he too had begun to take part in a movement to which his life was to be consecrated.

In August, 1835, he arrived in England. He had returned previously only for a few brief visits during the seventeen years since he left Ushaw as a boy. He broke his journey during the summer to make short stays with his friends in Munich and Paris, to renew his contacts with the leaders of the Catholic revival there. On his arrival in England in August, he went straight to Prior Park, where Bishop Baines was to discuss with him the projected establishment of a Catholic University. The Bishop was a Benedictine himself, and had formed his entourage from a group of monks who followed him from Ampleforth. But he had come into acute conflict with the Benedictines at Downside over the rights of the regular clergy in his District, and Wiseman, as his agent in Rome, was well aware of the friction that existed between the regulars and seculars. The reluctance of the English bishops to introduce religious orders, even when it was clear that they could undertake intensive efforts to open new missions in undeveloped

[1] *Life of Wiseman*, I, p. 132.

districts, had created an impression in Rome that the older Catholics were lacking in zeal, and that their obstructive attitude would have to be overridden. But Bishop Baines, while opposing the Benedictines in some of their plans in the west of England, had given ample proof of his desire to promote religious revival. He had bought Prior Park, and was full of ambitious plans for development. Moreover, he had heard of Rosmini's new Institute of Charity in Italy, and believed that its rules—though the Order was not yet formally approved by Rome—would provide him with the co-operation of zealous missionaries without encroaching upon the authority of the Bishop. Father Gentili, an ardent young priest of Rosmini's Institute, had met old Sir Harry Trelawney in Rome, and had accepted his invitation to open a mission in Cornwall, to be worked from Trelawney Castle, where Bishop Baines had permitted the opening of a private chapel since the baronet's conversion. Ambrose Phillipps had previously invited Dr. Gentili to start work in his neighbourhood in Leicestershire, but Trelawney's invitation meant breaking completely new ground, and Gentili went there with three companions to open his first English mission.

Bishop Baines had been so much impressed by Gentili that he wished him to leave Cornwall for the larger opportunities at Prior Park. Trelawney's death, early in 1834, led to family litigation over his will, which decided the founder of the Institute to accept the Bishop's offer, and Gentili accordingly went to Prior Park. He was already installed there when Wiseman arrived in August, 1835. He had been made Vice-Rector of the College and Spiritual Director, and had lost no time in introducing less reserved forms of devotion than had been customary in the past.[1] He distributed holy medals and devotional emblems among the boys, and encouraged them to wear them constantly. He inaugurated public devotions, particularly in honour of Our Lady, which were entirely in harmony with the ideas that Wiseman had practised in Rome. In these conditions, the prospect of collaboration between Wiseman and the Bishop seemed most favourable, when an

[1] See *Sequel to Catholic Emancipation,* by Bishop Ward, I, pp. 67-69.

unexpected estrangement developed in their personal relations. The Bishop had adopted a more cautious note than Wiseman expected in his discussions of the future. He now suggested that Wiseman should come to Prior Park only on an experimental basis for a year, and he made no further mention of the former intention to apply for his nomination as coadjutor bishop. Wiseman had taken everything for granted, and he talked freely of changes and improvements which he thought should be made. The Bishop resented his attitude, and after his departure wrote him a letter which Wiseman described long afterwards as " such a rebuff as I had never received before, and never have since." [1] All the hopes that he had based upon Prior Park were completely destroyed, and he went back to London to undertake his wide tour through England. He made his first stay with Bishop Bramston, the Vicar-General of the London District, in his house in Golden Square.

His first letters from London reveal a self-conscious diffidence in English surroundings. " Yesterday upon my arrival in Babylon I found your note," he wrote in an amusing letter [2] to Monckton Milnes in Italy. " My projects are as follows : in a few days . . . I set out on a species of tour, or rather *progress*, through England and Ireland, having made a resolution never to sleep in an inn or hostelry the whole way ; but I intend to quarter myself upon such of the nobility or gentry of these realms as can sufficiently appreciate such an honour. My first station will be in the neighbourhood of Birmingham and other Midland Cyclopean towns, where I have several short calls to make. Thence I proceed to the princely towers and enchanted gardens of Alton, and so forward to Sir E. Vavasour's, where, if you are in the neighbourhood, I hope I may have the pleasure of seeing you. . . . You could let me know by a few lines under cover to Lord Shrewsbury at Alton, Ashbourne." His intention of concentrating upon the " nobility and gentry " was not due to preference for luxury or high society. The Catholic Church in England had for generations been kept alive mainly through the loyalty of these old families, who maintained the clergy

[1] *Sequel to Catholic Emancipation,* I, p. 70.
[2] *Life of Wiseman,* I, p. 215.

as private chaplains in their houses and provided in their own
districts a centre where Catholic families lived in dependence upon
them. It was they alone who could be expected to provide the
means for church building or the opening of new missions, and
particularly for the promotion of such ambitious projects as the
foundation of a new Catholic University, which was Wiseman's
immediate concern in visiting England.

Moreover, it was they alone who could be expected to make
effective use of the new freedom and rights conceded to them by
the Catholic Emancipation Act. It had already enabled a number
of Catholic peers to take their seats as legislators in the House of
Lords, and had offered possibilities of election to the House of
Commons for some of the Catholic landowners whose estates gave
them an important position in their own counties. Wiseman had
been so immersed in Rome that he knew next to nothing at first
hand of the penalties and restrictions under which the English
Catholics had been persecuted and impoverished during the penal
laws. Yet the priests' hiding places in the great houses which he
now visited had been used in earnest within the memory of people
who were still alive. Those who offered him hospitality could,
and did, tell him endless stories of the disguises which had been
necessary even to enable priests to say Mass in obscure places.
Even now the Catholic clergy were still known as " Mr.," without
any designation of their religious title. Everywhere the tradition
of avoiding publicity in Catholic practices, and of conformity to
the conditions of a society which regarded Catholics with mistrust,
were still evident and overpowering.

But before Wiseman had time to gather his fuller impressions
of the state of the English Catholics through the country, he had
an opportunity to display his own gifts and to express his own
sanguine views before a London audience. The Italian priest who
was in charge of the Sardinian chapel in Lincoln's Inn Fields was
going to Italy, and asked Wiseman to deputise for him during his
absence. He could preach in their own language to the Italian
colony in London who attended the chapel, but he decided to use
the opportunity also for delivering a series of Advent lectures for

English audiences. The presence of an English Monsignor in London aroused considerable curiosity, and Wiseman's reputation among the numerous English visitors to Rome had made many people desire to see and hear him. He gave two lectures a week during Advent, and he was amazed by the success of his experiment. " The effect has been a thousand times beyond my expectations," he wrote [1] to a friend at the time. " The chapel is crowded to suffocation, every seat is occupied half an hour before the compline, and if it were three times as large it would be full. I have never preached less than an hour and a half, generally an hour and three quarters, yet no one has found it long, nor has attention once flagged. Last week I treated of Church authority, and this of the Real Presence ; next week, the Supremacy and Indulgences, etc. The common people say they can follow every word and I ' make them quite sensible ; ' the priests come in shoals, and they and all the congregation tell me that the whole system and the form of treatment throughout is quite new to them all. Indeed they wish that I would stay till Lent and give a fuller course, but this is out of the question. Nay, *entre nous*—for I write to you as a friend— they say I ought not to go back at all. But I am thus *vainly* full with you because it will convince you of what I have often said, that the method I have followed in school was as applicable to a congregation, if simplified and reduced to a popular form, and in this I always thought I could succeed. Everyone agrees that the most successful experiment has been made, and that proof has been given of the interest which may be thrown round the Catholic doctrines by a little exertion."

Impressions of Wiseman at the time record that he was jovial and good company, though always restless, in his private relations, but there was considerable suspicion of him among the older clergy. Dr. Bowdon, the President of Sedgley Park, for instance, met him during the winter, when he stayed at Oscott and with Bishop Walsh at Wolverhampton. Bowdon dined with him and the Bishop, and told [2] a friend that he was " distant and formal, the result of

---

[1] *Life of Wiseman*, I, p. 233.

[2] *History of Cotton College*, by Canon Buscot, p. 132.

Roman pomposity." But his name was "in everyone's mouth and his every movement is recorded." The Bishop afterwards brought Wiseman to call at Sedgley Park, which had been the first Catholic secondary school in England, bravely founded by Bishop Milner in disregard of the penal laws. Bowdon still found him "pompous and stiff with the dignity of a Roman prelate." But Bishop Walsh was "quite wrapt up in him," and made a special journey to Birmingham, to hear him preach at St. Peter's twice in one day. "I do not like Wiseman's writings nor his preaching," Bowdon wrote frankly. "It is not English and it is obscure. He appeals to the head and not to the heart. He cannot compare with Milner as a controversialist. I consider Baines and Lingard as the cleverest apologists we have." But in London his success was undoubted and most remarkable. Old Bishop Bramston prevailed upon him to stay until Lent, and he repeated his experiment of a series of popular lectures in St. Mary's, Moorfields. His audiences consisted largely of Protestants, and he addressed himself mainly to them. He set himself to enlist their attention by a sympathetic understanding of their difficulties, instead of meeting them with direct attack as the older apologists had done. "Here was a young Roman priest," wrote [1] one who attended the lectures, "fresh from the centre of Catholicism, who showed himself master, not only of the intricacies of polemical discussion, but of the amenities of civilised life. Protestants were equally astonished and gratified to find that acuteness and urbanity were not incompatible even in controversial argument. The spacious church of Moorfields was thronged on every evening of Dr. Wiseman's appearance . . . many persons of position and education were converted, and all departed with abated prejudice, and with very different notions about Catholicism from those with which they had been prepossessed by their education." His audience included many remarkable men, and among others who attended constantly was Lord Brougham. His success attracted considerable comment in the newspapers. Even Newman referred to it in an article in the *British Critic* which gave much offence to some of his friends, who accused him of

[1] *Life of Wiseman*, I, p. 234.

" making Wiseman a peg to hang your attacks on Protestantism on." But while Newman admitted willingly that " Romanism will spread among Dissenters and irregulars," he had no fears of any effect upon the right-minded of the Church of England. And in the following year [1] he contributed to the same review a vigorous attack on Wiseman's *Lectures on the Eucharist*, endorsing the verdict of Dr. Turton that " the author is subtle but not sagacious ; he is dexterous but not circumspect ; he is learned after the manner of a controversialist, not after that of a student. It would have afforded me great pleasure if I could have pointed out a single instance of fair, manly investigation in the course of his lectures, and I sincerely regret that he has not enabled me to pay him the compliment." Such criticism, Wiseman felt himself, was unfair ; for his lectures had been delivered to a mixed audience which included " a large proportion of poor, who yet stood out the longest of the discourses, apparently without much fatigue."

Another immediate effect of his lectures was a direct approach by Daniel O'Connell, who had been a great deal in London as Member of Parliament for Clare since soon after the Catholic Emancipation Act, to join with him in the founding of a Catholic quarterly review. O'Connell, with his customary generosity, offered to guarantee the costs of production, and for several years he bore the entire loss which the enterprise incurred. One of O'Connell's friends in London, a barrister and journalist named Quin, who was with O'Connell, one of the earliest members of the Reform Club, undertook to act as editor of the *Review* if Wiseman would collaborate in it. They met to discuss the matter at the old Spanish chapel in Soho Square, and it was decided to establish an organ of Catholic opinion and controversy, similar to the vigorous quarterlies which were then at the height of their prestige. The *Edinburgh Review* particularly had played a notable part in converting public opinion to the concession of Catholic emancipation, although its chief contributors regarded Catholic doctrines with unconcealed contempt and ridicule. But several of them, including Lord Brougham and Macaulay, were known

[1] *Life of Wiseman,* I, p. 243.

personally to Wiseman, and were indebted to him for hospitality and friendly offices in Rome. The new quarterly would be largely concerned with counteracting the Liberal doctrines which found expression in the *Edinburgh Review*, and for that reason, besides O'Connell's connection with it, it was to be called the *Dublin Review*. Wiseman was aware that his association with Daniel O'Connell would offend, and even scandalise, many of the old Catholic families in England. But he had never acquired their anti-Irish prejudices, and he was himself of Irish extraction, although he counted himself an Englishman. Moreover, he and O'Connell had many mutual friends and admirers, of whom Montalembert was one. Wiseman could not forget that he, personally, had been privileged to carry to the newly elected Pope the news that the Catholic Emancipation Act had become law as a result of O'Connell's tumultuous agitation in Ireland. He stipulated only " that no extreme political views should be introduced into the *Review*," and on that understanding [1] he considered himself " as associated (with the other two editors) to represent the theological and religious elements in the journal."

In May, 1836, the first number of the *Dublin Review* made its appearance. Wiseman had become keenly interested in its success, and he contributed various long articles to its early numbers. He was arranging for the inclusion of contributions by many of his distinguished Catholic friends on the Continent, and he stayed on in England through the summer until the second number had appeared. A whole year had passed since he left Rome in the previous summer, and he was to return to the English College a changed man, no longer the academic professor and college administrator, but a popular preacher and controversialist, who had discovered that he possessed unexpected powers of influencing and inspiring others. His impressions of the English Catholics had strengthened his desire to return to England, and awaken in them the courage and the ardent faith which had seemed so natural to him in Rome. The English Catholics, he wrote at the time,[2] had " just emerged from the catacombs." And in his recollections

[1] *Life of Wiseman*, I, p. 248.   [2] *Ibid.*, p. 216.

twenty years later, he was to write[1] concerning the Catholic Emancipation Act, " The generation still exists which had life and action before the momentous step. Many survive it who regret even bitterly the good old days of exclusion, which amounted to monopoly for them and theirs : some, too, remain whose shackles were removed, but not the numbness and cramp which they had produced. By degrees society will consist more and more, and then entirely, of those who have grown up side by side from infancy under the fostering of impartial laws, in the feeling of essential equality, without consciousness or pretension of this having been a concession. The remembrance of a condition of things, when one portion of the same community was a suppliant to the other for common rights, will have passed away ; and with it the pride of having refused or of having granted, and the humiliation of having long been spurned, and at last almost compulsorily relieved."

His outlook was so changed when he returned to the English College in the autumn of 1837 that unfriendly critics considered that his head had been turned by his success. But he was in fact a man of deep humility ; and in after years he related[2] to an intimate friend how, during the success of his lectures in the Sardinian Chapel, " I used to shed tears in the sacristy, fearing that whatever good the lectures were doing to others, they were filling me with vainglory." His friend Dr. Kyan records[3] also that he had once heard him complain that " I am totally misunderstood, and my motives and conduct are misrepresented. Everywhere I encounter a wall of reserve. I have my faults. I often do wrong, and if anyone would speak to me like a friend I should be thankful to have my errors pointed out and be glad to correct them." " He did not get credit for the high aims which inspired him," writes Father Kyan, " but was supposed, as it seemed to me, to be actuated by personal motives, such as vanity and ambition. Such a view of him was quite false, though perhaps he was not and could not be indifferent to fame." At least he was well aware already that his

---

[1] *Recollections*, p. 144. [2] *Life of Wiseman*, I, p. 233.
[3] *Ibid.*, p. 257.

success might make him vain and ambitious. And there is on record a copy of the earnest resolutions [1] which he made during his annual retreat in Rome after his return from England. Among these were the resolutions " to humiliate pride always, particularly when it arises under the form of good and tempting me with the pretext of doing something for the cause of God. . . . To crush vainglory, particularly when it comes in the practice of good works and in the exercise of my ministry ; and to try not only to endure but also to love humiliations and to rejoice in them."

In the later years his sensitive temperament was to be often pained acutely by such humiliations and discouragements. Bishop Baines had hurt him deeply by showing him that he was no longer desired as a coadjutor bishop and by dashing his hopes of great achievements in Prior Park. But before he left England that dream had vanished completely when the superb buildings of Prior Park were destroyed by fire, and the Bishop was left with a legacy of financial loss and debt which was to cripple development in the Western District for many years. Another disappointment followed in July, 1836, shortly before Wiseman's departure from England, in the death of old Bishop Bramston of the London District. He was succeeded at once by his young coadjutor, Dr. Griffiths, who regarded Wiseman with all the suspicion of the English-trained clergy, and was strongly of opinion that Wiseman himself was largely responsible for the mistrust with which the English Vicars-Apostolic were viewed by the authorities in Rome. Nevertheless Wiseman had found many who shared his enthusiasm, and who believed that their own hopes of religious revival and development could never be attained until he came back to England as their leader. Among these were the young converts from Cambridge, and another convert named Augustus Welby Pugin, who had become a Catholic almost as early in life as Ambrose Phillipps.

Pugin's early conversion was generally attributed to his enthusiasm for Gothic churches, just as Kenelm Digby had been attracted to the Catholic Church by his study of medieval chivalry.

[1] *Life of Wiseman*, I, pp. 261-264.

His family had indeed been Catholic for centuries, until his father abandoned the faith early in life. Augustus Pugin the elder came of old Catholic stock in Switzerland, but left his country during the revolutionary wars and found refuge in England as a young man and became an apprentice of John Nash, the architect who designed Regent Street. He made his name quickly as an architectural designer, and in 1827 was commissioned to prepare drawings for the new Gothic furniture at Windsor Castle. His son, Augustus Welby Pugin, had been working under him for some years, and the elder Pugin handed over to him, when he was only fifteen, the entire work of fulfilling the royal commission. The young man's work was so accomplished that he quickly became a celebrity. He married while he was little more than a boy and, his first wife having died in childbirth, he married a second time when he was only twenty-one. He built himself a house at Salisbury in the shadow of the cathedral, which inspired him to a fierce energy of architectural drawing. His devotion to Gothic art soon led him to revolt against the whole atmosphere of the Church of England as he knew it. In an autobiographical note[1] he explains how " the origin, intention and use of all I beheld around me was then perfectly unintelligible to me ; but applying myself to liturgical knowledge, what a new field was open to me ! with what delight did I trace the fitness of each portion of those glorious edifices to the rites for whose celebration they had been erected ! Then did I discover that the service I had been accustomed to attend and admire was but a cold and heartless remnant of past glories, and that those prayers which in my ignorance I had ascribed to reforming piety were in reality only scraps plucked from the solemn and perfect offices of the ancient Church. Pursuing researches among the faithful pages of the old chronicles, I discovered the tyranny, apostasy and bloodshed by which the new religion had been established, the endless strifes, dissensions, and discord that existed among its propagators, and the devastation and ruin that attended its progress : opposed to all this I considered the Catholic Church ; existing with uninterrupted Apostolical succession, handing down

---

[1] *Recollections of Pugin,* by Benjamin Ferrey, p. 103.

the same faith, sacraments and ceremonies unchanged, unaltered, through every clime, language and nation. For upwards of three years did I earnestly pursue the study of this all-important subject ; and the irresistible force of truth penetrating my heart, I gladly surrendered my own fallible judgment to the unerring decisions of the Church, and embracing with heart and soul its faith and discipline, became an humble, but I trust faithful member. I therefore hope that in Christian charity my conversion will not any longer be attributed solely to my admiration of architectural excellence ; for although I have freely acknowledged that my attention was first directed through it to the subject, yet I must distinctly state that so important a change was not effected in me but by the most powerful reasons, and that after a long and earnest examination."

Even so, he was only twenty-two when he became a Catholic, and it was a few years later that Lord Shrewsbury discovered him, after inquiring about the designer of some Gothic furniture which he had admired. Through Shrewsbury, he soon made the acquaintance of Ambrose Phillipps, who found him an even more vehement propagandist of Catholic revival than himself. His capacity for work and the rapidity of his execution were almost incredible, and the same exuberant energy overflowed in his conversation and in his writings. In 1836 he published his book *Contrasts*, which established his reputation immediately as a devastating critic of contemporary architecture and design, and as an expert with immense knowledge of Gothic art in all its forms. The book revealed also his uncompromising courage and vigour in denouncing the established Church. No publisher would have accepted it, and he had to print and publish it from his house in Salisbury. Not long afterwards he published a still more vehement *Apology for the Contrast*, in which he stated boldly the following theses :

" 1. That everything grand, edifying and noble in art is the result of feelings produced by the Catholic religion on the human mind.

" 2. That destruction of art, irreverence towards religion, contempt of ecclesiastical persons and authority, and a complete loss of all the nobler perceptions of mankind, have been the result of Protestantism, wherever it has been established.

" 3. That the degraded state of the arts in this country is purely owing to the absence of Catholic feeling among its professors, the loss of ecclesiastical patronage, and the apathy with which a Protestant nation must necessarily treat the higher branches of Art."

Pugin's *Contrasts* had been published during the period of Wiseman's tour in England, and Wiseman had already heard, through Lord Shrewsbury and Ambrose Phillipps, of his work and his vehement personality. Like Wiseman, Pugin had been dismayed by the supine attitude of the old Catholics, and particularly by the neglect of ceremonial and the miserable state of the Catholic churches and chapels. In later years he described [1] to his son-in-law, John Powell, his feelings concerning the Catholic places of worship at the time of his conversion. " Going into Catholic chapels (there were no churches then) what did I see ? The very tabernacle a Pagan Temple, the altar a deal sarcophagus, over which a colossal eye within rays looked down from a flat ceiling, artificial flowers under glass shades between the altar candlesticks, costly marbles produced in cheap paper, brackets painted with sham shadows supporting nothing ; and vestments, who can describe ? In the music gallery soprano and contralto soloists publicly emulating each other, lady vergers in feathers collecting the offertories. High Masses advertised as attractions. Even Bishop Milner's own chapel, he the Catholic pioneer of the revival, not exempt." But he had found an ideal patron in Lord Shrewsbury, who possessed many treasures of old Catholic days which were preserved among his family heirlooms, and whose home was pervaded by the atmosphere of culture and piety. Shrewsbury had become the sixteenth Earl, on succeeding his uncle in 1827, and he was already devoting a large part of his wealth to building and restoring churches and opening new missions. Bishop Walsh, the Vicar-Apostolic of the Midland District, was in full sympathy with his aims, and with Shrewsbury's generous aid he undertook to build a cathedral in Birmingham of which Pugin was to be the

[1] *Sequel to Catholic Emancipation*, I, p. 101.

architect. At the same time he proceeded to rebuild the college and seminary at Oscott. There, another architect had been employed at first, but Pugin's growing influence led to many criticisms of the earlier designs, and eventually Pugin was appointed to supersede him. Before the end of 1837 he had become still more closely attached to Oscott College as a member of its staff, with the title of Professor of Ecclesiastical Architecture and Antiquities.

CHAPTER VI

THE REVIVAL BEGINS

ALL hopes of persuading Ambrose Phillipps to abandon his change of faith had disappeared before he came of age in 1830. His father was thereafter chiefly anxious that he should marry and establish himself in life, before he might decide to take vows of celibacy and enter a religious order. He had made friends among the old Catholic families and among them he found his future wife. Laura Clifford was an orphan, and had been living for some years with her guardian and uncle, Lord Clifford, at Ugbrooke Park in Devonshire. Ambrose Phillipps married her after a short engagement, and under the existing law two ceremonies were necessary. The first took place at St. George's, Hanover Square, in 1833, and the religious wedding was celebrated at the Spanish Embassy chapel. His father made him an allowance of £1200 a year, and gave him possession of Grace Dieu manor, the second of his mansions in Leicestershire. The surroundings were most appropriate. Grace Dieu had been originally founded as a priory of Augustinian nuns nearly six centuries before. It had been suppressed and confiscated at the dissolution of the monasteries by Henry VIII, and had remained the property of the descendants of one of the Royal Commissioners, John Beaumont, until it was bought in 1683 by Sir Ambrose Phillipps of Garendon. The old priory church had fallen into complete ruin, and only a few traces of it still remained. The manor house had also fallen into ruin after being largely destroyed by fire, and Mr. Phillipps now undertook to restore and renovate it for his son after his marriage. The young people spent most of their time on the Continent, while a new Tudor style manor house was being built ; and their eldest son was born before they were able to enter into occupation of their home.

Ambrose had already conceived plans for reviving the monastic life on his new estates, and in the summer of 1835 he bought from Mr. Thomas Gisborne, M.P., some 230 acres of land in Charnwood Forest. He desired to present them to the Cistercian Order who, in pre-Reformation days, had owned at least part of the land, and his ancestors the De Lisles had been among the benefactors of their abbey of Garendon. His friends had taken for granted that he would lose no time in developing Catholic life in his neighbourhood. But the decision to commence his work for the Catholic revival in England by founding a monastery of contemplative monks seemed so fantastic that they could not refrain from protests. He had raised the £4000 needed for the purchase of the land from Bishop Walsh, on the condition that he need pay no interest on the loan unless he succeeded to his father's property ; but that the accrued arrears as well as future interest were to be paid by him yearly as soon as he inherited Garendon. Even the Bishop, who sympathised with his desire to become the founder of the first monastery built in England since the Reformation, was apprehensive of active opposition. He desired that the monks should on no account appear in public wearing their habits and cowls, and he even suggested that the place should not be openly called a Trappist monastery but an " agricultural and philanthropic community." Other friends who frankly disliked the idea of establishing a contemplative monastery in England besought him to employ the money to better purpose, by building small churches in the villages around Grace Dieu, where English priests trained at Oscott, and not foreigners, could take charge of them. Even if he insisted on introducing a monastery, they urged that he might do far better in introducing some order of preaching friars into the growing towns of the northern midlands, where a Catholic population was already forming with the immigration of labourers from Ireland.

Lord Shrewsbury had long been in correspondence with him, and shared both his generous instincts and his determination to spend his wealth in building churches throughout the country. Shrewsbury had at first been so much impressed by his zeal that he promised to follow his example by building another Trappist monastery at Alton Towers. But in September, 1836, while the enterprise at Grace Dieu was taking shape, and the four-roomed cottage which served Brother Augustine as his abbey was being built in the barren waste which he and his few monks had reclaimed, Shrewsbury wrote to report that the land he desired to buy himself could not be had. Meanwhile he had been thinking that more practical purposes might be served by introducing a different sort of religious community. "Could we unite the monks with an establishment of Christian Instruction?" he wrote.[1] "I am apt to think that a society of Brothers of Christian Instruction, with almshouses for the poor old people, would be more *useful* than a regular monkery. What think you? I begin to repent of my promise, not that I do not wish, nay ardently desire, to see a *religious* establishment on the premises; but I fancy we might have a much more useful one than a Trappist monastery. The new system of Poor Laws makes it once more highly desirable to have almshouses where the poor old forlorn wretches may find a comfortable asylum with the benefits of religion, instead of those horrid haunts the common workhouses. I think the brothers of Christian Instruction, by devoting themselves solely to one object, are fitter for the purpose than the silent Contemplative monk. I hope this is not treason. Tell me if it be."

But Ambrose Phillipps had formed strong views on the matter, and he countered Shrewsbury's objections with a long dissertation in reply. He was under the illusion that the Trappists would not only bring the complete religious atmosphere of their holy life, but would undertake active work in the surrounding country. He was to learn before long that they were forbidden by their rule to undertake such work, once their abbey had been fully constituted. "If you wish for an effective corps of Missionaries," he wrote, "I am certain that you cannot fix on a more serviceable class of Men than the Trappists, and I say this from experience. The Brothers of Christian Doctrine, I take for granted you are aware, are never in Holy Order; by their rule they can never be Priests; they are devoted solely to the education of the Poor, for which they are indeed invaluable; but then it is necessary that

[1] *Life of Ambrose Phillipps,* I, p. 69.

they should be in a Mission where there is already one or more Priests, consequently they would not in the least answer your object, as far as I understand it. The Trappists, on the other hand, have Priests in their Order, the more the better, for the grand object of their Rule is the singing of the Divine Office. They devote themselves to missionary duties, and to the *corporal* as well as spiritual relief of the poor and the sick, to whom they distribute medicines, etc.—and all this with a degree of ardour and assiduity which I never saw in secular Priests. Their abstemious life, their constant meditation, and their profound study of spiritual books qualify them admirably as spiritual Directors, while it forms a fine Commentary on the self-denying maxims of that Gospel which our Saviour came on earth to teach. Their houses are houses of spiritual retreat also for secular Gentlemen and Ecclesiasticks, and the good they do in this way is very great." A further considera-tion, on the practical side, was that a Trappist monastery could be established at far less cost than any other form of religious house. " You may support half a dozen Trappists," he pointed out, " on what would not satisfy one ordinary Priest ; only think that for many weeks the expenses of our good Neighbours at Mount St. Bernard did not exceed £1 a week for the whole community, which then amounted to eight individuals. Thus you will find that the 25 acres you contemplate purchasing would, with a very moderate little convent built upon it, support a community of 14, of whom in course of time 7 might be Priests. It is unnecessary to enlarge here on the immense benefit that must result to the Founder from such a number of Masses and other good works, in all of which he will have a very prominent share ; but unquestionably in a Missionary point of view, you could do nothing better or for a more moderate expense. I like your idea of Almshouses very much, and those you might have in your villages, and they might be visited and superintended in spiritual matters by your Monks. There is nothing contrary to their Rules in anything of this sort."

So the work at Mount St. Bernard was already in progress, while Wiseman was carrying out his tour in England. By October 1837 the monks had cleared a good part of the ground, and had built both their temporary home and the chapel. Bishop Walsh came to open it formally, and George Spencer came with him to preach a short sermon. The experiment had already won a surprising amount of sympathy in the neighbourhood, and assistance had been generously given to the monks from many unlikely sources. Before long they were at work already on the construction of their permanent Abbey, and Phillipps was able to tell Lord Shrewsbury that they had begun drawing the stone. One of the contractors for the Midland Counties railway had " given them enough iron rails to make a little Railway to their great granite rock from the spot on which the Monastery is to stand, so that by the help of a rope and a windlace with *only one horse* all the material except sand, lime, and freestone will be drawn." Another very handsome gift was from the proprietor of the lime-works at Barrow-on-Soar, who had " given them gratis all the lime they will want for the whole edifice." Other difficulties arose, however, and before long Shrewsbury was blandly suggesting that the monks should be transferred to Italy. Phillipps refused to be discouraged. " The sunny plains of Sardinia are out of the question for them," he replied,[1] " they must remain upon the heights of Charnwood, which are no longer the unproductive heaths you remember them, but are covered with some of the most flourishing crops in the county of Leicester, a specimen of agricultural skill and perseverance well worthy of the admiration of anyone who owns an estate. If you will only keep your promise and come here (if you do not I never mean to come to Alton again), I am sure you would be pleased to see what the good Monks have done. And to complete their Monastery would not take anything like what Pugin says. They have got four hundred pounds of their own already, and if one thousand or twelve hundred were added to that it would suffice not only to put them beyond the reach of temptation, but to make Mount St. Bernard as comfortable as it ought to be for Trappists, and a beautiful ornament to Catholicity in this country. . . . I beg you to pass a Sunday here, I want you to see our ceremonies, all is done precisely as in *parish churches* in England before the change of

[1] *Life of Ambrose Phillipps*, I, p. 76.

Religion, with this only difference that of course we follow the Roman and not the Sarum Rite : though of course you are aware the two hardly differ at all."

His appeal conquered Shrewsbury at once, and a letter soon came from him promising £2000 for the building of the Monastery, and a further £1000 if the monks would devote to the building all the sums which they had succeeded in collecting in France and at home. Phillipps immediately conveyed the " good Earl's " message to the monks, impressing on them his " Instruction that the donation was being made with the express understanding that it was to exonerate the Monks from the necessity of begging any more *either here or abroad* for the completion of their establishment." In a letter to his father Ambrose wrote delightedly that " Lord Shrewsbury is giving away great sums now to the Church in different parts of England, but his giving this princely donation to Mount St. Bernard he told me he did chiefly from affection for me and to please me. Pugin gives all his time, drawings, etc., gratis, and charges no percentage on the Outlay ; he says that with materials so close at hand he shall be able to astonish everyone with what he will build for the money. The monks will do all the carriage of materials themselves and a part of the carpenter's work, all the plane work. They desire me to thank you very much for the strawberry plants you sent them, which they said had flourished exceedingly."

Phillipps had kept up a constant correspondence with George Spencer since his marriage ; but for some three years Father Dominic Barberi received no word from him. A long letter which he wrote [1] after his marriage had apparently miscarried, and it was not until the spring of 1836 that they began to exchange letters again. Dominic Barberi was no longer provincial, but he was still fully occupied with the affairs of his Order in Italy as First Consultor. He was still dreaming of his future mission to England, and in March 1836 he wrote to Phillipps, reproaching him for his long silence and saying " is there any hope that I shall see you on this earth ? Is there any hope that I shall cross the sea and convey

[1] *Life of Dominic Barberi,* p. 101.

my body to that island whither, twenty-two years ago, I sent my heart?" He had received no news of George Spencer, either, for three years, and Phillipps replied at once from Grace Dieu to give him all the news of their activities in the interval. "You are always present in my heart," he wrote,[1] "and in the remembrance of you I find a sweetness and consolation which I cannot express. Moreover, I always continue to cherish the hope that one day, and that too through my means, however unworthy, you will come to establish your holy Order in England and will see that island for which you have for twenty-two years offered such fervent and loving prayers. I am confident that the extraordinary progress of the Catholic religion in England, during the last five years, is owing almost entirely to your prayers, and to those of your holy Order of Passionists. I assure you that there is nothing which would give me greater consolation than to establish the Order in England."

Wiseman's lectures in London had certainly attracted attention, but the signs of "extraordinary progress" were indeed little apparent except in the district where Phillipps himself had been at work. His outlook was largely influenced by the remarkable achievements in his own neighbourhood. He told Father Dominic of how he and Lord Shrewsbury had founded a Trappist monastery near Grace Dieu, and that a large number of conversions to the Catholic faith had already resulted. "In less than a twelve month more than three hundred Protestants have embraced our divine Faith in the parish of Grace Dieu alone; and in every part of England the Catholic religion is making great progress. The Protestant ministers are raging with a degree of hatred and violence which can hardly be expressed. In this mission of Grace Dieu we have already formed a Catholic school to educate children in the principles of the true Church, and it will console you to know that there are at present one hundred and sixty-six boys and girls in it. The most extraordinary thing is that these children are all born of Protestant parents, and these parents are well satisfied at seeing them educated in the Catholic Faith."

The letter virtually offered to assist Father Dominic in estab-

[1] *Life of Dominic Barberi*, p. 101.

lishing a Passionist foundation in England ; and its glowing report of the progress already achieved inspired him to immediate action. He drafted a reply at once,[1] but before sending it he showed it to his provincial who would not allow him to commit the Order so far. "Do not think that so much is required," Barberi had written, " to prepare a house for a few poor Passionists. I should be content to live in a house fit for a peasant built in some open field, or in a wood. Nay, I should be happy in a cabin made of straw, or in a cave dug out in some rock, at least till some little dwelling might be provided built of stone. We should not need, either, to go with a numerous community. We might come at first two or three in number, and with these commence God's work. Also, for us nothing is needed but only and simply a dwelling. There is no need to think of providing funds or income, as we live on the voluntary offerings of the faithful. I am perfectly confident that God would not suffer us to die of hunger if once we were there." The provincial was impressed by the fervour of Father Dominic's appeal, but he had reasonable doubts whether he could find others prepared to face the ordeal in the same spirit. "To trust in God is well," he wrote [2]: "but to send religious on such an enterprise without the necessary spirit and courage, is certainly not consistent with sound and holy prudence, which must never be separated from confidence."

A letter to Barberi from George Spencer in September of the same year gave a less sanguine view of the possibilities. But Spencer himself had been producing remarkable results since he returned as a priest to England four years earlier. Bishop Walsh had sent him to Walsall, where he was to begin work under one of the ablest priests in the district, Mr. Martyn, who was also the first priest to be entirely trained in England since the Reformation. The area surrounding Birmingham was beginning to develop new industries, and the population was growing fast. From Walsall the priest in charge had to cover a very wide district. "He was a good rider," according to the records,[3] "and on his little pony

---

[1] *Life of Barberi*, p. 104.   [2] *Ibid.*, p. 106.
[3] *Life of Spencer*, p. 69.

dashed along at a rapid pace to visit his flock, to attend the sick, and instruct converts, often at considerable distances." His dress bore no resemblance to that of the Continental clergy, for he wore " buckskin breeches, with top boots or overalls, and hair powdered : such was his ordinary costume, though he always wore a black coat, and generally a vest to match." Among the most populous parts of his large parish was West Bromwich, and he put George Spencer more or less in charge there while a new chapel was being built. Spencer's father had received him home with real affection, and had made a point of inviting Wiseman to Althorp during one of his brief holidays in England after Spencer came home. He made generous financial provision for him, and George Spencer was thus able to contribute £2000 to the building of the new church, which was to be his first mission as a Catholic priest. In November 1832 the new church was ready for its opening, and he invited Phillipps to come to the ceremonies.

Besides the Passionists, both Phillipps and Spencer had established close contact with the Institute of Charity which had been recently founded in Italy by Father Rosmini. Sir Harry Trelawney had already brought the first Rosminians to England before he died, and Bishop Bains had given them full scope at Prior Park. But the zeal and energy of Father Gentili had made the Bishop feel that he was losing control of his own college and Gentili was soon brought back to Italy by his superiors. George Spencer had kept in touch with him after his recall, and he now had hopes of bringing back the Rosminian fathers to work in the Midlands. In writing to inform Phillipps about the new church at West Bromwich, Spencer told him of what might be an immediate opportunity for bringing them in. The Dominicans at Leicester, who had assisted in Spencer's sudden conversion two years before, had just informed Bishop Walsh that they would be glad to hand over the mission there to him ; but it was so burdened with debts that he could not accept the offer. "When he wrote to say this to Mr. Martyn," said Spencer,[1] "I thought that if Rosmini could raise money for this debt (of which I know not the amount) what

[1] *Life of Spencer,* p. 70.

a beautiful footing for his priests. Mr. Martyn has written to the
Bishop to suggest this. If you came and talked it over, perhaps
we should have the long wished for establishment made without
further trouble, and in one of the best stations in England. . . . Oh !
come Ambrogio, and help us here."

The church at West Bromwich was duly opened, and Spencer
was placed in charge of the new mission. He worked with such
energy that within three years he had also opened three schools.
By the end of 1833 he had extended his activities to Dudley, and
there transformed a warehouse into a chapel, with two small
houses adjoining which served as a sacristy and a sitting-room for
the priest. He was already making converts in large numbers, and
by the end of 1833 seventy of them were confirmed by Bishop
Walsh in his new church. His social connections gave him a
certain celebrity in the district, but he was constantly subjected to
violent and coarse attacks. " I remember one morning," writes [1]
one of his first parishioners, " when he was going his accustomed
rounds to visit the poor and sick, he had to pass a boy's school,
at Hill Top. They used to hoot after him low names, but, seeing
he did not take any notice, they came into the road and threw
mud and stones at him : he took no notice. Then they took hold
of his coat and ripped it up the back. He did not mind, but went
on all day as usual through Oldbury, Tipton Dudley, and Hill Top,
visiting his poor people. He used to leave home every morning,
and fill his pockets with wine and food for the poor sick, and
return home about six in the evening, without taking any refresh-
ment all day, though he might have walked twenty miles in the
heat of summer. One winter's day he gave all his clothes away
to the poor, except those that were on him. He used to say two
Masses on Sunday at West Bromwich and preach. I never saw
him use a conveyance of any kind in his visits through the parish."

In another letter to Phillipps [2] he writes rather sadly that many
of his plans were being vetoed by either the Bishop or Mr. Martyn.
But in regard to his personal affairs he had at last persuaded the
Bishop to allow him to relinquish all control of his " earthly goods

[1] *Life of Spencer*, p. 75.   [2] *Ibid.*, p. 77.

and income," and place them in the hands of an administrator. "Thus I am free from almost all the inconvenience which a missionary must find in being a married man and am able to give up all my time to my spiritual functions. It is, however, as yet only make-believe or playing at voluntary poverty, as I yet am watched over in all things without asking. All my wish now is to become worthy of getting on to the reality of this counsel. I also hope I may be thought worthy of practising perfectly the counsel of obedience, and so leading a life (if it please God) uniting the advantages of a secular and religious course." He had been drawn more than ever towards the work of "evangelising," but both Bishop Walsh and Mr. Martyn were still opposed to it. Nevertheless, he persisted in testifying wherever he went. On a visit to London in 1835 he went to see his sister at Kensington Palace, who was governess to the future Queen Victoria, and succeeded in obtaining an interview with the Duchess of Kent and the young heiress to the throne. He had been obliged to start begging for a new church at Dudley, as the landlord had given him notice to quit the warehouse which he had used as a chapel. He thought of undertaking a begging tour in Ireland but that project also was discouraged, and a sudden breakdown in health made him abandon it.

When he resumed his correspondence with Dominic Barberi in September 1836 he let him know that the difficulties were greater than he and Phillipps had foreseen. "I knew what difficulties I must meet with in this work," he wrote ; [1] "but before I came to the point of encountering and feeling their weight I formed a very imperfect idea of what they are. I know that in a day God is able to change the face of the whole country, but I find it not easy to imagine this being actually done, while living in the midst of it, and seeing with my own eyes and in so many directions marks of worldly mindedness and the unbelieving proud spirit which Protestantism has engendered here. From a distance (as from Rome) one does not see these things so plainly. The carelessness of some, and the bigotry of others among Protestants are so great, so obstinate, so incurable, that it appears almost vain to attempt

[1] *Life of Spencer,* p. 86.

anything with them. As regards Catholics, we have to lament continually the coldness of the generality of our own body and the vices and scandals of a great many. I find from all these causes a great disappointment of the bright hopes of speedy progress which I entertained when I first came to England. Disappointed and baffled in my too sanguine expectations, I have had a hard struggle to keep up my spirits."

"Whether the Passionists will find a settlement here depends on God's will alone," he continued. "You must have heard that Phillipps has founded a monastery of Trappists, an order which would seem amongst the least likely to find their way into England. But here they are, and are flourishing, and looked upon favourably by all the people. An opening may soon be made for you as unexpectedly. I am fully in the disposition to assist in bringing you and some of your companions among us if the occasion is offered. In fact, after receiving your letter I was for some time revolving how this might be done." He mentioned Dudley, and his hopes that "a religious house might be placed there as well as anywhere else." At any rate the Bishop was sympathetic, because "Dr. Walsh is very desirous of seeing all sorts of religious orders established within the bounds of his jurisdiction. Some of our secular clergy give way unhappily to the jealousy which you will know does sometimes exist against the Regulars. The Jesuits particularly have been discountenanced in some quarters of England. Our Bishop has no feeling of this kind, and only desires to see Catholic missions established in all places by whatsoever persons are disposed to do it in due order. He is about to make a journey to Rome very shortly. . . . He will be mostly in company with Dr. Wiseman of our College. I do not see why you should not, without impropriety, lay your history before him, and tell him all the extraordinary things which seem to connect your Order with England, and let him judge what to say or do. I leave at his disposal all my property and means of all sorts. If he is induced to employ any of them on your behalf, he may. I will tell him, if I can, before he goes, that I have written to you this."

Dominic Barberi had thus received two definite invitations to come to England, from friends who were both in a position to give him financial assistance. Spencer and Phillipps had begun to discuss the project together, and they met on several occasions when Spencer was deputed to preach special sermons at the opening of new churches in the northern midlands. Moreover, they had derived new hopes from an unexpected quarter. The Passionists had now been definitely invited to found a house at Boulogne, where Mgr. Affreingue was building the large cathedral which replaced the ruins of its predecessor burnt out during the revolution. Spencer's cousin, Mrs. Canning, was one of the many English people living in Boulogne, and she had been assisting in the work. In the early summer of 1837 she had been in England, and George Spencer made a long journey to see her on the subject. To one of the Passionists in Rome she wrote [1] that he had told her of his plans for assisting the Passionists in England. At first he had hopes that they might open a house mission " a few miles from where he lived, without a church. He was ready to give either £100 a year for the mission or £2000 all at once to build the chapel. He added that if Lord Clifford gave what they said he intended to give, in England instead of at Boulogne, altogether there would be a nice little sum to begin with. His second project was, that Father Dominic should come with two or three others, and that all should live with him till Providence should open a way." He had even thought of anticipating the foundation at Boulogne by inducing the Passionists to come first to England, as there was delays over the Boulogne negotiations. In the autumn of 1838 Phillipps went on a holiday to Dieppe, and brought George Spencer with him to recuperate from another illness. They went on to Paris to visit Lord Clifford, whose niece Phillipps had married, and Clifford introduced them to the Archbishop of Paris, Mgr. de Queslen. They talked eagerly to the Archbishop of their dreams of England's conversion, and besought him to join his prayers with theirs and with those of the Italian Passionists. The Archbishop was genuinely impressed, and from that interview there arose their decision to promote a Crusade of Universal

[1] *Life of Barberi*, p. 117.

Prayer for the conversion of England. The Archbishop gave it his full support, and before long eighty of the French clergy in Paris alone had promised to say Mass once a week for that intention. Spencer had desired such a movement for years, and now he and Phillipps threw all their energies into promoting it. Wiseman gave his assistance in Rome, and it was soon active in many countries.

Meanwhile the Passionist foundation at Boulogne hung fire, and Spencer through his Crusade of Prayer enlisted a powerful ally in Mgr. Acton, who was a few years later to succeed Cardinal Weld as the English Cardinal resident in Rome. New influences were brought to bear upon the Passionist authorities, and in January 1839,[1] Mrs. Canning was asked by her friend, Father Ignatius, to inform Spencer and Phillipps that they should address a formal petition to the General Chapter of the Passionists before its next meeting. Mgr. Acton himself drafted the petition. It stated definitely that " Lisle Phillipps, a Catholic landowner, is willing to make the offering of a house in the county of Leicester which might lodge six or seven religious. A devout lady recently converted engages to give every year fifty pounds sterling—two hundred and twenty Roman dollars—and there are grounds to hope that further resources will not be wanting from the alms of the faithful." The petition was duly presented and accepted by a large majority of the Chapter. On April 12, 1839, Father Ignatius was able to write [2] to Mrs. Canning that " the establishment of the Passionists in England is determined on." Father Dominic's dream seemed to have come true at last. But his hopes were suddenly dashed by his unexpected election as a Provincial in Italy for a second time. Without him it was useless to proceed, and the project was held up for a whole year, while a new foundation at Ere in Belgium was being undertaken instead. But when Father Dominic set out from Italy for Belgium in May 1840 he was already convinced in his own mind that the new enterprise was to be only the stepping-stone to his eventual mission to England.

While Phillipps and Spencer were rejoicing that their plans

[1] *Life of Barberi*, p. 125.   [2] *Ibid.*, p. 131.

were so near to fulfilment, the project was regarded with very mixed feelings by some of their friends. Lord Shrewsbury had been superbly generous in helping Phillipps with his Trappist monastery. By relieving the monks of all further necessity to beg for alms, he had gone far towards removing the objection of the secular clergy to their encroachment upon the very slender resources of the Catholic community, which had to support the clergy and provide for extending new missions. Phillipps was well aware of his personal obligations to Shrewsbury in that matter, and he appreciated very fully the spiritual example which the " good Earl John " was giving to his contemporaries. Even to complete the monastery at Grace Dieu had been more than he could manage for some years, and in one dejected letter he had written [1] to Shrewsbury : " I think we must let the Church be put in abeyance for a season : it is quite useless for me to recommend the matter amongst any Catholick friends I possess. You are the only Catholick, almost, in England with any public spirit, certainly the only one with any of the devotional generosity of ancient Times —we must wait awhile until the *reunion* of the Anglican Church has put a little new blood into our degenerate body before we can expect such work as Abbey Churches to rise up. . . . I conclude you have heard of Mr. Watts Russell's noble donation for the repairs of Stafford Church—£5000 ! This as a specimen when they are still in schism, may serve to show what the Anglicans will do when the *reunion* shall once be fairly accomplished and when they shall have received the inconceivable grace of Catholick communion."

He consulted Shrewsbury constantly on his projects, and it was a serious matter that Shrewsbury disapproved entirely of his desire to introduce Italian missionaries into England. He could report most remarkable progress in conversions around Grace Dieu, but he realised that something much more ambitious was needed to make any impression on the whole country. He had kept closely in touch with Father Rosmini's Institute of Charity as well as the Passionists, and was determined to give him every encouragement.

[1] *Life of Ambrose Phillipps*, I, p. 51.

He kept Shrewsbury fully informed of what he was doing. "In our own mission," he wrote [1] to Shrewsbury at Easter, 1839, "we continue to make a few conversions amongst the poor, thus yesterday twenty were received into the Church, and three weeks before seven had the same happiness, and on the first Sunday in Lent Bishop Walsh confirmed twenty-seven converts in our chapel ; all this sounds pretty well and looks well at the moment, but it is slow work after all, and if we go on at that rate we may wait a great many years before we convert even the single Parish of Whitwick, containing as it does three thousand inhabitants." He had come to the conclusion that " it is quite useless to build any more chapels just at present ; what I should do, if I had large means at my disposal, would be to procure a considerable number of holy Missionaries from the Continent, who might be fixed somewhere for a time until they thoroughly understood our language, and then I would have them go about and preach everywhere on the foreign plan—in the fields or in the high roads even. If they were persecuted, if they were even put to death (which is vastly unlikely in these days), they would only resemble the Apostles and the primitive Martyrs, and their preaching would even have still greater weight on that account with the great mass of the people. I fear, however, such a plan is likely only to be laughed at as the offspring of a heated imagination ; and so I must candidly say that I do not expect to see any great things for some time to come."

To those who resented the frequent allusions to the Catholic Church as the "Italian mission" in England, the suggestion of importing from Italy priests who could scarcely even read English was far from agreeable. Lord Shrewsbury lived most of the year in Rome or elsewhere on the Continent, and was likely to be free from the usual prejudice against foreigners. But Shrewsbury consulted his English friends, and they threw buckets of cold water on the suggestion. To Phillipps he wrote in April, 1839 : [2] "I have seen Lord Clifford, Father Glover, and the Passionists. The former agree with me, or rather I with them, that it is an

[1] *Life of Ambrose Phillipps, I, p. 105.*   [2] *Ibid.*

impracticable scheme to think of working with them in England. Father Glover said, ' You will never get an Englishman into that order, so what good can you do with them ? They came to me (Father Dominic and another) to ask if I knew anything about the matter, as they were ready to go and take possession of the House you were so good as to offer them. I said they could not eat the house, and I did not know what was to feed them otherwise. They replied they trusted to Providence. Father Dominic spoke a little broken English, but could not understand a word of what I said to him. You will only bring yourself and others into trouble with these good people, and do no good. We must work in the *large* towns with *large* churches, in which we can influence the people by the splendour, etc., of our service." So much for the Passionists. As for Father Gentili, Shrewsbury declared flatly that " we are all against your *Gentili* scheme. It is beginning at the wrong end. Besides which, Gentili is not suited for England. We must have a new race of zealous English missionaries such as are now bringing up at Oscott, under the good Bishop and Pugin. There must be, as you say, perambulating preachers—this is of the *utmost* consequence ; but surely it is of no use preaching among people whom you must leave without any means of practising their religion." Nevertheless he confessed that he took great interest in the Order of Charity, and would gladly assist them, if he had not decided to " concentrate all my forces on building. There are numbers to contribute small sums to exigencies like these and to other works of charity, but few can afford to build."

Shrewsbury's generosity as a church builder was indeed heroic, and it became the absorbing passion of his life. In another letter to Phillipps a few years later,[1] he wrote to say that he would henceforward spend a large part of the year abroad with the deliberate purpose of saving money to build churches. " Anything I might do in England must be problematical in its results," he wrote, with a humility which showed how different was his outlook from the patriarchal attitude of many Catholic landowners whose hereditary status was far less important than his. " What I do

[1] *Life of Ambrose Phillipps,* I, p. 80.

from hence is positive and certain. £2000 each summer is half a small church or a whole monastery, or, indeed, all you want for your own church at St. Bernard's; and a church, or chapel, or monastery will endure (it is hoped) for many a long day and be *infinitely* more instrumental in the conversion of the people than any personal exertions we can make at home. Of course we must come sometimes, but I hope not often."

CHAPTER VII

PUGIN, AND THE "OXFORD MEN"

THE Trappist monastery which Phillipps was building at Grace Dieu had appeared to his friends rather as a pious hobby than as a serious effort towards restoring the Catholic Church in England. The work took much longer than he had expected, and the abbey was not, in fact, opened until the summer of 1844. But the monastery and the two other small churches which he built on his estate did much more than provide a focus for all his enthusiasms. The astonishing progress which was made in his neighbourhood confirmed his highest hopes of what might be done by a concerted effort to preach the Catholic faith and to found new religious centres. Organised opposition was, of course, aroused when the village chapels were built, and a protest meeting was held at Ashby de la Zouch. Sir Charles Wolseley presided at the Protestant meeting and Phillipps attended it. But he persuaded Wolseley to return with him to Grace Dieu after the meeting, and a friendship arose between them which resulted within a few years in the baronet's becoming a Catholic. Phillipps wrote [1] to Lord Shrewsbury after the meeting and told him that one surprising result of it had been that " a *very large number* of the most respectable *Protestant* Trades people of that Town have petitioned that a Catholic church be built in Ashby, in order that they may learn the doctrines of the Catholic Church from the lips of her own Ministers, and that if convinced of their truth they may embrace them ! In consequence of this petition we are taking steps to do that which these good people so earnestly desire, and I am at this moment making negotiations with my good friends the Jesuits, who I have the greatest hopes will undertake this most important Mission." In the meantime a series of controversial sermons had been arranged in the Grace Dieu chapel to be preached by " Mr.

[1] *Life of Ambrose Phillipps,* I, p. 103.

Hulme of Loughborough who is a very clever man." They drew surprisingly large crowds, and on one Sunday some 700 people were counted in the chapel ; while already ten men had come to the Prior of Mount St. Bernard to receive instruction. Phillipps was already convinced that before very long " the majority of this neighbourhood will be Catholick." There had certainly been a most remarkable response. Priests were badly needed, but the monks of Mount St. Bernard were preaching in the villages and making many more converts than could have been reasonably hoped.

The new monastery and the chapels provided Phillipps with many other interests besides. There was the excitement of planning and designing the buildings, of supplying the vestments and other ecclesiastical properties, and of arranging for the performance of ceremonies which he had been unable to find elsewhere. His early friendship with Kenelm Digby deepened while Digby was completing and publishing the eleven volumes of his *Mores Catholici*, which were almost an encylopædia of religious practice and tradition. He and Digby had made many pilgrimages together when they were in Rome, and they had the same love for ceremonial and for church music. Pugin was a still more ardent lover of ritual and sacred music, and he and Phillipps had become intimate friends and allies. In a lecture [1] which he prepared for his choir at Grace Dieu and Whitwick, Phillipps deplored the long neglect of Church art and music, and expounded his plans for helping in restoration. He explained how during the years of persecution " as the Catholicks of England gradually lost sight of the architectural glories of their country, so also from the same cause did they lose the beautiful and majestick ceremonial for which England in ancient times was renowned all over the earth. Men who were compelled to worship in garrets were not likely to use a grand ceremonial, their object was to preserve the essentials of Religion, and in so doing to avoid the cruelty of their Protestant Persecutors, who doomed to death the Priest who should dare to offer up the Eucharistick sacrifice. Intimately connected with this ceremonial

[1] *Life of Ambrose Phillipps*, II, pp. 187-198.

was the ancient Church musick, and for the same reasons, which led to the disuse of the former, this was abandoned also. In fact, the only places in which it was possible for a High Mass to be celebrated in England during the period I allude to, were the chapels of the various Catholick Ambassadors resident in London. And even at the present day, as far as I am aware, there is hardly a single Catholick chapel out of London, if at least you except the Chapels of our Episcopal colleges, in which a High Mass with Deacon and Subdeacon is ever celebrated. But I regret to say that, if the disuse of the antient Catholick ceremonial has become general, that of the antient Catholick Church Chaunts has become still more so."

Pugin deplored this state of affairs as keenly as Phillipps, and with the encouragement of Bishop Walsh at Oscott he had been taking every possible step to rectify matters. The Bishop gave him almost a free hand in attempting to revive the old Gothic vestments of pre-Reformation days, besides encouraging him to build and restore churches in the Gothic style. But the older clergy heartily disliked these changes. They resented especially the vehemence of Pugin's manner and methods, and the authority which he had obtained through the Bishop's support. The Bishop was well aware of the prevalent criticisms, but Pugin's eccentricity amused him. He began to speak of him as " Archbishop Pugens," partly no doubt because of his odd habit of signing his letters with an initial cross before his name. But the opposition soon found expression in strong protests to Rome, and at the end of 1839 a letter was received from the College of Propaganda, which referred directly to him as " an architect converted from heresy." In a characteristic letter [1] from Ramsgate on December 1, Pugin wrote at once to inform Phillipps of what had occurred.

" I suppose you have heard of the Censure passed by the Propaganda on the proceedings of our good Bishop. If you have not, keep the intelligence closely to yourself ; but it is of great importance that you should be acquainted with all that is going on against us. The Bishop shewed me the other day a Letter he had

---

[1] *Life of Ambrose Phillipps,* II, p. 222.

just received from the Propaganda censuring his proceedings and denouncing me in no very measured terms. This is the result of some diabolical falsehoods and misrepresentations made at Rome by our adversaries, and the Propaganda have actually given credit at once to this *ex parte* statement and have condemned the proceedings of the only Bishop in England who has really advanced the dignity of religion. Dr. Walsh found the churches in his district worse than Barns ; he will leave them sumptuous erections. The greater part of the vestments were filthy rags, and he has replaced them with silk and gold. For this he has been censured ! ! ! Is this to be believed ? can it be possible ? It is, and a blow has been struck at us, which, if persisted in, will be far more fatal to religion than all the attacks of the hereticks. I am filled with dismay and indignation ; but in this matter I blame those who caused these misrepresentations to Rome more than the Propaganda, who are utterly ignorant of the whole business and are only at fault in giving credit to the Lies and ignorance of these informers. I am disgusted beyond measure. It is madness in the present state of things to check the restoration of the dignity of religion. We have a detestable crew to deal with—ignorance, prejudice, timidity, tepidity. All combined—my dear friend, we have a sorry soil to plant in, and that not from protestantism ; actually protestants in many cases are better inclined to Catholicism than half the soi-disant Catholics of our days. Every attempt to restore religion to its antient dignity and glory is met with sneers, insult, and opposition from those who ought to be foremost in aiding the great work. . . .

" Mark my words. Your chapel service, which is perhaps the most devotional in England, will be shortly put down because it is different from what has been lately seen in the scrubby rooms called chapels where *one urchin* is frequently the only assistant at the holy sacrifice, which is offered up in a place and at an altar far more calculated to excite ridicule than devotion. I am sick at heart. The apathy of the Catholic body on these things is alarming. I had formed dreams of returning glory ; but if this censure of the Propaganda is persisted in after the remonstrance which has been sent, I shall abandon all my hopes. I see everything that we had hoped dashed to pieces. Do not deceive yourself, My dear friend, do not deceive yourself: the Catholics will cut their own throats, the clergy will put down religion. These are hard sayings, but they are twice mad fools; straining at gnats and swallowing camels, the very men who would not hesitate to violate rubricks every day to suit their convenience or their pockets, now swelling with indignation and horror at the idea of an ample surplice or flowing chasuble such as almost every Saint in the Calendar wore. Administer baptism out of an old physick phial; reserve the blessed Sacrament in *dirty cupboards*; say mass in vestment made out of an old gown; burn gas on the altar; have everything as *mean*, as *pitiful*, as *shabby* as you please; hire protestant performers to sing, *leave out every ceremony in the ritual*; do all this and you will be right. But if you venture to speak of antient glory and ecclesiastical dignity, oh, you are a man of extravagant opinions, an enthusiast, a visionary—and *ecclesiastical censure* awaits you. Again I say I am disgusted. *Rubrick* indeed! *Innovators!* I wonder those who have been doing all these things venture to name Rubrick and innovations. If their censure is acted upon and all our splendid vestments cut to pieces, I shall try no more. Our good Bishop has given in too soon. The Censure was based on a *wrong position*. He was accused of innovation. He should therefore have been firm; but he has suspended the use of the vestments everywhere. Thus the wretched old things are actually used in the new Derby Church while Lord Shrewsbury's splendid donations are shelved. This is tacitly acknowledging the charge. I feel cut up beyond measure, but I do not mean to let this business drop. I will set forth the antient glories of Catholicism and leave people to judge why the service now performed in the modern Catholic chapels is not a ghost of the antient site. There is nothing out of Oscott so good as the service in your chapel, and that will be *put down*. I know it will. You are a marked man for the vengeance of those who do not like *to be put out of the way*."

In a postscript he added: " Everything in modern chapels is bad—vestments, music, altars—and the present Race of Catholics are so used to the miserable expedients which have been resorted to, through necessity, that they will not avail themselves of better things now that they are offered them. I feel completely upset and dejected by this business. Pray write to Lord Shrewsbury on this business—the Propaganda have been shamefully deceived in their information. They little know what might be done in England if proper measures were resorted to. If the English Catholics were zealous and *really set forth* their religion England might be regained ; but under the present system never."

Pugin's anguished letter illuminates the whole period during which the Catholics in England were in Wiseman's words " emerging from the catacombs." But Wiseman himself kept up the courage of these convert pioneers. He came back to England again in the autumn of 1839, and it was now recognised that he would soon return for good. His previous visit had shown that the time was not yet come for any such ambitious departure as the founding of a Catholic University. To establish a quarterly review was as much as he could hope for in the circumstances, and even that modest venture had been made possible only by O'Connell's personal generosity in tiding it over the first years of financial loss. Bishop Baines in the Western District had given up all idea of having Wiseman as his coadjutor, and he was already working among the other bishops to have Wiseman superseded as their regular agent in Rome. But Bishop Walsh not only regarded Wiseman with full confidence. He had already applied to have him appointed as his coadjutor. And although Bishop Baines was much the ablest of the Vicars-Apostolic, there had been no such progress in the western as in the midland district, under Bishop Walsh. The most rapid developments had indeed been in the north, where many important industrial towns and shipping centres had grown remarkably since the introduction of railways and the development of the mining areas. Wiseman had realised this fully during his first tour of England, and he had convinced the Roman authorities that there must very soon be a redistribution of Districts, with more bishops than the four Vicars-Apostolic whose districts had divided England between them since the reign of James II. Wiseman had been actively concerned in conducting the preliminary discussions in Rome since his earlier visit to England. " In fact, this had become a matter of absolute necessity," he wrote afterwards.[1] " For example the northern vicariate comprised not only the four counties usually designated by that epithet, but Lancashire and Yorkshire besides. Since this first distribution of episcopal jurisdiction, cities and towns, like Manchester, Liverpool, Leeds and Newcastle had arisen from secondary rank to the dimensions of capitals ; without mentioning innumerable other manufacturing places, or rather districts, composed of clusters, or chains formed by busy seats of industry, with a growing population."

On his second visit in the autumn Wiseman had been busy with many engagements in the midlands, and he saw much of the activity and controversies in progress. There had been trouble, for instance, when he was present at the opening of the new church in Derby. Lord Shrewsbury had presented Bishop Walsh with a set of cloth of gold vestments which were intended for use at the opening of all new churches. They had been made to Pugin's design, and they incorporated a number of valuable medieval ornaments and crosses which Pugin had collected in different places. But at the opening of the church in Derby the vestments were not used, though the reason was not any objection from Rome but a misunderstanding.[2] " It appears that Pugin had understood that the Mass was to be sung to Gregorian chant by a surpliced choir, and he arrived with the Earl of Shrewsbury and Mr. Lisle Phillipps, looking forward to seeing for the first time in England a real medieval High Mass, which was to show to some of his friends from Oxford the full Catholic ritual in the surroundings of Gothic architecture and vestments. What was their dismay when on their arrival they found a full orchestra in possession, and a large choir, including females, in accordance with the custom of the day. Pugin protested in vain. Bishop Walsh was in the sacristy, ready vested, and said that it was too late to alter the arrangements.

[1] *Recollections*, p. 162.
[2] *Sequel to Catholic Emancipation*, I, p. 116.

Pugin appealed to the Earl of Shrewsbury, and not altogether without success. Being the donor of the vestments, he declared that they should not be used if there were to be lady sopranos and fiddlers. The Bishop, however, was inexorable ; so he exchanged his beautiful cloth of gold vestments for a dingy set of the French pattern, and the service proceeded. The three distinguished visitors drove away in high dudgeon, and took no part in the opening ceremony."

The ceremony, however, was extremely impressive, and Wiseman preached at it. In a letter [1] to his mother he declared that "It is without exception the most magnificent thing the Catholics have yet done in modern times in this country, and is quite worthy of ancient days. The church is all of stone with three aisles, a glorious tower and a very rich sanctuary ornamented with beautiful stained windows and rich broad hangings, all given, as well as very splendid vestments, by Lord Shrewsbury. There were about eighty boys in attendance, two bishops, and a great show of vestments from Alton and Oscott. On the whole it would not have done dishonour to Rome." Wiseman was being called upon to preach in many places during his visit. "When I have finished my engagements which will be before the end of the month," he told his mother,[2] "I shall not be sorry. By that time I shall have preached about ninety times in six weeks, averaging an hour each time, which I think you will say is pretty good. I have travelled, chiefly by railroad, 1600 miles since I came to England." In Yorkshire there had been more great ceremonies, particularly at Huddersfield, where "it was more like an Italian than an English day. The Guild Confraternity, with their tippets and badges, walking two and two, with their crucifixes canopied over like the Roman ones, the banners, lamps, crucifixes, or rather processional crosses, borne before the clergy, and acolytes with surplices, and the priests with copes, the whole preceded by a band of music, recalled my thoughts to Monte Porzio. . . . The people behaved admirably, the streets were crowded, notwithstanding every attraction in other directions had been held out, as

---

[1] *Life of Wiseman,* I, p. 310. [2] *Ibid.,* p. 311.

missionary meetings, teetotallers' feast, etc., and it was a work day ; they seemed to enjoy the sight and no expression escaped them collectively or individually which indicated unpleasant feelings. . . . Mr. K. himself was the curiosity of the day, wearing a Roman three-cornered hat, buckles, etc. In fact, he dresses like a Roman Abbate, and cares for no one. In the West Riding of Yorkshire they can do what they please, bigotry is at an end, and processions may walk the streets with no more fear of molestation than in Rome and the priests all wear the Roman collar and an ecclesiastical costume."

The awakening from the catacombs in these northern places was most remarkable. On the day before these celebrations at Huddersfield Wiseman had preached at the opening of yet another church, at Stalybridge, which had been built by Mr. Brown, the son of the Catholic bookseller. Two days later he had another lecture " to a still more crowded audience, the leading Dissenting ministers of the place and crowds of Protestants, including the most respectable inhabitants." From Nottingham he went on to Ushaw, his old school, and thence to Manchester before returning to London. He was sure now that he would soon return definitely to England. " Even if Rome should refuse to consent to this, my visits must be very frequent. In fact, Dr. Griffiths actually wants me to be in London for next Lent to preach, in London, etc., but this would indeed be too soon and I should hardly have had rest enough after this year's campaign. However, it seems to be quite a generally understood thing, both among clergy and laity, that I have to be in England again next year, if not for good, at least for a visit."[1]

His preaching had been much more than that of a public orator for state occasions. He was addressing himself constantly to Protestants as well as Catholics, and he had been following with always keener interest the development of the Tractarian movement at Oxford and in its ramifications through the Church of England. His articles in the *Dublin Review* had been largely occupied with theological controversies concerning their position, and in the

[1] *Life of Wiseman*, I, p. 313.

issue for July 1839, just before he came to England, he had published an essay which was to have far more important effects than
he yet knew. His previous contributions had been largely technical discussions, designed to prove that the Tractarian claim to
apostolical succession could not be upheld. In the July issue he
approached the subject from a different angle, in an essay on
Saint Augustine and the Donatists. Newman's wide knowledge
of the Fathers of the Church had given the impression of impreg-
nable strength. But Wiseman had now recalled a controversy in
which Saint Augustine had dealt with a schism which bore many
resemblances to the claims of the Tractarians. He had discovered
the analogous case of a local church which had claimed that it
possessed valid orders, and that it was orthodox in doctrine, but
which persisted in schism from the supremacy of Rome. The
Donatists had persisted in calling themselves Catholics, and they
had used precisely similar arguments to those of the Tractarians
in justifying their independent position. In showing how Saint
Augustine had dealt with these claims, Wiseman emphasised the
close analogy. Overriding all minor questions in dispute, Augustine
had given a verdict which was of immediate application to any
other local Church in a similar position : "*Quapropter securus
judicat orbis terrarum, bonos non esse qui se dividunt ab orbe terrarum in
quacumque parte orbis terrarum.*" Wiseman pressed the application
of that answer in all its bearings, and he concluded that "by the
Fathers the question was essentially considered one of fact rather
than of right : that is to say, the very fact of one particular Church
being out of the aggregation of other Churches, constituted these
judges over the other, and left no room for questioning the justice
of the condemnation."

Wiseman's article was of such direct application to current
controversy that it was soon being widely read among the Tractarians, who relied upon Newman to furnish the reply to this
new and formidable antagonist. In the *Apologia* [1] Newman
himself recalls that "in the spring of 1839 my position in the
Anglican Church was at its height. I had supreme confidence in

[1] *Apologia*, p. 58.

95

my controversial *status*, and I had a great and still growing success, in recommending it to others. . . . In January, if I recollect right, in order to meet the popular clamour against myself and others, and to satisfy the Bishop, I had collected into one all the strong things which they, and especially I, had said against the Church of Rome, in order to their insertion among the advertisements to our publications." In the April number of the *British Critic* he had published an article on "the state of Religious Parties," which he described afterwards as containing "the last words which I ever spoke as an Anglican to Anglicans," although he had no such intention in mind when it was written. It concluded with a renewed and powerful plea for "*some* Via Media which will preserve us from what threatens, though it cannot restore the dead. The spirit of Luther is dead ; but Hildebrand and Loyola are alive. Is it sensible, sober, judicious, to be so very angry with those writers of the day, who point to the fact that our divines of the seventeenth century have occupied a ground which is the true and intelligible mean between extremes ? Is it wise to quarrel with this ground, because it is not exactly what we should choose, had we the power of choice ? Is it true moderation, instead of trying to fortify a middle doctrine, to fling stones at those who do ? . . . Would you rather have your sons and daughters members of the Church of England or of the Church of Rome ? " This was precisely the question to which Wiseman, with a less direct appeal, was devoting himself in the pages of the *Dublin Review*. There was no other controversialist on the Catholic side who could hope to gain the same degree of attention from the Oxford leaders ; and there were indeed few Catholics who attached much importance to the controversies with the Tractarian leaders which Wiseman was conducting. Newman had by this time become so fully satisfied with his own position that he had [1] "put away from me the controversy with Rome for more than two years. In my Parochial sermons the subject had at no time been introduced : there had been nothing in my Tracts or in the *British Critic* of a polemical character." He had returned to his close readings of the Fathers, particularly con-

[1] *Apologia*, p. 70.

cerning the Monophysites, and he could feel that " my stronghold was Antiquity." It was at this stage that Wiseman's article on the Donatists was shown to him, shortly after its appearance, by some of his Oxford friends " who were more favourable to the cause of Rome than I was myself." But he was already familiar with the history of the Donatists, and when he read the article he " did not see much in it." He felt at once that " the case was not a parallel to that of the Anglican Church. St. Augustine in Africa wrote against the Donatists in Africa. They were a furious party who made a schism within the African Church and not beyond its limits. It was a case of Altar against Altar, of two occupants of the same See, as that between the Non-Jurors in England and the Established Church ; not the case of one Church against another, as of Rome against the Oriental Monophysites." That answer seemed sufficiently convincing, but Newman's friend,[1] who was " an anxiously religious man, now as then very dear to me, a Protestant still," pointed out the quotation from St. Augustine and repeated it again and again. " When he was gone," writes Newman, " they kept ringing in my ears : *Securus judicat orbis terrarum ;* they were words which went beyond the occasion of the Donatists : they applied to that of the Monophysites. They gave a cogency to the Article, which had escaped me at first. They decided ecclesiastical questions on a simpler rule than that of Antiquity ; here then Antiquity was deciding against itself. . . . Who can account for the impressions which are made on him ? For a mere sentence, the words of St. Augustine struck me with a power which I had never felt from any words before. To take a familiar instance, they were like the ' Turn again Whittington ' of the chime ; or to take a more serious one, they were like the ' *Tolle lege—Tolle lege* ' of the child which converted Saint Augustine himself. ' *Securus judicat orbis terrarum !* ' By those great words of the ancient Father, interpreting and summing up the long and varied course of ecclesiastical history, the theory of the Via Media was absolutely pulverised."

Newman could not conceal the distress which Wiseman's

[1] *Apologia*, p. 72.

article had caused in him. In a letter [1] to Rogers on September 22 he wrote : " I have had the first real hit from Romanism which has happened to me. I must confess it has given me a stomach ache. You see the whole history of the Monophysites has been a sort of alterative. And now comes this dose at the end of it. It certainly does come upon one that we are not at the bottom of things. At this moment we have sprung a leak ; and the worst of it is that those sharp fellows, Ward, Stanley and Co., will not let one go to sleep upon it. I seriously think this a most uncomfortable article on every account, though of course it is *ex parte*." Its effect went so deep that within a month he had " confided to Henry Wilberforce his suspicion that in the end he might find it his duty to join the Roman Catholic Church." [2] When he came back to Oxford after the vacation,[3] he " found a general talk on the subject of the Article in the *Dublin Review*," which had affected others as much as it had affected him. He still " felt no kind of certainty that the argument in it was conclusive," and he replied to it in the *British Critic* of the following January with an article on " The Catholicity of the English Church." In a letter to Bowden soon after he confessed privately that it had " made me for a while very uncomfortable in my own mind." But he had overcome his first shock of dismay, and other troubles had occupied his mind in the interval. He had been confronted in other quarters with a direct challenge to his conception of Anglicanism as " nothing else than a continuation in this country (as the Church of Rome might be in France or Spain) of that one Church of which in old times Athanasius and Augustine were members." Newman was firmly convinced that the doctrine of the Church in England was still unchanged, and that the Thirty-nine Articles were fully capable of being construed in that sense. On this matter compromise was impossible, and he set himself, in composing Tract 90, to establish his claim beyond all doubt. He realised that, if he should fail in the attempt, the result must be his retirement from the Anglican ministry. " I would not hold office [4] in a Church which would not allow my sense of

[1] *Letters of Cardinal Newman*, II, p. 286.

[2] *Life of Newman*, I, p. 68. [3] *Apologia*, p. 80. [4] *Ibid.*, p. 81.

the Articles." For this purpose he withdrew to Littlemore, which was some three miles outside Oxford but within the parish of St. Mary's. He had built a small church there some years previously, and he now went to reside there in order to complete his task in seclusion. He appointed a curate at St. Mary's and he was already considering the prospect of retiring. But he was persuaded by Pusey against resignation, on the grounds that it might appear to signify doubts as to the validity of his religious position.

Not until after his return to Rome at the end of 1839 did Wiseman learn of the deep impression that his article had caused. He was by now convinced that he would very soon leave Rome for ever, and find his life's work in promoting the Catholic revival in England. He was reporting to the Roman authorities on the urgent necessity for appointing more bishops in England so that a more intensive development of the Church could be undertaken. But his special attention had been attracted more than ever to the Oxford leaders, and to the profound influence they had exercised in fostering a new sense of religious life within the Church of England. Phillipps kept him informed from England of what was developing, and George Spencer had grown more sanguine than ever since he started his Crusade of Prayer for England's conversion. Before Wiseman went back to Rome Spencer had been transferred from his parochial work around Birmingham, to live at Oscott as spiritual director to the college. With more time at his disposal for public activities, Spencer likewise turned his attention to Oxford, and decided boldly to undertake a personal visit to the Tractarian leaders. He went there early in the new year to ask them to join, as Anglicans, in the Crusade of Prayer. But he met with a direct rebuff from Newman which would have daunted any less humble man. Newman described it all afterwards in the *Apologia*, in a passage which throws light on the complicated situation which confronted those few Catholics, including Wiseman, who desired to establish cordial relations with the Oxford Movement. The *Dublin Review* had undoubtedly established itself as an influential organ, and Wiseman's essays in it could not be ignored. But Wiseman had been directly associated with Daniel O'Connell in the foundation and the conduct of the *Review*, and Newman, in his own words,[1] " had an unspeakable aversion to the policy and acts of Mr. O'Connell, because, as I thought, he associated with men of all religions and no religion against the Anglican Church, and advanced Catholicism by violence and intrigue. When then I found him taken up by the English Catholics, and, as I supposed, at Rome, I considered I had a fulfilment of how the Court of Rome played fast and loose, and justified the serious charges which I had seen put down in books against it. Here we saw what Rome was in action, whatever she might be when quiescent. Her conduct was simply secular and political."

It was this antipathy towards O'Connell that led Newman " into the excess of being very rude to that zealous and most charitable man, Mr. Spencer, when he came to Oxford in January 1840, to get Anglicans to set about praying for unity. I myself, at that time, or soon after, drew up such prayers ; their desirableness was one of the first thoughts which came upon me after my shock ; but I was too much annoyed with the political action of the Catholic body in these islands to wish to have anything to do with them personally. So glad in my heart was I to see him, when he came to my rooms with Mr. Palmer of Magdalen, that I could have laughed for joy ; I think I did laugh ; but I was very rude to him, I would not meet him at dinner, and that (though I did not say so) because I considered him ' in loco apostatae ' from the Anglican Church, and I hereby beg his pardon for it." Newman relented quickly, and sent him a letter of apology for his rudeness. But he explained bluntly that, while he agreed entirely with the spirit of his search for unity, " your acts are contrary to your words. You invite us to a union of hearts, at the same time that you are doing all you can, not to restore, not to reform, not to reunite, but to destroy our Church. . . . In order to gain an end on which you set your hearts—an open stage for yourselves in England—you ally yourselves with those who hold nothing against those who hold something. This is what distresses my own mind so greatly, to speak of myself, that, with limitations which need not now be

[1] *Apologia*, pp. 76-77.

mentioned, I cannot meet familiarly any leading persons of the Roman Communion, and least of all when they come to me on a religious errand. Break off, I would say, with Mr. O'Connell in Ireland and the liberal party in England, or come not to me with overtures for mutual prayer and religious sympathy." So far as Newman was concerned, Spencer's mission had been a complete failure. He was even less successful in his efforts to hold his own in arguments with his friend Palmer. He was one of the leading exponents of the Branch Theory, and he left poor Spencer utterly bewildered and speechless by bombarding him with historical analogies and theological subtleties which were completely new to Spencer, and for which he could provide no sort of answer. In a letter [1] to Phillipps, Spencer reported sadly that " I was brought during the first days of fight to the most astonishing point not only of having my battery regularly silenced but of being in a complete maze in my own mind."

Wiseman alone of the group who had focussed their attention upon the Oxford Movement was a scholar and controversialist capable of meeting them on level terms. He realised this more than ever when he learned of the impression that had been made by his article on the Donatists, and he was impatient to return to England, so that he could continue the controversy at close quarters and establish personal relations with the Oxford men. He admired their great gifts, their earnestness and their profound learning, and he admired above all the intensely spiritual purpose of Newman and Keble and their followers. Phillipps admired them still more, and he was convinced already that the " Oxford Men " were not only an example and a reproach to the supine Catholic body, but the chief hope of all religious revival in England. The discouragement of Pugin's attempts to revive the pre-Reformation vestments and architecture had pained him deeply. " For God's sake, my dear Lord Shrewsbury," he wrote in December 1839,[2] " do speak out firmly, that these good men who have been so grossly deceived may be rightly informed : do urge Dr. Wiseman to use his influence. I can tell you that it is the same

[1] *Life of Spencer*, p. 112.   [2] *Life of Ambrose Phillipps*, II, p. 221.

party who are endeavouring to crush the restorers of Christian art, who have vowed that Wiseman shall never be Bishop in England. I know it, for they tried to make a tool of me, in that business, and it was at their instigation that I wrote to you what I said of him in the letter I sent to Dover. But I thank God upon that point I am now better informed. . . . Once more, my dear Lord Shrewsbury, I conjure you to speak out as the premier Earle of *England*, and as the restorer of the Church of God in his Kingdom : you have a right to speak and your voice will not be contemned." Pugin was as much impressed as Phillipps by the earnestness and piety of the Tractarians, and in one of many characteristic letters he wrote [1] to Phillipps : " Rely on it, these Oxford men are doing more to catholicise England and to work the real *internal change of mind* than all our joint body. I consider them quite as raised up by God in the present energency, for we seem sinking to utter degradation."

Powerful influences to prevent Wiseman's nomination as a bishop had, in fact, been at work in Rome, but without success. The preparations to increase the number of English bishops were now almost complete. In July 1840, some months after his return to Rome, the new arrangements were announced. Since 1688 the country had been divided under four Vicars-Apostolic, with jurisdiction respectively over the London, Midland, Northern and Western Districts. On July 3, 1840, the number was increased by Pope Gregory XVI to eight. The Vicars-Apostolic of the London and Western Districts, Bishops Griffiths and Baines, retained their former titles. The Northern District was divided into three parts, to be known as the Lancashire, Yorkshire and Northern Districts. Bishop Briggs, formerly Vicar-Apostolic of the whole Northern District, was now confined to the Yorkshire district. Two other new Districts, the eastern and the Welsh, were also formed. Bishop Walsh, formerly in charge of the whole Midland District, was to be Vicar-Apostolic for a smaller area called the Central District ; and Wiseman, as Bishop of Melipotamus, was to become his coadjutor. Wiseman was consecrated in May, two months before the fuller announcement was made, and it was known that he was

[1] *Life of Ambrose Phillipps*, II, p. 225.

to leave Rome to become President of Oscott. When the new arrangements were published, it was announced that he was to combine the presidency with the rank of coadjutor to Bishop Walsh.

At Oscott Wiseman would be within close range of Oxford, and his hopes ran high as he left Rome after twenty-two years of residence in the English College. He had become rooted there [1] " till affection clung to every stone like the moss that grew into it," but his heart was set upon his future work in England, and he went with a full sense of having vast labours to perform. On September 16 he made his official entry to the College as its new President. " The boys met their new President [2] at the lodge gates and dragged his carriage up to the College. He was received at the College with the symbolical ritual congenial to his tastes and his Roman education. The professors of the College, headed by his old friend, Father Spencer, met him, according to medieval Catholic custom, at the door, and vested in cassock and surplice, and walked with him in full procession to the chapel, intoning the antiphon always used in honour of a bishop of the Church : ' *Ecce sacerdos magnus, qui in diebus suis placuit Deo.*' A formal address of welcome followed, and a reply from the new President, before the party passed to the usual greetings of the nineteenth century." In a letter [3] to his friend Bagshawe, before his departure at the end of his last tour in England, he had written : " When I look back at what I have got through in England, it appears to me like a dream. I feel completely at a loss to discover what can have gained me the influence I have been able to exercise upon others, or what I have done to make my presence desirable. For everything I have done has fallen wonderfully short of my desires, and everything I have acquired or effected has gone wonderfully beyond my expectations." His reputation had indeed extended far over the Continent, besides Rome and England. The Paris *Univers*, in an article [4] on him before his consecration, had said, he " has fixed on him the eyes of Europe. . . . He goes to take his place among the new Augustines whom a new Gregory sends forth to achieve a second time the conquest of England."

---

[1] *Recollections*, p. 163.   [2] *Life of Wiseman*, I, p. 345.
[3] *Ibid.*, p. 335.   [4] *Ibid.*, p. 346.

CHAPTER VIII

WISEMAN AT OSCOTT

WISEMAN'S desire to establish direct contact with the Oxford Movement had been only increased by what he learned of George Spencer's unlucky attempt to gain Newman's co-operation in his Crusade of Prayer. He sympathised fully with the Crusade, and had used his influence at Rome and among his friends in France and Germany to further it. But these attempts at fraternising with the Tractarians were regarded with deep disapproval by the older Catholics, who regarded them as being avowed and insidious enemies of the Catholic Church. Bishop Baines of the Western District had openly denounced Spencer's movement in his Lenten pastoral while Wiseman was encouraging it in Rome. The Bishop's attitude scandalised the Pope, when he was informed of it, and he was soon afterwards summoned to Rome to defend himself. He was obliged, very reluctantly, to modify his opposition, but his attitude was shared widely in England. Wiseman was well aware that Spencer, with his lack of theological or historical knowledge, had been a hopeless messenger for such purposes in Oxford. He himself could have met the most learned Tractarian leaders on their own ground, and he was impatient for an opportunity to make the attempt. But Spencer, as spiritual director at Oscott, was almost alone among the College staff in sharing Wiseman's sympathy for their movement. Wiseman had provided himself with another ally by appointing Dr. Logan, who was also a convert from Cambridge, as his vice-president, and that appointment had rather increased the atmosphere of suspicion. Pugin also was constantly at Oscott, and he was definitely in touch with the Oxford Movement. As an ecclesiastical architect he was being constantly employed in many places by High Anglicans, who could appreciate without reserve his efforts to restore the older forms of church architecture, and who were strongly attracted by his enthusiasm for Gothic vestments.

Ambrose Phillipps also had established personal relations with some of the most active Tractarians at Oxford, particularly with Bloxam and Bernard Smith. And soon after Wiseman's arrival at Oscott Phillipps was engaged in making preparations for a personal visit to Oxford. For several years he had been in constant correspondence with Bloxam and other members of the movement, and he had been writing with increasing insistence of his desire to visit Oxford and bring about personal discussions between the Tractarians and some of his Catholic friends. " My great desire and object," he wrote [1] to Bloxam from Grace Dieu early in 1841, " is to contribute what little so humble an individual as myself is able, towards producing a good understanding between the Catholick and Anglican Churches, with a view to the ultimate restoration of that happy and blessed Unity which formerly existed between them for more than a thousand years, and which I am perfectly certain will one day be restored." He hoped particularly that he might himself " be the means of introducing to Oxford some foreign Theologians, who I assure you thoroughly appreciate the Catholick movement there, who admire your admirable treatises, who fully understand the difficulty of your position, who see that humanly speaking the great result to which we look must be distant, the fruit of much labour, much patience, much tribulation, but who feel that God holds in his hands the hearts of Men, and that to humble earnest persevering prayer He will refuse nothing." His visit to Oxford was fixed for Easter week ; and in the meantime Bloxam communicated his letters to Newman, who still refused to have any direct dealings with Catholic controversialists, and insisted that his views must be communicated at second hand.

In a written statement [2] which Bloxam was thus charged to convey to Ambrose Phillipps, Newman answered that it was " impossible to read his letter without the deepest sympathy where our sympathies are so much the same. Why should we be separate, except that there is a strong body in both churches whose antipathies are more powerful still, and because this body has the

[1] *Life of Ambrose Phillipps*, I, p. 203.   [2] *Ibid.*, p. 205 *et seq.*

governing authorities on its side?" But he came to the crux immediately by declaring that in his view the attitude of Rome made any agreement unattainable. "This I feel most strongly and cannot conceal it, viz. that, while Rome is what she is, union is impossible. That we too must change I do not deny. Rome must change first of all in her spirit. We must see more sanctity in her than we do at present. Alas! I see no marks of sanctity, or if any, they are chiefly confined to converts from us. 'By their fruits shall ye know them' is the main Canon our Lord gives us to know true Pastors from false. I do verily think that, with all our sins, there is more sanctity in the Church of England and Ireland that in the Roman Catholic Bodies in the same countries. I say not all this in reproach, but in great sorrow. Indeed I am ever making the best of things before others when the Roman Catholics are attacked, but I cannot deny this great lack. What Hildebrand did by faith and holiness they do by political intrigue. Their great object is to pull down the English Church. They join with those who are further from them in creed to oppose those who are nearer to them. They have to do with such a man as O'Connell. If they want to convert England, let them go barefooted into our manufacturing towns—let them preach to the people like St. Francis Xavier—let them be pelted and trampled on—and I will own that they can do what we cannot. I will confess that they are our betters far. I will (though I could not on that ground join them), I *would* gladly incur their reproach. This is to be Catholics —this is to secure triumph. Let them use the proper arms of the Church, and they will prove that they are the Church by using them."

Although Newman was unaware of it, Phillipps could claim with more personal knowledge than almost anybody else, that there were already Catholic priests in England, introduced by his personal persuasion, who were already engaged in just those works of faith and charity in face of ridicule and persecution which Newman demanded. Newman admitted at once that, while "I can feel nothing but distrust and aversion towards those who offer peace yet carry on war," he felt grateful to Ambrose Phillipps because " *He* has taken the opposite course and in taking it has exposed himself to obloquy from those whom he is opposing." " What a day it will be," he continued, " if God ever raises up holy men, Bernards or Borromeos, in their communion. But even if this were done, difficulties would not be at an end, though I think Sanctity being secured, everything would ultimately follow."

It would be a sin, he was deeply convinced, " for any of us to *leave* our Church. We must make our Church move." The statement continued with detailed complaints of the " sadly degenerate state of Rome," and it concluded with the general warning, " Their success rests with themselves. The English never will be favourably inclined to a plotting intriguing party, but faith and holiness are irresistible." Phillipps replied at length, and in regard to the complaint concerning " the tone of their periodical publications," he made a startling disavowal of some of Wiseman's controversial writings. " I have effected a stoppage of the circulation of Dr. Wiseman's Tracts against the High Church claims in this neighbourhood," he told Bloxam. " I have no right to judge a Bishop, but I confess I thought the publication of those Tracts ill timed from the first moment I heard of them, and I was not aware till a few days ago that any had been circulated hereabouts ; for the future it is stopped. I should deem it ungrateful to circulate such things now, after the glorious vindication of the Pope of Rome from the absurd charge of his being the anti-Christ which appeared in the last No. but one of the *British Critick*."

Although Newman's extremely low opinion of the English Catholics was certainly not shared by Phillipps, it was among his Continental friends he had been most impressed by the evidence of real holiness. " I sympathise with Mr. Pusey," Phillipps replied [1] for Newman's information, " not because I think we have no Men like him in our Church, but because I think he is so like the Men in our Church. If Mr. Newman was acquainted with such Ecclesiasticks of our communion as the late Monseigneur Queslen, Archbishop of Paris, as the present Archbishop of Bordeaux, as de Bonald, the present Archbishop of Lyons, as

[1] *Life of Ambrose Phillipps*, I, p. 211.

Dr. Forbin Jansen, the present Bishop of Nancy, as a multitude of other saintly prelates whom I have had the consolation of knowing on the Continent, or even as my own immediate superior, the Rt. Rev. Dr. Walsh, V.A. of the central District, he would know that we have some Men amongst not only our Clergy but even our *Bishops* possessed of a spirit akin to that of Dr. Pusey." As for " the *political* connexion between the Irish R. Catholick body and the English Dissenting body," Phillipps wished Newman to know that he entirely agreed in regretting it. He would use any influence he had among the English Catholics to discourage it. But " let Mr. Newman in return endeavour to break up the political connexion between the High Church Party in England and the Manichean Orangemen in Ireland."

Wiseman's relations with Phillipps were still intimate, and it is unlikely that Phillipps failed to inform him that he had banned the circulation of some of his tracts in his own neighbourhood. He showed Newman's communications to Wiseman, and Wiseman soon replied with a public letter to Newman on the various points which he had raised. But Newman's position was becoming extremely delicate at Oxford, and he had no desire to be drawn into further direct correspondence with these Catholics who were angling for his soul. He had just published Tract 90 as a fully considered statement of the relations between Anglican and Roman belief, and Bloxam wrote from Oxford to Phillipps in March saying that their attention was absorbed by the excitement which the Tract had aroused. " There is a heavy storm brooding over us ; it is difficult to foretell how it will terminate ; certainly we are not in a state at the present time to consider calmly your propositions, however some of us may wish and pray for the Reunion of the Churches. At the present time such a proposal on your side, if supposed to be connected in any way with Oxford, would materially diminish, in my humble opinion, the hope of future success."

The storm over Tract 90 resulted in the immediate discontinuance of the series. Newman openly admitted its authorship, and in a public letter to Canon Jelf took steps to reply to various charges of Roman leanings. Bloxam sent a copy of the letter to Phillipps, who immediately expressed his strong objection to various statements it contained. But Newman replied to his criticisms only with a very brief letter, acknowledging that Phillipps was " full of earnestness and charity," but avoiding any detailed argument. The time for Phillipps to visit Oxford was fast approaching, but the storm over Tract 90 had made all further approaches impossible. Newman now wrote direct to Phillipps from Oriel on April 8 : " Your letter just received is kind far above my deserts ; but, I assure you, you do but do me justice when you imply that the unity of the Church Catholic is near my heart. Only, I do not see any prospect of it within our time, and I despair of it being effected without great sacrifices on all hands. Were the Roman Church in Ireland different from what it is, one immense stumbling block would be removed. . . . You have no cause to be surprised at the discontinuance of the Tracts. We feel no misgivings about it whatever, as if the cause of what we hold to be Catholic truth would suffer thereby. . . . No stopping of the Tracts can, humanly speaking, stop the spread of opinions which they have inculcated. One is apt to be sanguine, but I trust that the fire is kindled, and will make progress even though the original torch is extinguished. But you will observe that it is *not* extinguished. The Tracts are not *suppressed*. . . . I am afraid that in one respect you may be disappointed, if you will allow me to say it. It is my trust, though I must not be too sanguine, that we shall not have individual members of our communion going over to yours. What one's duty would be *under other circumstances*—what one's duty ten or twenty years ago—I cannot say ; but I do think that there is less of private judgment in going with one's Church than in leaving it. I can earnestly desire a union between my Church and yours ; I cannot listen to the thought of your being joined by individuals among us."

A week later Newman wrote again to acknowledge another letter in which Phillipps had assured him of Dr. Wiseman's prayers. He was determined to remove any slightest hope that he might be a party to negotiations, or that he believed that they should be attempted. " I cannot help writing at once for another reason.

I am very anxious lest you should be entertaining sanguine hopes in which you may be disappointed. You overrate our exertions, our influence, our tendencies. We are but a few, and we are what we are. Many times before now in the course of the last 300 years has a hope of concord arisen among Christians, but as yet it has ever come to nothing. When was a great schism ever healed? Why should ours cease, if that between the East and West has continued so long? And if a growth in sanctity be the necessary condition of it in both parties, what stipulation can be more costly, more hopeless? No, I feel that both parties must resign themselves to dying in their estrangement; but that is no reason why they should not, though they be a few against many, both pray and labour against it."

Newman could not have expressed himself more plainly. But Phillipps, though deeply disappointed, was still convinced that the reunion of both Churches was fast approaching. He wrote a long letter to Lord Shrewsbury in Rome, urging him to use his influence there to prevent any move which might discourage the Oxford men. He drew attention to a letter from one of their number which he had succeeded in publishing, after it had been translated by Bloxam, in Louis Veuillot's *Univers*. "You will see from it that the leading Men in the Anglican Church are determined to reunite their Church in the Holy See. But in order to effect this a little time is required. The Archbishop of Canterbury and the Bishop of Oxford approve of the design, but *as yet* the other Bishops stand out, and some of them violently: to gain them requires immense management: they already see that they cannot much longer resist the movement, still they have great prejudices, and to remove these is a most laborious task. . . . Meanwhile I beseech you to give us all the assistance you can. Urge at Rome the necessity of immense prudence and forbearance, to do everything to *encourage*, nothing to *damp :* not to call upon these Men to quit their communion to join ours, but to proceed on courageously with our holy and glorious intention of reconciling their CHURCH to OURS : remember this involves the reconciliation of the *kingdom*, of the *aristocracy* with all its wealth and power, of the

Nation. A false step would spoil all, would produce a protestant reaction, and would defeat the hopes of the Holy See for another century. . . . Urge upon all the necessity of doing everything to forward matters *gently* and not *precipitately*."

After his visit to Oxford had been prevented, Phillipps continued his correspondence with Bloxam and Bernard Smith. His letters were usually passed on to Newman, and in June Newman felt compelled to write [1] once more in firm discouragement. " I must ask your leave to repeat on this occasion most distinctly that I cannot be a party to any agitation ; but mean to remain quiet in my own place, and to do all I can to make others take the same course. This I conceive to be my simple duty ; but over and above this paramount consideration I believe it to be the wisest and most expedient course for the eventual unity of the Church Catholic. I will not attempt to reap before the sowing ; I will not set my teeth on edge with sour grapes. I know it is quite within the range of possibilities that one or another of our members should go over to your communion ; though, I trust, it will not be the case as regards the individuals you specify. However, if such an event were to happen it would be a greater misfortune to you than a grief to us. If there is any one thing calculated more than another to extinguish all hope of a better understanding between Rome and England, by discrediting us with our own people and rendering us suspicious of yourselves, it would be the conversion by you of some of our members. If your friends wish to put a gulf between themselves and us let them make converts ; but not else.

" Some months since, I ventured to say in a letter to Mr. Bloxam, which was sent to you, that I felt it a painful duty to keep aloof from all Roman Catholics, however much to be respected personally, who came with the intention of opening negotiations for the union of the Churches ; when you now urge us to petition our Bishops for a union, and lay down the terms, this, I conceive, *is* very like an act of negotiation."

Newman's letters had been so emphatic that Wiseman could

[1] *Life of Ambrose Phillipps*, I, p. 228.

not entertain any hopes of the friendly relations which he had desired. Moreover, it had been intimated to him very plainly that Newman disliked some of his controversial writings, and felt no special tenderness towards him personally. So Wiseman prudently refrained from taking advantage of their previous acquaintance in Rome. When he wrote his public letter to Newman, in reply to Newman's explanatory letter to Canon Jelf, he said openly that he would not presume upon that passing acquaintance, but was actuated only by the " earnest anxiety to convince " a man who had shown so much candour and sincerity. Newman declined to answer Wiseman's letter, and a wall of silence seemed to have arisen between Oxford and Oscott. Only through Phillipps and the eccentric Pugin was it possible to retain contact with what was being thought and said. But the warmth of Wiseman's feelings towards the " Oxford men " is shown in the letter which he wrote to Phillipps at the beginning of April, while Phillipps still hoped to pay his visit to Oxford. " Let us have an influx of new blood," Wiseman wrote [1] from Oscott ; " let us have even a small number of such men as write in the Tracts, so imbued with the spirit of the early Church, so desirous to revive the spirit of the ancient Fathers—men who have learnt to teach from St. Augustine, to preach from St. Chrysostom, and to feel from St. Bernard : let even a few such men, with the high clerical feeling which I believe them to possess, enter fully into the spirit of the Catholic religion, and we shall be speedily reformed, and England quickly converted. I am ready to acknowledge that in all things, except the happiness of possessing the truth, and being in communion with God's true Church, and enjoying the advantages and blessings that flow thence, we are their inferiors. It is not to you that I say this for the first time. I have long said it to those about me—that if the Oxford Divines entered the Church, we must be ready to fall into the shade, and take up our position in the background. I willingly say to any of them ' *Me oportet minui.*' I will willingly yield to them place and honour, if God's good service require it, I will be a co-operator under the greater zeal and abilities of a new leader."

[1] *Life of Wiseman*, I, p. 385.

The ardent generosity of Wiseman's attitude was scarcely even discouraged by Newman's determined refusal to enter into any conversations or correspondence. Newman not only refused friendly intercourse and discussion. He was still using all his powers of persuasion to restrain others from moving in the direction of Rome. One chief object of his writings was to prove that the Roman Church had no claims to allegiance in England and was definitely in error. It is not surprising that the older Catholics had no patience with what they regarded as the mistaken sentimentalism of Wiseman's attitude. They believed that he was not only condoning but encouraging open antagonism to the Catholic Church. So far as the Tractarians were concerned, they were disgusted by what seemed to be an attempt on their part to have the best of both worlds, by claiming that the Thirty-nine Articles were susceptible of a Catholic interpretation, although everybody knew that they were not so interpreted by the mass of Protestants. Inevitably, this twisting of doctrine to give it a meaning which had for centuries been denied, had the appearance of an insincere and unworthy attempt to retain the material advantages of the Anglican ministry without facing the necessity of open revolt. Some of the older Catholics were already writing openly in this sense. Mr. Rathbone's pamphlet entitled " Are the Puseyites sincere ? " was only one of similar outbursts which imputed dishonest motives to the Oxford men. More disturbing to Wiseman was a letter from Dr. Lingard, his old friend and former schoolmaster at Ushaw, who reminded him of the false hopes that had been raised in the time of Laud, and recalled the long series of similar disappointments among Catholics who had hoped vainly for a return to Catholic orthodoxy after the Reformation. But Wiseman refused to abandon hope. While doing all in his power to encourage individual conversions, he certainly did hope for the secession of large numbers if the leading men could be won over. But he never accepted the view of Ambrose Phillipps that individual conversions should be discouraged, either to avoid annoying Newman or in order that the leaven might work more strongly in the Established Church, until the time was ripe for a spontaneous and general reunion with Rome. Wiseman's attitude on this matter was made plain in a letter [1] which he wrote to Dr. Russell, the President of Maynooth, who was one of the very few who showed genuine sympathy with his efforts :

" I can assure you that what appears on the surface is nothing to what is working in the deep ; and the Catholic movement is not merely as some imagine, in the outward forms and phrases adopted by the Tractarians, but is in their hearts and desire. They are every day becoming more and more disgusted with Anglicanism, its barrenness, its shallowness, and its ' stammering ' teaching. Their advance is so steady, regular and unanimous, that one of two things must follow : either they will bring or push on their Church with them, or they will leave her behind. The first is their great object ; the second may be their gain. If their Church repel them and attempt to damp their efforts, they will abandon her, for their hearts have allowed Catholicism to take too deep a root in them for it to be plucked up by the *telum imbelle sine ictu* of Anglo-episcopal authority. In the meantime many of them are as yet terribly in the dark as to their *individual* duty, in their present state of feeling ; and it seems to me that, if consulted by any *one* as to what *he* should do, I should of course tell him to go forth from his father's house and kindred and come into the land which God's grace shows him, by *at once* yielding to his convictions and securing his own salvation. But when (as in every case that I as yet know of them) they have not been so far enlightened by faith and grace as to feel that it is a risk to their own salvation to remain united to the Anglican Church, though they consider it a duty of that Church to bring itself into communion with the Catholic Church, all we can do is to push them forward in their view so as to make them diffuse it in every direction, and to invite them towards us rather than to repulse them, as some seem inclined to do. I should like to see them become Catholics at once and one by one ; but, if they will not do that, I should be sorry to check them in their present course.

" Let me entreat you to join me in my determination to devote

[1] *Life of Wiseman*, I, pp. 387-388.

my life and all the little energy and power that God has given me to forward this Divine work. Get prayers on every side for it : inspire as strong an interest as possible in the hearts of the young clergy of Ireland for the reunion of this country to the Catholic Church. Above all things, do your utmost to quell violent political feeling. What a mortification before God will it be to any of us if we be found in the end to have been thwarting *His* work by our violence, our political antipathies, or even our negligence."

Meanwhile he could only wait and continue to observe from a distance that gradual progress towards Rome, which he had recognised even in the disappointment of Hurrell Froude and Newman when they had visited him at Rome eight years before. His duties at the College kept him fully occupied, and as Bishop Walsh's coadjutor he was involved in all the plans for expansion and for new church building in the Central District, with its rapidly growing towns and centres of industry. More than ever he believed in the necessity of introducing religious orders, to supplement the activities of the secular clergy, whose hands were more than full in their local missions. He had kept in touch with Father Dominic Barberi since his departure for Belgium, and he lost no time in assisting his desire to make a first foundation in England. Father Gentili of the Rosminians had been so successful at Prior Park that Bishop Baines found that his authority in the College was being undermined. Many of his clergy had expressed the desire to join the Rosminian Institute, and the Bishop decided that he must assert himself by removing Gentili from the College and placing him in charge of other work outside it. His superior was not satisfied, and recalled Gentili to Rome, but Phillipps was so distressed at his departure that he arranged for his return. Having built three churches in his own neighbourhood which were virtually under his control, Phillipps decided to remedy matters by bringing Father Gentili to Garendon as his personal chaplain so that he could make a start from there. However much the old Catholics might dislike the importation of foreign missionaries, Gentili could at least speak English fluently, and he showed remarkable courage in face of public insults when he preached in the open. Going outside the villages immediately served from Grace Dieu, Whitwick and the abbey, Phillipps got him to preach publicly among the labourers in and around Shepshed. He hired a hall for him at Osgathorpe, where he " gave instruction three times a week and preached in the open air." [1] Two schools were also opened at Osgathorpe, one for Sundays and one for weekdays. Father Gentili's success in making converts was so rapid that Protestant opposition was soon organised. At Shepshed he was pelted with mud and came home covered with filth. He had been wearing his religious habit openly, as the Trappist monks also had been doing for some years. At Osgathorpe a demonstration was organised at which Gentili's effigy, dressed in robes like his, was paraded through the streets and then set on fire and thrown into the river. But Gentili went back next day, treating the demonstration as a joke, and continued his preaching. Soon afterwards he vindicated the right to hold a Catholic procession by leading his assistants and the school children from the chapel at Grace Dieu to Osgathorpe singing litanies as they went.

In the meantime Phillipps had been hastening preparations for Dominic Barberi also. Wiseman, as coadjutor bishop, was now sponsoring his earlier invitation, and went specially to Belgium to see Father Dominic. He had got Bishop Walsh to agree that the Passionists were to take over a house and mission at Aston Hall, near Lord Shrewsbury's home. There had been difficulty in persuading the priest who was there to give up the house, and a temporary delay resulted, but Dominic Barberi was to come over early in November and prospect. He was in Boulogne, where his new foundation was now firmly started, and on the day before his journey to England he climbed the tower of the new rebuilt cathedral [2] to catch a glimpse of the English coast. In writing to his General in Rome, he announced that, for the first time, he had been obliged to discard his Passionist's habit. " I am dressed in secular clothing. If you only saw me you would smile. But I think that God recognises me well enough in these garments."

[1] *Life of Ambrose Phillipps,* I, p. 110.
[2] *Dominic Barberi in England,* by Urban Young, C.P., p. 29.

In November he arrived in London and went on to Oscott, only to find that Wiseman urged him *pro bono pacis* that he had better not visit the house intended for him until it had been vacated.

He stayed for some months at Oscott, learning English diligently and observing all that he could of conditions in England. The students were accustomed to many strange visitors whom Wiseman brought to the College, but Father Dominic was one of the strangest they had seen. One of them, who afterwards became Wiseman's Vicar-General at Westminster as Mgr. Searle, has left his impressions of Barberi at this time.[1] "He had an eagle eye ; could blend sarcasm and irony in the most simple and apparently harmless observation ; his grave demeanour when he spoke of heaven made him seem compound of all that was humble and sublime in human nature. When he came to see us in recreation he amused us immensely. When we went to speak to him in confession, or to have our vocations decided, we came away in admiration ; he possessed marvellous sway over us all, and could do what he liked with us."

His Passionist superiors had impressed on him that the foundation in England should not be involved in taking over parochial duties, but Wiseman had said this would be quite impossible.[2] "He explained, among other points, that wherever a Catholic priest is stationed in England at present the Protestants around come in numbers for instruction, like bees to their hive ! So that in any case, apart from hereditary Catholics, a parish very soon grows up." That statement had reflected Wiseman's sanguine temperament, but there was certainly evidence to support it in the districts where Lord Shrewsbury and Phillipps had been building churches. Dominic Barberi went on to Grace Dieu to stay with Phillipps, and found Father Gentili there at work already. He records a remarkable instance [3] of the effect which Gentili was already producing. "On that occasion a poor Protestant walked seven miles to hear Father Gentili preach ! More than that, he stayed on all day in the Church, shivering with cold, and only a

[1] *Life of Dominic Barberi,* p. 32.
[2] *Dominic Barberi in England,* p. 31.   [3] *Ibid.,* p. 31.

piece of bread in his pocket, for the sole purpose of trying to persuade Gentili to go and preach in his own town. At the same time he offered the priest his own house as a place for meetings, and so on. The poor missioner could not make him any promise, as he was already fully occupied in towns and villages nearby. And be it noted that, in the town from which this Protestant came, there is not a single Catholic! Poor people—to make them Catholics all they want is someone to instruct them with combined zeal and charity. Ah! If there were only many good missioners! But the labourers are few."

Dominic Barberi had to go back to Boulogne, to wait for nearly a whole year more. But he had seen at Garendon that a religious revival in England was already in progress. It was, in fact, much more widespread than he could have imagined from his concentration upon the Tractarians at Oxford. Phillipps himself, in a letter [1] to Shrewsbury in January 1841, was reporting that although he certainly regarded " the Catholick movement at Oxford as the brightest symptom of England's re-conversion," he could thank God that it was not the only one. " There is a general movement among the lower classes, which is most consoling." All over the Midland District during the previous Christmas season there had been great numbers of individual conversions. In his own neighbourhood around Garendon " during the octave of Christmas our good Father Gentili received sixty-seven most promising and interesting converts, forty-three of whom in one body made their solemn profession of Catholick Faith after the third High Mass on Christmas Day itself. The whole of these conversions have been from the single little town of Shepshed, which contains a population of more than four thousand souls, and is peculiarly interesting to me, as they are almost entirely the tenants of this estate. Since the reception of these, there has been such a movement, such a demand for Catholick instruction amongst the whole population, that Father Gentili ventures to hope that after a few months we may count our converts even by thousands." At Whitwick likewise there had been sixteen converts received on Christmas Day, and

[1] *Life of Ambrose Phillipps,* I, p. 107.

others were under instruction, and the figures for Loughborough was still larger. In these three missions alone Grace Dieu, Loughborough and Whitwick, fully two hundred Protestants had become Catholics since the previous October. From Leicester, Derby, Hinckley, Atherstone and other places not far away he had received similar most encouraging reports " whilst scarcely a week passes without isolated straggling conversions taking place in the intermediate villages, which again become the focus of a new colony." They had established new missionary stations in several of the nearby villages, and Father Gentili was preaching at them regularly. Once again Lord Shrewsbury came forward to build another little church, guaranteeing the interest on a loan of £500 from Bishop Wiseman so that a chapel could be erected at Shepshed. Phillipps made himself personally responsible for the loan, and Pugin was commissioned to build a chapel at the lowest possible cost. By the end of 1842 he was able to tell[1] Lord Shrewsbury that " Thank God we have now more than 1000 Converts in our own villages ! and every day they are becoming more and more organised."

Meanwhile the monastery had become a centre of attraction in Leicestershire, to an extent far beyond what Phillipps had imagined. " It is perfectly astonishing what crowds of people come to see the monastery from all parts of England," he wrote[2] to Lord Shrewsbury in 1842. " The other day *again* more than 300 visitors were counted and no less than 50 carriages. The Church is generally crowded at the hours of Nones and Vespers, by persons who come through curiosity. I believe this Monastery will do more good than any mission."

[1] *Life of Ambrose Phillipps,* I, p. 109. [2] *Ibid.,* p. 81.

CHAPTER IX

TRIALS AND DIFFICULTIES

WISEMAN had much to learn, and many disillusionments to face, in the years after his triumphal arrival at Oscott. As agent for the English bishops in Rome, he had been aware of the disagreements among them on many matters, and that Bishop Walsh had often been in opposition to the other three. As Bishop Walsh's coadjutor at Oscott, he encountered the full force of that opposition, and it was to some extent increased by suspicions of his own views after so many years absence from England. His zeal for reforms, and his desire to introduce many practices which were general in Catholic countries but had fallen into disuse in England during the centuries of persecution, were construed as criticism of the old Catholics. This distrust of his attitude and dislike for his foreign training was intensified by his undisguised sympathy with the Tractarians and his association with Phillipps and Pugin and Father George Spencer. But Bishop Walsh had definite plans and persisted bravely with them. Moreover, he had practical support of a kind which was very difficult to obtain elsewhere, in the generosity of Lord Shrewsbury and Phillipps and their friends. He did not share the dislike of Bishop Baines and some of the other bishops for the religious orders, and he was willing to receive assistance from foreign missionaries. He had welcomed the arrival of Father Gentili in his Central District when he came back to England under the patronage of Ambrose Phillipps, and he was prepared to welcome the Passionists also if they could see their way to establish an English foundation. In early August 1841, he accompanied Wiseman to Brussels to meet Father Dominic Barberi and conclude the arrangements for his coming to England. By early October everything had been settled, and Father Dominic went straight to Oscott, to remain there for some little time until the house at Aston was vacant. The weeks grew into months, but at last in

February 1842, he was able to write to his General from his new home, with spacious grounds and a church with a small congregation.

During his stay at Oscott Father Dominic had learnt to speak English with reasonable fluency, though with a marked foreign accent, before he went to Aston. He caused suppressed laughter in his new church on the first Sunday there, by reading the English prayers after Mass, and he was in tears as he returned to the sacristy.[1] But he had come prepared for ridicule and hostility, and he would make no concessions to avoid it. He wore sandals, as well as the Passionist robes, with the large emblem of the Sacred Heart sewn on his tunic. Within a few weeks of his arrival he began giving his first mission, and by Good Friday he had received his first convert. Before long he had managed to hire a room in Stone also, where he could say Mass and preach in public, and crowds gathered most surprisingly. " The concourse of people is immense," he wrote,[2] " especially in the evening when they come to hear the controversial lectures. The other evening there must have been four to five hundred Protestants listening to me with the closest attention. About fifteen presented themselves for instruction." The Protestant clergy began to organise services and meetings at the same hours so as to withdraw people from him. " They have started house to house visiting with the sole object of exhorting the people not to come to me. They have opened a new church close to our own and placed a new minister in charge. But not one of them has come face to face with me personally. I hear that they are afraid and have some idea that I am a very learned person."

But his success was obtained only at the cost of constant personal insults and humiliation. " In all things beginnings are difficult," he wrote [3] to his General. " I am seeking to prepare the way for our successors. So far as I am concerned, I foresee that my life will always be led amid difficulties and trials of every description. Of these, the most terrible can be known to God alone." Some

[1] *Life of Barberi*, p. 202.
[2] *Dominic Barberi in England*, p. 82.   [3] *Ibid.*, p. 86.

idea of these sufferings may be gathered from the description of a contemporary who writes : [1] "Hell was let loose against him ; the Protestants, with their ministers in the forefront, rose in arms and declared implacable war. Every conceivable weapon was used in the diabolical warfare : sermons, commands, threats, satire, calumny, plots, derisions, insults, contumely and even blows. How he escaped with his life was a miracle. . . . Among the epithets hurled at him were : the stuttering Papist, Father Demonio, etc., etc. He was made the laughing stock of Stone. He used to walk to the Crown Inn, leaving Aston before six in the morning. As the people saw him in the distance cries of ' Here is the Demon— the Demon ' arose on every side. The very children joined in the mad onslaught. As he entered the town itself the crowds rushed out to gape at and insult him as if he was a savage wild beast. Hat in hand and in perfect calm he walked slowly along bowing to all and with a kind word for all. Behind him surged a rabble of all the local wastrels, from whose mouths came words of ribald and unrepeatable insult. . . . Stones and mud rained upon him. Once at a later time he was asked how he had got the terrible scar on his forehead. It was, as he at last confessed, caused by a violent blow from a stone used as a weapon. Once a huge beam hurtled by his head, missing him by inches." Only heroic fortitude could have endured it, and Dominic Barberi felt every humiliation to the full. "Crosses and difficulties multiply so quickly," he wrote [2] to a friend in Italy, "and seem so endless that I felt myself at the last extremity and was about to go back to Italy. God has assisted me up to this, and I hope He will continue to do so. Ah my God, how much I have to suffer. Although I have been preparing myself for imaginary trials for twenty-eight years, I find that I was not half well enough prepared for the dire reality. The will of God alone keeps me up." Soon after he confided to another friend : "My God, for what distress and sorrow you reserved me. I spent so many years before coming to this Island preparing myself at all times for suffering. And now it seems to me that if I had ever foreseen all that awaited me I should never have had the courage

---

[1] *Life of Barberi*, p. 207.   [2] *Ibid.*, p. 213.

to step on board ship. Such sufferings, and of every kind too, would be too much for a giant. Last Sunday I broke down and wept bitterly. I can do no more. The cross is too heavy. My God, if you intend to increase it you must increase my strength too."

Through all his trials and humiliations his chief consolation was the knowledge that he had gained the confidence of at least one of Newman's close friends at Oxford. Dalgairns, a young fellow of Magdalen, had sent to the *Univers* in Paris a French translation of a letter composed by W. G. Ward, explaining the attitude of the Tractarians, which was published in April 1841. Dominic Barberi had read it with great emotion, and had at once composed a long reply while he was still in Belgium. Its length was that of a pamphlet [1] rather than a letter, and it covered most of the ground in dispute with a sustained argument, combined with earnest and most sympathetic appeal. Dalgairns showed the reply to Newman, who was impressed by it, and said [2] that the author must be " a very sharp, clever man." George Spencer had sent copies of it to his Oxford friends, and Bloxam answered with a reply so appreciative that Spencer could write,[3] " you have already begun your work for us by this correspondence with Oxford." The correspondence continued more or less regularly after Father Dominic's arrival in England ; and in the years when Newman retired to complete seclusion at Littlemore, and all direct access to him and his friends was impossible for Wiseman and his English associates, Dominic Barberi was almost alone in retaining contact with them. He was working incessantly at Alton, and was already planning to build a new church at Stone, while he continued to say Mass there in the inn. But progress was very slow, and the opposition he aroused was overpowering. " Up to date I have received seventy-five Protestants into the Church," he wrote [4] in July 1843, " including adults and children. I have between twenty and thirty under instruction. If we could only build the new church I feel sure this

[1] See Appendix A, *Life of Barberi*, pp. 357-391.
[2] *Life of Barberi*, p. 186.   [3] *Ibid.*, p. 188.
[4] *Dominic Barberi in England*, p. 89.

number would be greatly increased. The obstacles are many. The greatest is the selfishness, the self-seeking, against which we have to contend unceasingly. I mean, not only the selfishness and self love of the Protestants, but of very many Catholics, too. And yet, some of the latter are most fervent and give me much help, poor as they are. Our alms-giving gives much edification, and causes much astonishment too, among the Protestants, who cannot understand how people who are so poor themselves can give so much alms. *Melius est dare quam recipere*. The ministers keep on declaiming against me but do not gain much credence." By November he could report to his General that " the new chapel and school at Stone are almost finished, but not paid for. When the building is opened we shall be able to do much more than we have done up to now. The ministers are very angry and threaten to pull down the Chapel. As regards the Protestant people, some are on the side of the ministers, others are indifferent. To make Catholics is not easy for the good reason that they have to be made Christians first, and that is precisely the difficulty. . . . Insults and mockery of every description are our lot, and conversions are few."

Wiseman's hopes had run high after the storm over Tract 90, but Newman had withdrawn into complete silence and was more than ever careful to avoid giving any impression of further advance towards Rome. Wiseman had been particularly anxious to reassure him concerning O'Connell, and he wrote to him, when an opportunity offered, to give evidence that O'Connell was less aggressive than he had appeared to be. Newman replied expressing gratification at what he was told, but he took occasion to raise another matter which upset Wiseman gravely. " I received a most distressing letter from Newman," he wrote [1] to Phillipps, " which has thrown me on my back and painfully dispirited me ; so that I have kept back a long letter which I had written to Cardinal Mai, for fear I may be myself deceived and may be misguiding the Holy See." Newman had in his letter referred quite gratuitously to the Catholic devotions to Our Lady, and had expressed " his

[1] *Life of Wiseman*, I, pp. 392-393.

regret that I should have attempted to vindicate the invocations of the B.V. used in the Church—and augurs it as a bad omen that we do not give them up. Now really if his expectation was that the Church, or that we, should give up our tender and confident devotion towards the Holy Mother of God, or that the least of her pastors would join (on his private judgment) with Mr. Palmer in condemning expressions sanctioned and approved by her Pontiffs, how high indeed must be his demands of condescension before we can hope for reunion." Wiseman had even hoped to meet the Oxford leaders when he was going there to administer confirmation in the summer after the Tracts were discontinued. But Bloxam conveyed clearly that it would be a mistake. " I own," wrote [1] Wiseman to Phillipps, " that I sometimes am inclined to feel like a man trying to reach the shore and beaten back by a wave every time he fancies he has secured his footing or caught hold of something that will help him."

Bloxam was by nature so cautious and timid that Newman could rely absolutely on his avoiding any step that might compromise the Oxford men. He had postponed the visit which had been arranged for Ambrose Phillipps at Easter, because of the excitement over Tract 90, and he had tactfully informed Phillipps that a meeting between Wiseman and Newman during his stay in Oxford must be declined for " motives that will easily suggest themselves to you." But he had shown his personal friendliness by promising that he would one day accompany Phillipps on a visit to Wiseman at Oscott. And after an interval of some months he arranged that Phillipps should come to Oxford during Newman's absence in London. He took Phillipps to see various churches [2] where the ritualists had already introduced startling innovations— " fitted up in a very Catholick way with large candelabra in front of the altars and great wax tapers besides 2 candlesticks upon the Altars themselves and the cross, flowers, etc." But what delighted him most, in his report to his wife, was to discover that " they have lately printed (but not published) a beautiful translation of

---

[1] *Life of Wiseman*, I, p. 393.

[2] *Life of Ambrose Phillipps*, I, p. 248.

the Roman Breviary in English, with everything precisely as it is in the Latin. The *Hail Mary* full length, the *Confiteor*, the *Salve Regina, Sancta Maria succurre miseris*, etc., with not an expression changed!!! Is not this wonderful? Nothing can be more determined than they are to *reunite their Church* to the Catholick : but they will not hear of individuals joining us from *them*, though they wish *us* to convert as many *dissenters* as possible ; and they are very glad to hear of Dr. Gentili's doings in that way—even I think they do not object to our converting such of the Church of England as do not hold Catholick views, but they deprecate any noise about it, and above all, they deprecate anything like warfare against the Church of England herself. . . . Many here would like to come to an understanding *with the Pope at once*, that so they might be in active communion with him, and yet remain in the Church of England to labour for the reconciliation of their whole Church. This is to be taken into solemn consideration ; I proposed to them last night that Father Rosmini should come to England and visit Oxford with me with a view to conveying their sentiments to the Pope himself. The proposition was well received ; but nothing is settled, nor will be yet. They think that the Bishop of Oxford may possibly come into it ; it is to be proposed to him. We must not, however, expect much just yet."

In his enthusiasm he reported this fantastic proposal fully to Wiseman, who was so rejoiced that he promised to inform the Pope through Cardinal Mai. But Wiseman had misgivings[1] at assuming " the responsibility of becoming (as I at the same time earnestly desire to become) the organ of intercourse between the Holy See and our Oxford friends." He felt the need for " clear and distinct instructions, such as I feel cannot be satisfactorily given except on full explanations, and by word of mouth. Again I should like something to emanate from the Pope towards encouraging our views—recommending mildness, prayer, calling on the Bishops for reforms, etc., and particularly checking all alliance with Dissenters." But Wiseman was never free from doubts as to Newman's real intentions. In one letter[2] to Phillipps he wrote

---

[1] *Life of Ambrose Phillipps,* I, p. 255.   [2] *Ibid.,* p. 288.

bluntly, " I think Mr. Newman is a timid man, and one who looks forward to reunion as a mere contingency." Still less did he agree with Phillipps in thinking that there should be any slackening in the attempt to promote individual conversions. He had heard from the Catholic priest in Oxford, Mr. Newsham, that [1] " the undergraduates are constantly coming to him privately, and he says he knows about forty who are ready to go abroad to study for the Church. If this should prove correct, who would venture to repel them or tell them to stay where they are ? I should tremble for myself were I to think of it. The Catholic doctrine is that each one must take care first of *his own soul* and not peril that for any consideration of good to others. Must they remain without sacraments, without active communion with the Church Catholic on the ground that, through their remaining in schism, a future generation may be brought to unity ? I of course do not speak of such as Mr. Newman or Bloxam, who feel convinced that they are safe in their present position ; but only of such as have had their conviction shaken and are impelled by conscience to make this enquiry. Our duty seems to enjoin two things ; first, with the latter class, we must be open and candid and ready to receive them and encourage them to come, when, where, and how grace calls them, be they one or be they a thousand. Second, with respect to the former, we must be most careful not to encourage them with the idea that they are justified in remaining in a state of schism for any consideration, although we may not feel it our duty to urge them forward faster than their own convictions carry them. These, if sincere, will justify them before God, but we must be on our guard against actively encouraging them, we may be running a great risk."

Direct contact with the Oxford men was what Wiseman desired most, and Phillipps had at last succeeded in bringing it about. He was overjoyed at hearing that Bloxam had agreed to visit Oscott, and he hoped that others of the group would accompany him. " I think Mr. Bernard Smith's observations very true," he wrote,[2] " that his friends at Oxford all speak and think of

[1] *Life of Ambrose Phillipps,* I, p. 287.   [2] *Life of Wiseman,* I, p. 394.

Catholic practices and institutions as things past or possible, not as things actually existing and acting." The visit took place, and was soon followed by others with startling result. R. W. Sibthorpe, a fellow of Magdalen, went to Oscott soon after, and decided to become a Catholic before he returned. A few months later he was confirmed at Grace Dieu, where Ward and Oakeley and others of the Movement had also been paying visits to Ambrose Phillipps.

Bishop Griffiths of the London District had been aware of Wiseman's sympathy for the Tractarians for some years before his return to England, and he differed strongly from Wiseman's attitude. He also feared, not altogether without reason, that Wiseman was influencing the Pope against the English bishops by creating an impression that they were neglecting a great opportunity to promote conversions among the Anglicans. It was scarcely a mere coincidence that when he contributed a foreword to the annual *Catholic Directory* for 1841, within a few months after Wiseman's arrival at Oscott, he alluded more or less openly to the tendencies then at work in Oxford. "At their first separation," he wrote, "some leaders of schisms have denied a greater number of revealed truths, whilst others have rejected only a few. In their progress they have generally increased the number of their errors, and have been again divided into other branches, as hostile to each other as to the Catholic Church, which they had deserted. As time has rolled on we occasionally find them acknowledging some truths which they had formerly rejected as errors, and approaching in particular tenets nearer to the true Church which they had abandoned ; but scarcely shall we find a body of schismatics returning with sincerity to the true faith." This provocative statement was very soon brought to the notice of the Pope, when he had received a petition sent to him by most of the London clergy. In his reply the Pope referred to it most forcibly.[1] "For in truth . . . no belief is more deadly," he wrote, "none can prevail among you more likely to quench the admirable zeal for church building, than that maintained recently by your Bishop in the

[1] *Sequel to Catholic Emancipation*, II, p. 102.

Catholic Directory, namely that it has never been heard of that a nation torn by schism from the Holy See ever returned of its own accord to the bosom of the Church. To what can it tend, such an opinion as this, utterly unsuited to the present time, except to check and discourage that noble band of Catholics, which with such effort of soul, such generous abundance of gifts, presses forward the building of churches? What, I repeat, can be the result of your Bishop's remarks but to hold back spirits eager for conversions, spirits more lofty than his own?"

These were hard words, and the Pope proceeded to contradict the Bishop's contention in still stronger language. But Bishop Griffiths was not alone among his colleagues in believing that the Pope had been misguided, in his ignorance of real conditions in England, and that Wiseman personally was responsible for the misunderstanding. His view of the Oxford Movement was clearly expressed a year later, in a letter which he wrote [1] to the priest in charge of the German church in London, to supply information which had been requested by Wiseman's friend, Prince Hohenlohe of Munich, who afterwards became Bishop of Sardica. "Several of the clergy of the Protestant Church in England," he wrote for the Prince's information, "are endeavouring to introduce Catholic practices which the pseudo-reformers in Elizabeth's reign rejected as superstitions and to accord, even by forced interpretations, the articles of their creed with the doctrines and decisions of the Catholic Church. They reject the name of Protestant and wish themselves to be called a branch of the Catholic Church. . . . They apply opprobrious epithets, and attribute false doctrines to the Catholic Church in general, and consider the Catholics in England as schismatics because not united to the Established Church in England. The leaders of this party seem to have no leaning to the Catholic Church itself, but to wish to recover as much as they can of Catholic doctrine and practice without submission and union to the true Church. . . . The principles, however, which guide their writings necessarily vindicate Catholic practices, and remove prejudices more extensively and more effectively than the writings

[1] *Sequel to Catholic Emancipation*, II, pp. 96-97.

of the Catholic clergy, because they are read and believed as coming from the enemies of the Catholic Church. Hence there have been many conversions to the true faith ; even some of the Protestant clergy have abandoned their errors, and their worldly prospects. The numbers however are small when compared with the population. About six Protestant parsons have been converted and a few hundreds of the laity. We have sufficient reason to thank Almighty God for the removal of prejudices in some quarters, and for the recovery of many lost sheep ; but when we look at the whole population, and consider the progress of conversion, we cannot say there is a reasonable prospect of England's reunion to the Church of Christ. The population of Great Britain is nearly nineteen million ; of this number about 900,000 are Catholics. The annual number of conversions is about 2000 or 3000 ; many years therefore, without the special interposition of Divine Providence, must elapse before any great progress is made in the conversion of the country ; particularly as we annually lose many Catholics from neglect, from allowing their children through worldly motives to be educated in error, etc., etc."

These discouraging views were impressed upon Wiseman with persistence from many sources, and a less ardent temperament than his would have been discouraged from further perseverance. But he made no secret of his deep interest in the Oxford Movement. In the autumn of 1841 he published a letter to the Earl of Shrewsbury which was intended to show his sympathy openly, after the protests against Newman's Tract 90 had thrown the leaders of the movement into open conflict with the Anglican bishops. "I see an approximation," he wrote, "not merely towards individual Catholic practices or doctrines but towards Catholic union. . . . It seems to me impossible to read the works of the Oxford divines, and especially to follow them chronologically, without discovering a daily approach towards our holy Church both in doctrine and in affectionate feeling. Our saints, our popes, have become dear to them by little and little ; our rites and ceremonies, our offices, nay, our very rubrics, are precious in their eyes, far alas ! beyond what many of us consider them ; our monastic institutions, our charitable and educational provisions, have become more and more objects with them of careful study; and everything, in fine, that concerns our religion deeply interests their attention. . . . I need not ask *you* whether they ought to be met with any other feeling than sympathy, kindness and offer of hearty co-operation? Ought we to sit down coldly while such sentiments are breathed in our hearing and rise not up to bid the mourner have hope? Are we who sit in the full light to see our friends feeling their way towards us through the gloom that surrounds them, and faltering for want of an outstretched hand or turning astray for want of a directing voice; and sit on and keep silent, amusing ourselves at their patient efforts, or perhaps allow them only to hear from time to time the suppressed laughter of one who triumphs over their distress? God forbid!" "Is this a visionary idea?" he had asked earlier in the same letter, "is it merely the expression of a strong desire? I know that many will so judge it; and perhaps were I to consult my own quiet I would not venture to express it. But I will in simplicity of heart cling to hopefulness cheered, as I feel it, by so many promising appearances."

Lord Shrewsbury was the most influential supporter of Wiseman's attitude in these matters, although he reacted strongly against it from time to time. But he was now resident in Italy or other foreign countries for more than half the year. In England Wiseman had to rely chiefly upon Ambrose Phillipps, who believed so enthusiastically in the imminence of Anglican reunion with Rome that he was already half convinced that individual conversions should be discouraged unless in extreme cases. Pugin, however, was too uncompromising an individualist to hold that view, and he "had no patience with the hesitations of those who felt drawn towards Rome but dared not take the final step." But Pugin shared to the full the belief that the Oxford Movement contained more real religious feeling than was to be found among the hereditary Catholics. "Rely on it," he wrote[1] to Ambrose Phillipps in February 1841, "these Oxford men are doing more to catholicise England and to work the great *internal change of mind* than

[1] *Life of Ambrose Phillipps*, II, p. 225.

all our joint body. I consider them quite as raised up by God in the present emergency, for we seem sinking into utter degradation."

Pugin had received a great shock to his hopes of Wiseman soon after his arrival at Oscott. Wiseman had gained the reputation in Rome of being a connoisseur in ecclesiastical art, and he had a most earnest desire to improve the condition of Catholic churches and make them resemble what had won his admiration in Rome. But Pugin regarded Roman architecture as being simply pagan, and he would admit no art as being Christian unless it were pure Gothic. He was quite unprepared for any opposition from Wiseman to his campaign for introducing rood screens into the Catholic churches—and particularly in the new cathedral of Birmingham—in order to emphasise the separation of the sanctuary from the people. Within a few months of Wiseman's arrival at Oscott he was writing [1] in agony to Phillipps in December 1840: " An affair has happened in Birmingham which has gone through me like a stab. We have had a tremendous blow aimed at us, and that from the centre of our camp. Dr. Wiseman has at last shown his real sentiments by attempting to abolish the great Rood Screen after good Mr. Hardman has given £600 for its execution. I say attempted, because I immediately wrote to John Hardman to this effect, that if the screen was suppressed I should not remain architect to the church *one day* longer. You know how decidedly I act on these occasions, and you know how I can sacrifice anything to the advancement of Catholic principle. I am now resolved to live or die, stand or fall, for the *real thing* and nobly act for the real thing. Yesterday I was informed the screen was not to be allowed, but what a miserable state of things, the grand division between sacrifice and the worshippers, between priest and people to be abolished by those who should be foremost in their restoration. My dear Phillipps, we nearly *stand alone* if we except the Oxford men, for among them I find full sympathy of feeling. But the real truth is the churches I build do little or no good for want of men who know how to use them. Your observations on Derby are quite applicable to all the rest.

[1] *Life of Ambrose Phillipps*, II, p. 213.

" As you say, till the old Gregorian Music is restored nothing can be done, but now I almost despair—I do indeed. I built a solemn church at Southport. It was opened with a perfectly disgusting display and a bill ending with an Ordinary at 2 o'clock, 3/6 each. Keighley was opened the other day with a most horrible scene. Not only was all decorum violated, but a regular Row took place between the musicians, who quarrelled about their parts in the church, and after an hour's delay one priest drew off his singers and a Miss Whitwell—whose name appeared in the bill in gigantic letters—quavered away in most extraordinary style. There was *no procession*. Every building I erect is profaned, and instead of assisting in, conversions only serves to disgust people. The church at Dudley is a compleat facsimile of one of the old English parish churches, and nobody seems to know how to use it. The present state of things is quite lamentable, and were it not for the Oxford men I should quite despair."

Wiseman's difficult position among the older clergy was by no means helped by his association with Pugin. Dr. Bowdon, as Rector of Sedgley Park, was one of their leading figures in the Midland District, and he spoke his mind freely with all his natural honesty. On the subject of retreats for the clergy on the Italian model, which Wiseman had desired to introduce after the synod of 1841, he expressed[1] the feelings of many. He spoke of them as " solitary confinement for ten days in darkened rooms and reflecting seriously on the state of our interior, I do not think that I can go through with it." As for Pugin, Dr. Bowdon wrote to one friend, " I do not like St. Chad's or any of Pugin's work. The episcopal palace is the most gloomy place I ever saw." He was frankly irritated by the influence that Pugin had acquired over old Bishop Walsh, and he declared roundly that " if Archbishop Pugens comes here I shall not do anything he advises." Wiseman had been taken aback by the explosion of Pugin's wrath when he tried to forbid the rood screen in St. Chad's Cathedral. He withdrew his opposition, and the completion of the cathedral proceeded until it was formally opened on June 20, 1841. Wiseman loved ritual,

[1] *History of Cotton College,* pp. 153–154.

133

and had the knowledge of an expert on all its details. Years afterwards,[1] while he lay dying, he was to say : " I have never cared
for anything but the Church. My sole delight has been in everything connected with her. As people in the world go to a ball for
their recreation, so I have enjoyed a great function." Few such
functions can have given him such intense pleasure as the opening
of Pugin's cathedral in Birmingham, the first Catholic cathedral to
be built in England since the Reformation. The ceremonies were
made the more impressive owing to the accidental discovery of the
relics of St. Chad, which had been stored away by Mr. Fitzherbert
of Swynnerton and forgotten until they were unearthed by the
priest at Aston Hall. Their authenticity was examined and verified
in time for the opening of the new cathedral, to which it was
desired that they should be transferred. They were brought to
Oscott and from there to Birmingham, where Bishop Walsh
celebrated the solemn high mass of consecration for the cathedral
and Wiseman preached. No less than thirteen bishops were
present, one from the United States and one from Australia, as
well as two from Scotland, with some 150 clergy. The question
of vestments for the occasion arose once more, and Bishop Baines
wrote in advance to ensure that no dispute should occur. But
Lord Shrewsbury's cloth of gold vestments satisfied all concerned ;
and Pugin, who had collaborated with Wiseman in perfecting
every detail of the arrangements for weeks beforehand, agreed
to waive his insistence on Gregorian music when it was decided
that a Mass by Haydn should be performed.

In another part of the Midland district in the meantime there
had arrived a young Benedictine, William Ullathorne, who had
returned to England after ten years as a missionary in Australia.
His scathing reports on the degrading conditions which were
prevalent under the convict system had at last aroused the Government to take action, and definite encouragement was being given
to the formation of a Catholic hierarchy in Australia. Ullathorne
himself had been mentioned prominently as one of the future
bishops as soon as the hierarchy was formed, but he had deter-

[1] *Life of Wiseman,* II, p. 510.

mined to refuse. At the mission in Coventry, where he arrived in November 1841, he found work that occupied all his energies. A blunt Yorkshireman, he undertook his parochial duties with a spirit no less ardent than that of the foreign missionaries whom Wiseman and Phillipps had been introducing into the Midlands. Coventry was still an old-fashioned provincial town with some 30,000 inhabitants, but its population was already growing fast. Its old industries of watch-making, silk-spinning and ribbon-weaving were being modernised and extended. There were less than a thousand Catholics in the neighbourhood, and the mission had been in the hands of the Benedictines for nearly forty years. " I found the mission of Coventry under the care of a young girl, and in a desolate condition," wrote Ullathorne in his *Autobiography*.[1] The chapel was " very small, in a very naked condition, and though not so many years built, the walls were cracked through, and exhibited considerable rents. As to the little bit of a house, there was scarcely space for anything in its little rooms but for myself and a small table." But there was a good schoolroom. The mission had suffered through the inability of its last priest, an old Benedictine, to do any active work, and Ullathorne set himself to bring back those who had lapsed and to make new converts. He had brought with him as his housekeeper a lady who had lived for some years in Bruges, and who had been recommended to him while he was in Rome. She had become a Dominican Tertiary, and was already known as Sister Margaret Hallahan. Within a few years Ullathorne had enabled her to form the nucleus of a community of Dominican nuns, and as Mother Margaret Hallahan she was to become one of the most remarkable women of the Catholic revival. " Foundress of a congregation of the great Dominican Order," Ullathorne wrote [2] of her afterwards, " she trained a hundred religious women, founded five convents, built three churches, established a hospital for incurables, three orphanages, schools for all classes, including a number for the poor."

With her help Ullathorne had quickly galvanised the little

[1] *Autobiography*, p. 198.
[2] *Life of M. Margaret Hallahan*, p. xiv.

mission to new life, and he began the building of a new church to replace the old one, which was threatening to collapse. He had hopes already of founding a Benedictine priory, with a full choir of " habited monk missioners." To raise money for his new church he undertook begging tours in every likely place, and he wrote [1] from London in 1840 that " hitherto begging has been pleasant enough : I suppose I shall find its pleasures diminish as time goes on. I walk some twenty miles a day on the London pavements without any excessive fatigue, because I have nobody to talk balderdash about it at the end." He had made his reputation as a preacher among the convicts in Australia, and he was preaching with his full vigour in his own parish. " When will the preachers of the Cross come forth as of old ? " he wrote in the preface to his sermons in 1842.[2] " Those men of prayer—those men of penance—those ardent lovers of God—those patient sufferers impassioned of the Cross ? When shall we see them in the midst of us ? Moved with sorrow and compassion for a people, who like sheep lie about without pastors ; who, always seeking and never finding, fill the air with their anxious questionings—they would go forth to the lowly and the poor, and to every spirit that suffers need. . . . The Apostles waited not for men to come together and build up roofs for their especial accommodation. They went about ; the very sight of men moved them and they spoke." Intensely English as he was in his temperament and outlook, he acclaimed the work of Dominic Barberi and of the Rosminians as an example to the English clergy, and he gave them his full support. He was the most outstanding figure in the younger generation of the English clergy who felt as Wiseman felt, and were to regard him as their leader.

[1] *Life of Archbishop Ullathorne,* by Abbot Butler, O.S.B., I, p. 126.
[2] *Sermons,* p. 58.

CHAPTER X

NEWMAN CAPITULATES

BERNARD SMITH, who was one of Newman's closest friends and formerly his curate at St. Mary's, had made the acquaintance of Pugin when he was carrying out some restorations at his rectory in Lincolnshire. Their friendship resulted in Bernard Smith visiting Wiseman and Bishop Walsh in Birmingham. He accompanied some of the Catholic clergy on their visits to the poor, and was astonished by the candour as well as the simplicity of the priests he met. His Roman leanings had definitely increased, and had found outward expression before his bishop came to inspect the rectory church at Leadenham at the end of 1841, pronounced all his innovations to be "unmistakably Roman" and forbade their continuance. Upset and distressed by this prohibition, Bernard Smith went to Oscott for consolation, and there [1] found Wiseman publicly receiving a Jew and a Socinian into the Church. He undertook a retreat at once, and at its conclusion was received as a Catholic, leaving his parish without a rector and without services. This sudden defection had been directly caused by the Bishop of Lincoln's condemnation of his ritualistic practices and the Bishop would not allow the challenge to his authority to go unanswered. He even attempted to contrive Smith's imprisonment, but the Archbishop of Canterbury declined to give him the necessary support. The Bishop's challenge, however, affected the position of Newman, and Smith's many friends in Oxford, who had been pleading with him to avoid any hasty decision. They might deplore his impetuous action, but they could not ignore the Bishop's open repudiation of their efforts to restore Catholic practices in the country parishes.

This crisis, following upon the conversion of Sibthorpe and

[1] *Life of Wiseman*, I, p. 413.

several others, revived hopes which had been overcast during Wiseman's first year at Oscott. It was a grievous personal blow to Newman. But Wiseman had learned by this time that Newman's position would scarcely be affected by the decisions of any of his friends. Nevertheless, the scandal which Smith's desertion had caused in the Church of England had compelled Newman to defend himself. Bernard Smith had been his curate, and had also been an inmate of his house at Littlemore. Furious complaints were made to Newman's bishop in Oxford that he was exercising an insidious influence, and in April 1842, the Bishop wrote directly to Newman to draw his attention to the charges which were being made against him. He mentioned particularly [1] a newspaper report to the effect that a " so called Anglo-Catholic Monastery is in process of erection at Littlemore, and that the cells of dormitories, the chapel, the refectory, the cloisters all may be seen advancing to perfection, under the eye of a Parish Priest of the Diocese of Oxford." The Bishop had too much confidence in Newman's good faith to believe these stories, and in his letter he declared that he " at once exonerated him from the accusation." But he felt it imperative to call upon Newman to provide him with a sufficient answer to such statements. At Littlemore, Newman had, in fact, been subjected to a persistent persecution by hostile or merely inquisitive visitors. " One day when I entered my house," he writes in the *Apologia*,[2] " I found a flight of Undergraduates inside. Heads of Houses, as mounted patrols, walked their horses round these poor cottages. Doctors of divinity dived into the hidden recesses of that private tenement uninvited, and drew domestic conclusions from what they saw there. I had thought that an Englishman's house was his castle ; but the newspapers thought otherwise, and at last the matter came before my good Bishop." In the circumstances he could not but welcome the opportunity to state how matters stood.

" It is now a whole year," he wrote [3] in reply, " that I have been the subject of incessant misrepresentation. A year since I submitted entirely to your Lordship's authority ; and with the

---

[1] *Apologia*, p. 107.   [2] *Ibid.*   [3] *Ibid.*, p. 108.

intention of following out the particular act enjoined upon me, I not only stopped the series of Tracts, on which I was engaged, but withdrew from all public discussion of Church matters of the day, or what may be called ecclesiastical politics. I turned myself at once to the preparation for the Press of the translations of St. Athanasius to which I had long wished to devote myself, and I intended and intend to employ myself in the like theological studies, and in the concerns of my own parish and in practical works. With the same view of personal improvement I was led more seriously to a design which had been long in my mind. For many years, at least thirteen, I have wished to give myself a life of greater religious regularity than I have hitherto led ; but it is very unpleasant to confess such a wish even to my Bishop, because it seems arrogant and because it is committing me to a profession which may come to nothing. . . . As to my intentions, I propose to live there myself a good deal, as I have a resident curate in Oxford. In doing this I believe I am consulting for the good of my parish, as my population at Littlemore is at least equal to that of St. Mary's in Oxford, and the whole of Littlemore is double of it. It has been very much neglected ; and in providing a parsonage-house at Littlemore as this will be, and will be called, I conceive I am doing a very great benefit to my people. At the same time it has appeared to me that a partial or temporary retirement from St. Mary's Church might be expedient under the prevailing excitement."

So far as Littlemore was concerned, the explanation was complete. But there were other grave accusations against Newman, particularly concerning Bernard Smith. It was being said freely that Newman had " advised him to retain his living after he turned Catholic." One newspaper editor applied to Newman direct for a statement on the subject, and he replied [1] telling him to give the story " as far as I was concerned an unqualified contradiction. Whoever is the author of it," he wrote, " no correspondence or intercourse of any kind, direct or indirect, has passed between Mr. S. and myself, since his conforming to the Church of Rome,

[1] *Apologia*, p. 112.

except my formally and merely acknowledging the receipt of his letter, in which he informed me of the fact, without, as far as I recollect, my expressing any opinion upon it. You may state this as broadly as I have set it down." That disclaimer was written in March 1843. Newman had already decided that he could not continue much longer in the Anglican ministry. In the previous months he had already written in the *Conservative Review* what he calls in the *Apologia* "a formal Retraction of all the hard things which I had said against the Church of Rome." In September he took the more definite step of resigning the living of St. Mary's, which included Littlemore. "The ostensible, direct, and sufficient reason for my doing so," he writes in the *Apologia* [1] "was the persevering attack of the Bishops on Tract 90. A series of their *ex cathedra* judgments, lasting through three years, and including a notice of no little severity in a Charge of my own Bishop, came as near to a condemnation of my Tract, and so far, to a repudiation of the ancient Catholic doctrine, which was the scope of the Tract, as was possible in the Church of England. . . . I had refused to suppress it, and they had yielded that point. . . . All my then hopes, all my satisfaction at the apparent fulfilment of these hopes, was at an end in 1843."

The news of Newman's resignation from St. Mary's increased the high hopes which Wiseman and his friends still held of Newman's early surrender to Rome. But while his position had been profoundly shaken, he desired above all to be left in peace and quiet. "For two years," he writes in the *Apologia* [2] concerning the period after his resignation, "I was in lay communion, not indeed being a Catholic in my convictions but in a state of serious doubt, and with the probable prospect of becoming some day, what as yet I was not. Under these circumstances I thought the best thing I could do was to give up duty and to throw myself into lay communion, remaining an Anglican. I could not go to Rome, while I thought what I did of the devotions she sanctioned to the Blessed Virgin and the Saints. I did not give up my fellow-ship, for I could not be sure that my doubts would not be reduced

---

[1] *Apologia*, p. 128.   [2] *Ibid.*, p. 114.

or overcome, however unlikely I might consider such an event. But I gave up my living ; and for two years before my conversion, I took no clerical duty. My last Sermon was in September 1843 ; then I remained in quiet for two years." In his craving for that quiet which had been so long denied to him, every attempt made from outside to provoke him into controversy could only incur repulse and drive him to closer retirement. More than ever he avoided contact with Catholics. Yet he had one Catholic friend already of whom he was to write [1] that " he had more perhaps to do with my conversion than any one else." He was at a safe distance in Ireland. Dr. Russell of Maynooth, who afterwards became President of the College, had been a constant contributor to the *Dublin Review*, and had for some years taken Wiseman's place as its editor. He had become acquainted with Newman quite informally, and had scrupulously avoided any theological discussions, with a tactful sympathy which won Newman's confidence and friendship. " He called upon me, in passing through Oxford in the summer of 1841, and I think I took him over some of the buildings of the University. He called again another summer, on his way from Dublin to London, I do not recollect that he said a word on the subject of religion on either occasion. He sent me at different times several letters ; he was always gentle, mild, unobtrusive, uncontroversial. He let me alone. He also gave me one or two books, Veron's Rule of Faith and some Treatises of the Wallenburghs was one ; a volume of St. Alfonso Liguori's Sermons was another." This latter volume reached Newman in November 1842, and his letter of acknowledgment states with special clearness the difficulties that still created a gulf between him and the Church of Rome. " I only wish your Church were more known among us by such writings," wrote Newman.[2] " You will not interest us in her, till we see her, not in politics, but in her true functions of exhorting, teaching, and guiding. I wish there were a chance of making the leading men among you understand, what I believe is no novel thought to yourself. It is not by learned discussions, or acute arguments, or

[1] *Apologia*, p. 121.   [2] *Ibid.*, p. 120.

reports of miracles, that the heart of England can be gained. It is by men 'approving themselves' like the Apostle, 'ministers of Christ.' . . . There is a divine life among us, clearly manifested, in spite of all our disorders, which is as great a note of the Church, as any can be. Why should we seek our Lord's presence elsewhere, when He vouchsafes it to us where we are ? What *call* have we to change our communion ? Roman Catholics will find this to be the state of things in time to come, whatever promise they may fancy there is of a large secession to their Church. This man or that may leave us, but there will be no general movement. There is indeed an incipient movement of our *Church* towards yours, and this your leading men are doing all they can to frustrate by their unwearied efforts at all risks to carry off individuals. When will they know the position, and embrace a larger and wiser policy ? "

Dr. Russell was an intimate friend and supporter of Wiseman, and he showed that there could be no immediate encouragement from Newman's side. And in October 1843, just after Newman's resignation from St. Mary's had revived his hopes, there came the most direct blow he had received. Sibthorpe, one of the most conspicuous of his converts, apostatised and rejoined the Church of England. Wiseman had received Sibthorpe as a Catholic himself, during one of those first exciting visits at Oscott from the more adventurous Tractarians. He had been freely criticised for having acted too impetuously, and his critics had now scored a decisive victory against him. Phillipps had shared the blame with him, for Phillipps had brought Sibthorpe to Grace Dieu and had him confirmed there in his own chapel, and there had been plans for active collaboration between them. Yet Phillipps might claim that Sibthorpe's relapse justified his own view that individual conversions should be discouraged, in order that Catholic influences should operate as strongly as possible within the Established Church. But Wiseman, though utterly dejected, remained un- shaken. In a letter to Phillipps soon after he had received the news, he impressed upon him [1] that " were a Catholic who had the opportunity of bringing anyone into unity, to neglect it, on the

[1] *Life of Wiseman*, I, p. 418.

ground that Providence seemed to work by exceptions in the present state of things here, he would certainly sin ; for he would be violating a clear and positive duty, in favour of his private judgment and views regarding which he had no authority from revelation or tradition. This, of course, would be most uncatholic and sinful. Our duty is clearly to bring everyone, singly or with others, as his case comes before us, into the bosom of the Church, and when God does not bless our efforts, adore His counsels, and beg of him to continue the work as most to His glory and the salvation of souls." " Mr. Sibthorpe's unfortunate fall" would probably give encouragement to those who had refrained from going the full length that he had gone. " But to us this is and ought to be no more a weakening of our views and proceedings than the fall of an apostle or a first deacon is of our convictions respecting the authority of the Church." Meanwhile he had been consoled by encouraging news elsewhere. He had just received a letter " exciting in me better hopes than ever, and urging me on to more exertions." Moreover, a new convert from Oxford had just arrived at Oscott, an Oriental scholar of great distinction, who would find in Wiseman a colleague with a European reputation. The conversion of Seager, another fellow of Magdalen, was at least some compensation for the loss of Sibthorpe.

His critics did not conceal their real gratification that Sibthorpe's desertion had been a stern lesson to him in his concentration upon the Oxford men. He was acutely sensitive at all times, and a feeling of loneliness and discouragement weighed heavily upon him. In a memorandum [1] which he wrote a little later he set down his thoughts in a mood of great depression. " I came to England and into this district and college without a claim upon anyone's kindness or indulgence, with over-rated abilities, exaggerated reputation for learning, overestimated character in every respect. I was placed in a position of heavy responsibility and arduous labour. No one on earth knows what I went through in head and heart during my years of silent and solitary sorrow. In the house I have reason now to know that *no one* was working with me, thought

[1] *Life of Wiseman,* I, pp. 447-448.

with me, or felt with me. Many an hour of the lonely night have
I passed in prayer and tears by the lamp of the Sanctuary ; many a
long night has passed over sleepless and [sorrowful]. . . . How
seldom has a word been spoken which intimated that those who
entered the College considered it as more than a mere place of
boys' education, or [saw in it] a great engine employed in England's
conversion and regeneration.   What a different place it would be if
all had laboured with this view, and for this purpose ! . . . How few
sympathised (Mr. Spencer did, certainly) with the tone of soothing
and inviting kindness which from the beginning Roman education
had taught me to adopt, the voice of compassion and charity. . . .
Newspaper assaults, remonstrances by letter (and from some of our
most gifted Catholics) sharp rebukes by word of mouth . . . were
indeed my portion, as though I compromised the truth and
palliated error ; as though I narrowed the distance between the
two by trying to throw a bridge over the hideous chasm, that
men might pass from one to the other.   Hence, when one (and
thank God ! the only one) of our good converts fall back after
receiving orders, I was publicly taunted with it in the newspapers,
and privately in every way, and when struck down and almost
heartbroken by it I was told by a friend that he was glad of it,
because it would open my eyes to the false plan on which I had
gone.   And yet I had been careful to consult the Holy See through
Propaganda before acting in his case."

He had come to realise, after so much waiting, that Newman
was not to be approached by argument, and that the revival of
religious feeling in the Catholic body was the chief hope of
influencing him in his retirement. The work of the foreign
missionaries whom he had helped to make foundations in England
was exercising more influence than all his own sermons and articles.
Reports of the work being done by Father Dominic Barberi and
Dr. Gentili had already made a deep impression upon the hermitage
at Littlemore.

The open wearing of the religious habit by Father Dominic
and his colleagues aroused mixed feelings of admiration and ridicule
everywhere. " I preached in my habit with the crucifix on my

breast all exactly as in Italy," Dominic Barberi wrote [1] to Rome in April 1844, after conducting one very successful mission. "The wearing of the sandals seemed to give great edification. At least, so I was told, and I was advised by one who was present to wear both habit and sandals on all future occasions of this kind." The Passionists, under Wiseman's instructions,[2] always preached in it, though they were not to wear it "in towns, but only in country places near the house, for short walks." On preaching expeditions they were to go out in ordinary secular dress, but they put on the habit when they reached their destination. In June at Oscott he took part in the Corpus Christi procession, with "triumphal arches, altars and a sermon preached out of doors," and on the following day fully a thousand Protestants had attended. But these bold proceedings always provoked opposition, and Dominic was still suffering acutely from the organised hostility that he aroused. "If you could send me," he wrote [3] in March, "a young Religious from Rome it would be a good thing. It does not matter whether he has great talent or not. What *does* matter is that he should have plenty of good will, and be prepared to suffer many things— derision, mockery and contempt. That would to a great extent be his lot here. Those who come must not look for comforts but a full meal of insult and outrage of every kind. If I had great virtue I could become a great saint here, but virtue is wanting, and at times I almost tremble for my salvation. . . . The crosses that come my way are almost unbearable and many of them from unexpected quarters."

Father Dominic had learnt much in the few years since he came to England. "I must tell you," he said [4] to his General, "that the whole situation and attitude of this country is very different from that which holds good in Italy. Italian ideas about things are of almost no use here and in any case are for the most part, impossible of execution." And a little later: [5] "In England haste is not wanted. Before taking one step they must take all possible measurements. But once the measurements are taken and the first step is made

---

[1] *Dominic Barberi in England*, p. 99.   [2] *Ibid.*, p. 105.
[3] *Ibid.*, p. 94.   [4] *Ibid.*, p. 95.   [5] *Ibid.*, p. 113.

they are strong and brave. I am exceedingly fond of their character, although so contrary to my own. For I always want to do things in the twinkling of an eye. I can tell you I have to keep my haste and hurry in check here." And in December of the same year : [1] " Here we don't want so much great talents but good will, good health and good example. That is all. I have never come in contact with a more reasonable nation. They do not ask for eloquence but a good heart, clear, well reasoned discourse, and personal good example." It was these qualities that had enabled him to retain contact, when all others had failed, with the disillusioned hermits at Littlemore. He was still in correspondence with Dalgairns since their exchanges of letters in the *Univers* of Paris. Their private correspondence grew more frequent during 1844, and in October Dalgairns wrote to him again. [2] " God who has brought us so far will not leave us where we are if it be His will that we go farther. Pray for us and make others pray, that we may see our way out of this perplexity." The letter concluded with a shy request for information as to where the community at Littlemore could procure " shirts or girdles of haircloth," and also a " discipline such as ordinary persons would use."

In June 1844 he was at last able to visit Littlemore in person. He had been invited to give a mission near Oxford and his record of it was characteristic. " You could not believe the impression our habit makes when we go to preach anywhere," he wrote [3] to his General. " The people kneel down in crowds just to receive my blessing. We do more preaching here with the bare feet and religious restraint and modesty than with the tongue. Somebody told me once that they had been converted at my first sermon although they did not understand a word I said. Protestants and Catholics alike come in crowds. Last month I preached in a hay loft, somewhere near Oxford, to about five hundred Protestants." He had gone on from there to Littlemore at the invitation of Dalgairns, and had met Newman there, and had a long talk with them. " Many vague rumours are flying about concerning him

---

[1] *Dominic Barberi in England,* p. 115. [2] *Ibid.,* p. 219.
[3] *Ibid.,* pp. 102-103.

and his possible movements," Dominic wrote [1] to his General, who had been under the impression that Newman was the head of Oxford University. "I am full of hope and keep up continual correspondence by letter with the house at Littlemore. The obstacles in their path are very great." Even he had not been prepared for the extreme austerity which Newman had introduced at Littlemore. "You may have thought of it as a kind of Monte Cassino," he wrote to his General later. [2] "I assure you I have never seen any monastery so poor. It is simply a long outhouse or hay shed with a ground floor only. You could touch the roof with your hands. The small cells are partitioned off from each other by rough bricks only. Inside the cells the furniture consists of a little straw bed and one or two chairs of the poorest kind. To pass from one cell to the other you have to go outside, almost in the open air. Our Retreats are palaces compared to this! Inside this outhouse there have been gathered together for several years past the greatest luminaries in the religious world of England."

External happenings could have little influence on the decisions of men immured in such austerity and seclusion. In another letter to Dominic Barberi, a few months after his visit to Littlemore, Dalgairns impressed on him that "as I am so much more open with you than I should be with almost anybody else, I must beg of you not to show my letters to anyone." "Those amongst us," he wrote, [3] when a new crisis had arisen in Oxford itself, "who have our eyes fixed on Rome care but little about such external things ; we have never had any hope of influencing authorities in the Church of England, and were most of us averse to making the attempt. . . . But this you will easily understand, that those who think deepest amongst us are generally averse to all riotous proceedings, which make a noise in the world. Their great hope is quietly to influence good people by gradually working away all Protestant prejudices, and gaining their intellect to Catholicism through their hearts and spiritual nature. I hope the *Lives of the*

[1] *Dominic Barberi in England*, p. 115.   [2] *Ibid.*, p. 144.
[3] *Ibid.*, p. 221.

Saints[1] do much to this. But we must not boast; prayer and mortification must do most." By the time that letter was written, the University at Oxford had been thrown into a ferment by the publication in June 1844 of Ward's *Ideal of a Christian Church*. Newman was deeply engaged in his own writings, and at Littlemore he and his friends had done all in their power to keep outside public controversies. But the storm which Ward had deliberately provoked sent its boisterous echoes even into the hermitage, where a Carthusian silence was observed through most of the day. There was news of further secessions to Rome among their closest associates in the Movement; and the solemn assembly of Convocation to discuss whether Ward should be deprived of his degree was a challenge which could not be ignored. In February 1845, while the storm was approaching its climax, Dalgairns wrote to Dominic Barberi a letter which lifted, for him alone, the curtain behind which they had retired. " I must not conceal from you," he wrote,[2] " that matters are in a dangerous state with us. I do not allude to anything that is taking place in Convocation in Oxford. I state what is my deliberate conviction when I say that I do not believe that such matters as have just now taken place at Oxford about Ward advance the real question much, whichever way they turn out. It is not therefore about such matters that I would have you pray. God's work is a silent one, going on in many hearts of whom you know nothing. There are difficulties in the progress from error to truth, of which you happily have no experience. Depend upon it that there will be many who will make shipwreck of their faith before all is over. . . . Pray for all who are in spiritual darkness. There are many who are just now balancing between Catholicism and scepticism, and one precipitate measure may plunge them irrevocably into the depths of heresy or indifference. These are the things you must pray for, rather than for the success of any public measures."

This agony of conscience was not afflicting all the former

[1] Newman and his friends had been publishing a planned series of Lives of the Saints.

[2] *Dominic Barberi in England*, p. 222.

Tractarians with equal force. Ward particularly had always favoured, and never been afraid of, precipitate measures. His restless interrogations had undoubtedly forced the pace, even for Newman, at an earlier stage. Phillipps had brought him into contact with Wiseman at Oscott, and with other Catholics, and he had no patience with the restraints that Newman's caution imposed on his closest friends. He had written his book with his customary provocation, and in the winter of 1843 he had already let Wiseman know its thesis. "Its object," Wiseman told Phillipps at the time,[1] "will be to show that Rome is the great exemplar to which they must study to approach, and he will not admit the existence of a single practical corruption." Its publication shattered the Tractarian Movement irrevocably, and it was received at Oxford as an open challenge. Convocation met on February 13, 1845, and the whole situation which he had compelled it to consider was frankly reviewed. By a vote of 777 to 391, it was declared that Ward could not in good faith subscribe to the Thirty-nine Articles while holding such opinions. By a vote of 569 to 511 he was formally deprived of his degree. Newman's Tract 90, which he had never withdrawn and which was still regarded by his followers as the basis of his creed, became a main subject of the debate ; and its formal condemnation was only averted by the veto of the Proctors, who decided that it could not then be considered. The cleavage of opinions had become so definite that even Pusey was obliged to dissociate himself from Newman's attitude. That Newman should still remain silent seemed unbelievable, and Wiseman lived in suspense from day to day, waiting to hear of his final withdrawal from the Established Church. At Littlemore the determination to escape being drawn into controversy was still sustained, but not all of Newman's little community possessed his immense capacity for self-control.

While the University had thus condemned Ward's book, and had deprived him of his degree, Ward had not yet come into direct collision with the authorities of the Anglican Church, and he still considered himself to be one of its ministers. But he had already

[1] *Life of Wiseman*, I, p. 422.

decided upon another step which gravely disturbed the peace of Littlemore. Ward was preparing to marry, and the fact was already known to Dalgairns when he wrote the last quoted letter to Dominic Barberi, a few days before the condemnation. " I must tell you what may disappoint you," Dalgairns had written,[1] " and yet serve to convince you how little you know from external signs what is going on in individual minds, that my friend Ward is on the point of being married. I cannot say that I approve of it, but yet you must not judge him hastily. There are circumstances, which I cannot explain, to palliate it." Others of Ward's friends, who had attended the meeting of Convocation to vote in his defence, were no less pained when they saw the news publicly announced a few weeks after the proceedings. Ward heard of the criticisms, and at once wrote to the *Times* to defend his action.[2] " He had certainly upheld celibacy as a higher state than marriage ; but he had never considered himself called to that higher state ; and when he offered himself for ordination he had done so knowing that the Anglican Church did not *de facto* insist on celibacy for her clergy. In private, however, he went further, and admitted that he did not believe in Anglican Orders and did not consider himself a priest." But his further decision was already imminent, and in August he wrote personally to the *Oxford Herald*, to announce that he was about to be received into the Catholic Church.

Since Newman's retirement to Littlemore, Ward had become the most conspicuous figure in the Tractarian Movement, and his submission to Rome made it certain that others would follow his example. He was received by the Jesuit Father Brownbill in London on September 5, and within a few weeks several of the Littlemore community had decided that they must do likewise. Dalgairns had not written to Dominic Barberi since February, but on September 20 he sent him an urgent letter[3] from Littlemore : " I am by God's grace going to become a Catholic," he wrote. " I am very desirous of being received into the Church in a quiet

---

[1] *Dominic Barberi in England,* p. 223.
[2] *Sequel to Catholic Emancipation,* II, p. 113.
[3] *Dominic Barberi in England,* p. 223.

place, and I can think of none better than your house. The uniformly kind expressions which you have ever used towards me make me feel sure that I shall be welcome." But he earnestly begged that Father Dominic should for the present mention the fact to "no one whatever." Newman himself had in the meantime reached a point at which his destination could no longer be doubted. Eighteen months before, in February 1844, he had written to an old friend who was then near to death,[1] "I could not come to see you; I am not worthy of friends. With my opinions, to the full of which I dare not confess, I feel like a guilty person with others, though I trust I am not so. People kindly think that I have much to bear externally, disappointment, slander, etc. No, I have nothing to bear, but the anxiety which I feel for my friends' anxiety for me, and their perplexity." Of his own feelings during that summer of 1844 he writes in the *Apologia*:[2] "My difficulty was this: I had been deceived greatly once; how could I be sure that I was not deceived a second time? I thought myself right then; how was I to be certain that I was right now? How many years had I thought myself sure of what I now rejected? How could I ever again have confidence in myself? As in 1840 I listened to the rising doubt in favour of Rome, now I listened to the waning doubt in favour of the Anglican Church. To be certain is to know that one knows; what inward test had I, that I should not change again, after that I had become a Catholic? I had still apprehension of this, though I thought a time would come, when it would depart. However, some limit ought to be put to these vague misgivings; I must do my best and then leave it to a higher Power to prosper it. So at the end of 1844, I came to the resolution of writing an Essay on Doctrinal Development; and then, if at the end of it, my convictions in favour of the Roman Church were not weaker, of taking the necessary steps for admission to her fold."

He had ceased even to make a secret of his state of mind by the end of 1844. "As far as I know myself," he wrote[3] to a friend in that November, "my one great distress is the perplexity,

[1] *Apologia,* p. 141.   [2] *Ibid.*   [3] *Ibid.,* p. 142.

unsettlement, alarm, scepticism, which I am causing to so many; and the loss of kind feeling and good opinion on the part of so many, known and unknown, who have wished well to me. . . . And as far as I know myself, my one paramount reason for contemplating a change is my deep, unvarying conviction that our Church is in schism, and that my salvation depends on my joining the Church of Rome. . . . I have no visions whatever of hope, no schemes of action, in any other sphere more suited to me. I have no existing sympathies with Roman Catholics; I hardly ever, even abroad, was at one of their services; I know none of them, I do not like what I hear of them. And then, how much I am giving up in so many ways! and to me sacrifices irreparable, not only from my age, when people hate changing, but from my especial love of old associations and the pleasures of memory. Nor am I conscious of any feeling, enthusiastic or heroic, of pleasure in the sacrifice; I have nothing to support me here."

In March 1845 he had written [1] to another friend that he intended to give up his fellowship in October, " and to publish some work or treatise between that and Christmas." In July one of the Anglican bishops announced openly that it was well known that Newman was " preparing for secession; and when that event takes place, it will be seen how few will go with him." Meanwhile his continuous work on the Essay on the Development of Doctrine had cleared his mind so far that " I ceased to speak of the Roman Catholics and boldly called them Catholics." Before he got to the end of the book he had formed his final resolution to be received into the Catholic Church.

Rumours of this increasing decision had reached Oscott, and Wiseman could restrain his eager impatience no longer. Bernard Smith, as Newman's former curate at St. Mary's, believed that he would still be greeted with kindness if he went to Littlemore, and he was not mistaken. The little community consisted of Dalgairns, Ambrose St. John, E. S. Bowles, and Richard Stanton, besides Newman himself; while Albany Christie and John Walker, fellow of Brasenose, were frequent visitors. When Smith came to see

[1] *Apologia*, p. 142.

them in the July of 1845 they received him with undisguised friend-ship. Newman was deliberately frigid at first, and soon left the room.[1] The others were full of inquiries concerning his experi-ences, since he left them to become a Catholic at Oscott. In the evening Newman joined them again for dinner, and his former curate recognised immediately the sign which it was intended that he should note. Newman was wearing grey trousers, and by this solemn act he revealed for the first time that he no longer regarded himself as being a clergyman in Anglican Orders. " I know the man," Smith reported to Wiseman afterwards,[2] " and I know what it means. He will come, and soon." Only a few weeks later came the news that Ward was to become a Catholic at once, and the Littlemore community could wait no longer. Dalgairns and Ambrose St. John each went off for a holiday, and St. John was received into the Church at Prior Park. Dalgairns had already sent his letter to Dominic Barberi asking him to fix a day so that he could be received. It was arranged that he should go to Aston, and there Dominic Barberi received him into the Church on Michaelmas Day. He had no misgivings in returning at once as a Catholic to Littlemore, and he had arranged that Father Dominic was to visit him there within the following month. Stanton also had in the meantime left Littlemore for Stonyhurst to become a Catholic there. Only Bowles and Newman now remained, and they felt that their isolation could not continue. Newman wrote to Stanton at once after Dalgairns came back, asking him to come home so that they could both be received at Littlemore by Dominic Barberi, whose arrival was now expected on October 8. " Come back on that day," he wrote. In the meantime he was closing his accounts. On October 3 he resigned his fellowship at Oriel, and all day on October 5 he prepared his general confession.

Father Dominic had not yet been told that he was to receive Newman into the Church when he came to visit Dalgairns. But on the eve of his arrival Newman wrote to tell Henry Wilberforce his intentions : " Father Dominic the Passionist is passing this way on his way from Aston in Staffordshire to Belgium, where a

---

[1] *Life of Wiseman,* I, p. 427.   [2] *Ibid.,* p. 429.

Chapter of his Order is to be held at this time. He is to come to Littlemore for the night as the guest of one of us whom he has admitted at Aston. He does not know of my intentions but I shall ask of him admission into the one true fold of the Redeemer. Father Dominic has had his thoughts turned towards England from a youth, in a distinct and remarkable way. For thirty years he has expected to be sent to England, and about three years since was sent, without any act of his own, by his Superior. . . . On Thursday or Friday, if it be God's will, I shall be received." Even Dalgairns had not yet been told, when he prepared to walk across the fields to the Oxford " Angel " to meet the coach. He was taking up his hat and stick when Newman spoke to him : [1] " When you see your friend will you tell him that I wish him to receive me into the Church of Christ ? " Dalgairns answered simply " Yes," as he set out in pouring rain. The coach brought their guest, and Dalgairns broke the great news to him at once. Father Dominic was drying himself by the fire when Newman entered and fell on his knees before him. In the evening he made his general confession, and was so exhausted that St. John and Stanton had to help him out of the little oratory. Having finished with Newman, Dominic Barberi received the submission of both Stanton and Bowles ; and in the following morning all three, together with Dalgairns and St. John, assisted at Mass and received Holy Communion together at his hands, in the oratory of Littlemore.

To his General in Rome Barberi reported the news when he reached Tournai some days later : [2] " Those who know Mr. Newman and his companions," he wrote, " will be in a position to judge and weigh the results of such an event. Newman has been up to now what I might term the Pope of the Protestants, their oracle, the soul of the Puseyite party, which is the most widely diffused in the Church of England, and embraces all that is serious and devout in the Protestant Church. He is reputed to be the most learned ecclesiastic in England. In my judgment he is one of the most humble and loveable men I have met in my life. Let

[1] *Life of Barberi,* p. 258.
[2] *Dominic Barberi in England,* p. 140.

us hope that the results of such conversions may be incalculable. All that I have suffered since I left Italy is well compensated by such a happy event as this. I pray that all good Religious everywhere may be spurred on to pray more fervently than ever for our most dear England ! Once she was the island of saints, and so may she be once again ! This daughter of the Church, who for three centuries has strayed from the path, will surely return full of vigour to her mother the holy Catholic and Apostolic Roman Church. So may it be ! I trust that your Paternity will deign to make further sacrifices for England, and send me more good subjects to labour in the great cause. As yet I have not seen the new house offered us by Dr. Wiseman. He has been away from home. Our chapel at Aston threatens to fall and another must be built, and God will see to this also. Let us one and all pray hard for England."

CHAPTER XI

CONVERTS AND IMMIGRANTS

NEWMAN'S sense of loneliness after he had taken the final plunge was overwhelming. He had no friends among the English Catholics, and he had reason to believe that few of them were likely to be congenial to him. Even Wiseman, who had suffered so much through his encouragement of the Oxford Movement, seemed to the small group of disciples at Littlemore an incorrigible controversialist who was continually trying to break in upon their seclusion. But Wiseman was consumed with the desire to help them, and he had far more tact and considerateness than they had believed. The proximity of Oscott to Oxford made it inevitable that they should be quickly brought together, and it was soon arranged that Newman was to go to Oscott to receive confirmation at Wiseman's hands. Their first meeting was embarrassing to both sides, and they scarcely spoke beyond exchanging formal courtesies. But Bernard Smith was there also to receive them, as well as George Spencer ; and Newman came accompanied by Ambrose St. John and Walker, who had become a Catholic almost at once after Newman's submission. Oakeley came also to join the group, who were to be confirmed together at Oscott on All Saints' day. Wiseman, with his impulsive generosity, had been thinking out plans for their future, and he at once offered them the use of the old college buildings if they should wish to continue their communal life together there.

From Rome also Newman received a letter of warmest greeting from Cardinal Acton, the English Cardinal in Curia and a man of charming temperament and wide culture. He offered all his personal assistance for Newman's future plans. But Newman was still set upon retirement. " Did your Eminence know me," he wrote in reply,[1] " you would see that I was one, about whom

[1] *Apologia*, p. 146.

there has been more talk for good or bad than he deserves, and about whose movements far more expectation has been raised than the event will justify. . . . If I might ask of your Eminence a favour, it is that you would kindly moderate those anticipations. Would it were in my power to do, what I do not aspire to do ! At present certainly I cannot look forward to the future, and, though it would be a good work if I could persuade others to do as I have done, yet it seems as if I had quite enough to do in thinking of myself." He intended, for the time being at least, to " betake himself to some secular calling," although Wiseman had hoped to arrange immediately for his ordination to the Catholic priesthood. He gladly accepted Oakeley as a permanent resident at Oscott, but he found that Newman wished first to complete his book on the Development of Doctrine. " The work was all written while an Anglican," Wiseman wrote [1] to Dr. Russell at Maynooth, " when he did not contemplate joining us, at least immediately, and gives the history only of the mode in which he was led to his own convictions ; but at the end he will state that now he is a Catholic, and holds his faith on the authority of the Church and believes in all things as she teaches, etc."

But it was inevitable that Newman himself should soon find his life's work in the Catholic priesthood. The number of Anglican clergymen who had become Catholics was increasing year by year, and with Newman's submission a stream of others followed. " We had *ten* quondam Anglican clergymen in the chapel," Wiseman wrote to Dr. Russell,[2] in describing Newman's confirmation " Has this ever happened before since the Reformation ? " Their number grew very rapidly in the following months. Faber, who had won a large following as a country parson, had become a Catholic a few months after Newman, and he also brought his friends in his train. He undertook to unite them in a community of St. Wilfrid's at Cotton Hall, while Newman and his friends accepted Wiseman's hospitality at Old Oscott, which they renamed Maryvale. " You may think how lonely I am," Newman wrote [3]

[1] *Life of Wiseman*, I, p. 434.   [2] *Ibid.*, p. 433.
[3] *Apologia*, p. 146.

to a friend towards the end of January. "*Obliviscere populum tuum et domum patris tui* has been in my ears for the last twelve hours. I realise now that we are leaving Littlemore, and it is like going on the open sea." He spent the last few days there entirely by himself, and then said goodbye to a number of his closest friends in Oxford, before leaving the city for good on February 23. But Wiseman's warm friendliness soon made him feel more at home, and before long Wiseman was able to write [1] to Dr. Russell : "You cannot think how cheerful Newman now is, and how at home he makes himself amongst us. This is his second visit. He was going from this to Ushaw with Faber, but the latter was prevented, so Newman is gone to Prior Park, and he has been to Old Hall. He will thus be soon known to all the clergy, and become popular among them." Meanwhile other convert clergymen were flocking to Oscott, where Wiseman had become the recognised focus for their reception.

Letters from Wiseman to Ambrose Phillipps at this time record the names of many. They reveal the new anxieties which were arising, through the need to provide for married men whose families were left destitute by their relinquishing their positions in the Established Church. In December 1845, he wrote [2] to Phillipps a letter typical of many others : "I am anxious to learn whether you have come to any arrangement with or about Mr. Coffin, who of course, you know, has been received into the Church. I have not said or written to Mr. Marshall on the subject, but I know that he is reduced to great straits, and is suffering cruel persecution from friends and family. He has, however, brought over seventeen of his parishioners, including the district surgeon, and he has several others under instruction. As Mr. Coffin is unmarried and staying at Prior Park, he possibly may intend to remain there, and study for orders. Mr. Marshall will be in Birmingham to-morrow. Mr. Glennie, and Mr. Watts Russell, and probably Mr. Woodmason are coming to settle in Birmingham, where Mr. Faber has also formed a society of young men, his converts, who live in community. So that we shall have quite a colony of converts near us,

[1] *Life of Wiseman*, I, p. 433.   [2] *Ibid.*, p. 443.

On Sunday last Mr. Stokes, late secretary of the Camden Society, was received at St. Chad's, and next Sunday Mr. Hutchinson of Trinity, Cambridge, will be received. He talks of seven more coming."

This sudden influx was producing an immense problem which had not been foreseen. Many of the new converts had to sacrifice their livelihood by their change of faith, and their families were in immediate need. "Scarcely a day passes," Wiseman wrote [1] to Mr. Walker of Scarborough about this time, "that I do not hear of someone who is on the point, or in the thought of, joining us and losing often their all. In their number are several married clergymen who are unfit for secular employment, and yet with their livings lose everything. This is a serious matter weighing heavily upon us. I have taken some preliminary steps towards meeting the most pressing exigencies of this state, but it is really only beginning and a trifle. . . . The question is not of providing an asylum for the celibates and Littlemorians, but of assisting, at least temporarily, those who, in coming over, give up all, and are from circumstances unable to do anything for themselves. There are one or two very able men in that painful position. The same is to be said of ladies who lose their situations by becoming Catholics. . . . The spirit of inquiry and dissatisfaction among clergymen and educated persons in the Anglican Church is spreading in every direction, and we cannot know how it will end."

The enthusiasm which greeted all this tide of conversion in the Midlands was by no means shared to the same extent in other places, where hostile suspicions still lingered. These Anglicans who had for years been using all their talents and influence to discredit the Church of Rome, and to prevent others from submission to it, were regarded as being, at best, on probation in their new surroundings. Wiseman was fully aware of how much they depended upon his personal encouragement and aid. When insomnia and illness overtook him during 1846 he was constantly anxious about what might happen if he should be unable to continue his devoted attentions to them. Matters were eased for him when

[1] *Life of Wiseman*, I, p. 444.

it was arranged that Newman and several of the leaders should go to Rome to study for the priesthood. He was able to keep in touch with them by correspondence, and to promote their plans for the foundation of a Society of the Oratory, to be formed when they returned to England. But other problems arose through the uncompromising zeal of Faber and other converts, who believed that it was their mission to arouse the old Catholics to greater devotion and activity. They began to propagate Italian practices and devotions, just as Father Gentili had done at Prior Park until Bishop Baines severely restrained them. Bishop Walsh had for years been in a minority among the English bishops in encouraging such changes, and some of the bishops, particularly Dr. Baines and Dr. Griffiths in London, resented strongly the implied suggestion that the Church had been neglected and needed reform. They had been in trouble in Rome already on account of their aloofness, and their unwillingness to accept proposals which emanated from the Holy See. Pope Gregory XVI had been Prefect of Propaganda before his election, and in that capacity had acquired a close knowledge of English affairs, through handling the communications which had passed between England and the Holy See. He had been particularly grieved by their apparent refusal to allow the religious orders to undertake work in England. Being a Benedictine himself, he had become convinced that they were obstructing all efforts to introduce a new vitality into the Church when Catholic Emancipation had opened a new era of great possibilities.

Misunderstandings between the English bishops and the Holy See had, in fact, become so acute in 1840 that the decision to increase the number of Vicars-Apostolic from four to eight was taken in spite of their opposition and without their knowledge. They had been isolated for so long that they acted more or less without reference to Rome on many matters which Rome considered to require frequent consultation. Both as Prefect of Propaganda and as Pope, Gregory XVI had found that matters upon which he expected to be consulted were settled without even any formal intimation of what had been done. Wiseman had received many direct complaints on the whole position while he was their official agent in Rome, and in February 1839, particularly, he was summoned for an interview, which he had to report to the bishops in the clearest terms. It was pointed out, for instance, that the Vicars-Apostolic had issued decrees on their joint authority without either submitting these decrees to Rome for approbation or even seeking permission ; whereas the American bishops, at a much greater distance, regularly reported to Rome when they held their synods every three years. A bishop's authority, it was emphasised, was confined to his own diocese or district. There was no suggestion that such action had been intended as a defiance of discipline or Papal authority, but it was symptomatic of the neglect to keep Rome informed. Still more the Pope had complained [1] " that he never had any communication from the Vicars that could console him, as of the progress of religion, the state of the Districts, etc., but that he had to learn what he could from newspapers, etc., while all correspondence was of a disagreeable nature." Such letters as he did receive were, moreover, strangely informal, although Roman custom throughout the Church was that they should be written in certain forms. Dr. Griffiths in London even wrote his letters [2] " with a carbon copier, so that the letters had the appearance of being written in pencil. Not infrequently when no definite answer seemed called for, the receipt of the letter was not even acknowledged."

A further cause of complaint was that the English bishops very seldom came to see the Pope on *ad limina* visits, with the result that suspicions as well as misunderstandings arose on both sides. Complaints on this matter had been made to Wiseman while he was Rector of the English College in 1837, and he had felt obliged to write a letter [3] to Bishop Griffiths to report an interview in which the Pope had spoken strongly on the subject. "He spoke of Dr. Walsh's intended visit with great pleasure, and said he wished the other Bishops would also make it a point to come to Rome, observing what a number of Irish and American Bishops have come, but none from England. This he said he would wish were there

---

[1] *Sequel to Catholic Emancipation,* I, p. 150.
[2] *Ibid.,* p. 168.   [3] *Ibid.,* p. 125.

no other reason, for the sake of keeping up the connexion with the Holy See. . . . The Pope expressed himself as much hurt that neither Dr. Bramston nor Dr. Penswick had ever answered his letter written in reply to one signed by the Bishops." Wiseman had tactfully urged the Bishop to undertake the journey, which could be made " in a very short time and at a very small cost." He drew his attention to the fact that steam packets were now running regularly on the principal rivers in France, so that " the only land travelling need be from Boulogne to Paris, and from Musteron to Chalons, all the rest by sea and rivers to Civita Vecchia." The real explanation of the misunderstanding lay in the fact that the four English Vicars-Apostolic were in charge of districts which were much too large. Until they were subdivided they could not possibly be supervised and developed, as the times required, when the population was growing very rapidly, and a constant influx of Catholics from many sources was transforming the whole character of the Church in England. Overworked, and lacking adequate resources for the developments which were urgently needed, they had no time for general discussions. They were constantly irritated by the critical suggestions which were being urged from Rome, under the influence of foreign missionaries and of wealthy converts who had little understanding of their enormous difficulties. There was no lack of respect or deference towards the central administration in Rome, still less towards the personal authority of the Pope. But they were immersed in their own problems ; and the atmosphere which they had always known in England strengthened their natural inclination to concentrate upon their own surroundings, while Rome still seemed a remote and picturesque place where no appreciation of the abnormal conditions in England could be reasonably expected. What they asked of Rome was to introduce some definite system which would give them real authority over the clergy in their widely scattered districts. Even parishes were the exception rather than the rule, and a large proportion of the clergy were practically private chaplains attached to the old families which had maintained Mass centres in their houses through the penal times. In other places the religious orders, particularly the Benedictines, had been in charge of the local missions for many years, and these missions had been growing rapidly in importance.

In the North the growth of Catholic population had been so rapid that Rome had decided to divide the former Northern District into three districts in 1840. But even in London conditions had been developing out of all comparison with previous times. Bishop Griffiths was very much aware of the extent of the growth under his own jurisdiction. When he and Bishop Walsh went to Rome together, while the creation of new vicariates was in preparation, he had mentioned [1] more than once to Bishop Walsh " that the number of Catholics in and about London was equal to the whole population of the Eternal City." But when he intimated this to the authorities in Rome, they felt all the more that the time had come for a more enterprising outlook than the Vicars-Apostolic appeared to entertain. Some three years later Bishop Griffiths wrote [2] to Dr. Baggs, who had succeeded Wiseman as agent for the bishops in England : " You can inform his Eminence Cardinal Fransoni that the accounts he has received agree with my own statements, that there is great want of more and larger chapels or churches in London, and that much more good might be done if we had a greater body of clergy. But after stating these facts to his Eminence, let him understand distinctly, 1st, that the providing of churches and pastors requires much money : 2ndly, that the Catholic body, although contributing liberally according to their means, cannot on account of their general poverty do all at once ; 3rdly, that the most destitute parts must first be attended to." He explained that he had recently acquired six new sites for churches, to be built as soon as funds could be collected, that he " had paid himself, independent of local subscriptions, £16,000 towards the building of other churches during the last five years," and that in many congregations the priests could not be supported without generous help from other places. The Catholics, he insisted, although they were mostly poor people, " have to support their churches, to support their pastors, their schools, their charitable

[1] *Sequel to Catholic Emancipation,* I, p. 155.
[2] *Ibid.,* pp. 171-172.

institutions ; every want of religion has to be supplied by their contributions." Particularly Cardinal Fransoni should understand " that of the Catholics of London three-fourths are the poorest and least religious of the Catholics in Ireland, who emigrate continually to the large towns of England. The surprise is not that much room is wanted for the poor but that so much has been provided." He cited instances of " the most destitute parts of London " which show how overwhelming the problem was. At Saffron Hill there were now about 4000 Catholics, with only a temporary chapel made out of two rooms. At Hackney a temporary chapel in a schoolroom had to provide for some 1400, and at Deptford the same for some 3500. At Poplar there was a chapel which might hold 800 people for a congregation of 5000, and at Virginia Street, where the chapel could hold 1200, there was now a congregation of 21,000.

Even in 1838, before the influx from Ireland grew so rapidly in the forties, the Vicars-Apostolic had issued a joint pastoral appealing for funds to assist the education of the clergy. Much had been done already since the Emancipation Act to provide a native clergy trained in England, and the majority of the Vicars-Apostolic even at that time were former presidents of English seminaries. Dr. Walsh had been president of Oscott, Dr. Briggs of Ushaw, and Dr. Griffiths of St. Edmund's, while Dr. Baines in the Western District had founded his own seminary at Prior Park. " Consider how rapidly our holy religion is again spreading its branches over this kingdom," they wrote in their joint pastoral in 1838—seven years before Newman's surrender to Rome, and before the stream of Anglican converts had assumed large proportions : " What numbers have recently returned to the bosom of the Catholic Church ; how many new missions have been established and how many of the old established congregations have so far increased as to require an additional supply of labourers ; and above all how many large bodies of Catholics, especially in the Western District, are left without a pastor, being too poor to maintain one, and too distant to be visited by any other missionary. Hence not only are their children left without instructions, but no priest is found to administer to them the sacrament of Baptism, nor to impart to the dying the last consolations of religion." The problem grew more difficult each year as the influx of poor Catholics from Ireland increased. Dr. Griffiths estimated [1] that during the first seven years of his episcopate the number of Catholics in the London District alone had risen from 145,000 to 195,000. That was an average increase of about 7000 a year, of whom some 500 were converts, and the remainder, after allowing for natural increase, were chiefly immigrants. In Moorfields, the principal centre of Catholic life in London for many years, there were then four priests, who had to care for a Catholic population of some 30,000, besides attending to the charity schools and 24 workhouses and numerous hospitals. In other places the conditions were scarcely less exacting. New churches were being provided at a rate which seems astonishing in view of the prevailing poverty. In his nine years as Vicar-Apostolic for the London District Dr. Griffiths himself had opened eighteen new missions, he had built new churches in nine others, and had twelve more in course of erection, besides enlarging four more and acquiring sites for eight others.

Such conditions were very unlike the quiet work of the clergy in most parts of the country during previous generations, with their thinly scattered congregations over a wide area. But the industrial revolution had resulted in the growth of great cities all over the north and the midlands. Dominic Barberi's letters from England during the early forties describe a much more rapid expansion even than in London. He was giving missions in the crowded centres of Lancashire during the months before Newman made his final decision at Littlemore. "In Liverpool there are about eighty thousand Catholics, fifty thousand of whom are Irish, so we shall have plenty of work," he wrote [2] on the last day of 1844. In the following August he was in Manchester and wrote [3] to his General : "I could never make you realise the needs of this Island, and the well-grounded hopes there are of great good to be done. Let me tell you one thing about what has happened and is still happening

---

[1] *Sequel to Catholic Emancipation*, I, p. 177.
[2] *Dominic Barberi in England*, p. 123.   [3] *Ibid.*, p. 133.

at Manchester, where I have been this week. Forty-five years ago there were in this city forty-four Catholics. At this moment the Catholic population is in the neighbourhood of a hundred thousand. For this number there are just twelve priests, who work like heroes, hearing confessions at times from three o'clock in the afternoon till after midnight. Nevertheless about forty thousand Catholics have not yet made their Easter ' duty,' for sheer want of someone to hear their confessions. Apart from Catholics, these priests are called continually to assist dying Protestants, and they often find themselves faced with the dilemma—either to abandon Catholics in order to give some spiritual aid to poor helpless Protestants who call for their assistance, or to let these Protestants die without any hope whatever. One case happens particularly often—namely that of a Protestant who was quite willing to live outside the Catholic Church, but is unwilling to die outside it. . . . Now what I say about Manchester, which contains almost half a million of inhabitants, may be said proportionately of other populous cities— Liverpool, Birmingham and the rest. In all these places the Catholics are daily increasing in numbers, and the increase would be even greater if some definite encouragement were given. I therefore beseech you once again to see if you could not send a few more good men ready to suffer, to be mocked and despised for the love of our Lord and His Church in this land. Consider that if we win England for the Faith it would mean the sure and certain expansion of our holy religion throughout the world. English influence, English energy and might, far surpass that of any other nation. Besides the nation is already so accomplished in every way that the one thing it lacks to become the finest nation in the world is the possession of the Catholic faith. Send then all the men you can, and I will see to their expenses."

This promise that he would himself provide for the expenses of the missionaries is a true measure of Dominic Barberi's heroic faith. Utter poverty had been his experience since he reached England, yet he had somehow contrived to build several houses for his Order, and to open a number of missions. The sufferings of " Mr. Newman's victims "—as the convert parsons and others who had been left destitute by their conversion were soon called—were less severe than what the Passionists and other missionaries cheerfully faced from the day of their arrival. Married clergymen were a problem with which the Italian missionaries had scarcely reckoned. They had counted rather upon the convert clergymen to increase the supply of priests for work in England. "The conversions are going on splendidly," Father Dominic reported [1] to Rome in December 1845, after he had received Newman into the Church. "More than thirty Protestant clergymen have embraced the Catholic Faith in a few months. I had already foreseen that Newman's decision would be an epoch-making event. The well-known Mr. Faber was here yesterday. He is the author of several learned works, and became a Catholic a few weeks ago. He has left here two young men, converts both of them, who have had to fly from the wrath of their relatives in consequence of their change of religion. They will stay here about a week. How these poor converts suffer! They are real martyrs for the Faith." A few weeks later he wrote again [2] about the general conditions in England. "Crosses, heavy and grievous, are not wanting, but patience and perseverance can do wonders. Beginnings are always difficult and painful. Never mind! . . . How much all founders have suffered. Here in England our work may be regarded as an entirely new foundation. . . . We must never lose courage. For myself I can say that for thirty years I prepared myself to suffer in England, and I am bound to admit that my sufferings here have far surpassed anything I could have expected. And what am I to expect for the future? Crosses—and still more crosses. And of what kind? I know not and I do not care to know; God will support me."

In February 1846, he was unexpectedly offered another house for a new Passionist foundation. Another Oxford convert, Mr. William Leigh, of Brasenose, had become a Catholic in the previous year, and he wished to offer them a house in the Western District, where he could build a church for them. He had bought Woodchester Park in Gloucestershire for the purpose, an ample place

[1] *Dominic Barberi in England*, p. 145.   [2] *Ibid.*, p. 146.

three miles from the nearest town, but in a thickly populated district, where " we would be as it were in the centre of a circle with a circumference of about a hundred miles, where there is not a single Catholic chapel." Mr. Leigh would build a house for them as well as a church, and in the meantime he would rent a building for them. Before Easter Dominic Barberi had completed the arrangements. Since the days of Henry VIII there had been no Catholic chapel in all the district around, but the Passionists were already celebrating the full ceremonies of Holy Week in their new home. Barberi himself was preaching to a congregation of Protestants who crowded the chapel to its doors, while others stood outside to see through the windows. For months the crowds continued to come, though the converts were very few. But there were requests for other chapels in the surrounding country and in time converts were received.

In August another of his long-cherished hopes was fulfilled, when he heard from George Spencer, who had decided that he must enter some religious order and asked for admission as a Passionist. It was nearly twenty years since they had first met in Rome, with Ambrose Phillipps and Kenelm Digby, and no man had done more to inflame his desire to work in England. " He is the noblest and perhaps the man of holiest life among the priests in this country," Barberi wrote [1] to Rome. " My hopes are that he will be for this branch of our Congregation what St. Bernard was for Citeaux, and that he will bring many with him under the standard of the Passion. He has assured me that his choice of our Congregation was determined by our poverty, not only in our Rule, but in our observance of it. And he gave me clearly to understand that if we contemplate any change whatever in our mode of life, garb, etc., he would not join us. I replied that I hoped nothing of the kind would happen. He must now put his affairs in order, a matter of some weeks' delay. I have told him to leave any money he has in the hands of his Bishop, and to bring nothing to us. He will do so, and of his money we shall retain nothing. If the Bishop should then desire to give us something by way of an alms or to build the

---

[1] *Dominic Barberi in England,* p. 166.

Church at Aston we shall receive it." Spencer's accession to the Passionists was all the more welcome because they were still a small community of Italian priests who made themselves understood with difficulty in English. He was not only an Englishman, but with social connections which brought them in touch with many benefactors and future converts. His family had treated him with great kindness since he became a Catholic ; and his brother, on inheriting the Earldom, had continued to make him a generous personal allowance. He discontinued it, however, when Spencer took a vow of poverty, and neither the Bishop nor Dominic Barberi was to receive any further assistance from that quarter. But George Spencer always kept up affectionate relations with his relatives, and early in 1846 he had again paid a visit to his sister, Lady Lyttleton, who was then governess to Queen Victoria's children. On entering the Passionist novitiate his personal freedom was restricted, and he was put to scrubbing stairs and the other menial duties which the novitiate requires. He was soon to be engaged in work among the poor Catholics of the Potteries, of a kind which threw an unprecedented strain upon the overworked clergy of the Midlands and the North.

The Irish influx had become an acute problem in the cities, before the Chartist riots drew attention to the growing misery of the industrial workers. Carlyle had already recognised it as one of the chief factors in the prevailing distress when he published his essay on Chartism in 1839. " Crowds of miserable Irish darken all our towns," he wrote.[1] " The wild Milesian features, looking false ingenuity, restlessness, unreason, misery and mockery, salute you on all highways and byways. The English coachman, as he whirls past, lashes the Milesian with his whip, curses him with his tongue ; the Milesian is holding out his hat to beg. He is the sorest evil this country has to strive with. In his rags and laughing savagery, he is there to undertake all work that can be done by mere strength of hand and back ; for wages that will purchase him potatoes. He needs only salt for condiment ; he lodges to his mind in any pig hutch or dog hutch, roosts in outhouses ; and

[1] *Critical Essays*, VI, p. 127.

wears a suit of tatters, the getting off and on of which is said to be a difficult operation, transacted only in festivals and the hightides of the calendar. The Saxon man if he cannot work on these terms, finds no work. He too may be ignorant ; but he has not sunk from decent manhood to squalid apehood ; he cannot continue there. . . . And yet these poor Celtiberian Irish brothers, how can they help it ? They cannot stay at home, and starve. It is just and natural that they come hither as a curse to us. Alas, for them too it is not a luxury."

The stream of immigration from Ireland which had been increasing steadily for years assumed far greater proportions as a result of the famine in Ireland which followed upon the failure of the potato crop in 1845. The crop failed again in 1846, and for a third successive year in 1847, until the emigration assumed the character of a national exodus. Literally millions of starving and plague-stricken people sought escape in England or overseas. By the end of 1846 the situation had become extremely serious, and appeals for relief funds were being widely made in England.

Dominic Barberi was so moved by the accounts of starvation in County Kerry that he sent from his own little community a subscription of £4, which they saved " by denying themselves some things which our holy Rule allows them." But the demands upon them for the relief of Irish distress became overwhelming, when the Irish refugees flocked into the towns surrounding Aston and established themselves in his mission. A larger church became a necessity, while he and his priests spent their days ministering to the starving people in the streets of the industrial towns. In Liverpool particularly, where swarms of immigrants arrived on their way to America, or in the dim hope of finding work and refuge in England, the " famine fever " which they brought with them was spreading fast. There also Dominic Barberi was being called upon to give missions and to assist in places where the priests had died after contracting typhus. In June 1847, he was [1] in Liverpool " giving the spiritual exercises to the holy priests who are sacrificing their lives at present for the unfortunate Irish people

[1] *Dominic Barberi in England*, p. 177.

there ravaged by the plague. And priests are dying of the plague in other parts of the country. At Stone we have about a hundred Irish, of whom about half have been infected by the plague, and all are in want. I am terribly afraid we may lose some of our own men, but what can be done?" In September he was writing [1] from Aston that " for the past three months Father Gaudentius has not been able to go out on missions, as he has been kept constantly at work among the Irish emigrants at our doors. The plague is still here, and I don't know where it will end. Father Gaudentius has been, and still is, exposed daily to the terrible danger of contagion. . . . Personally I have not a moment's rest, amid all the work of every kind." He was being required to give retreats to the clergy in many places, from London to Liverpool or York. " I go straight ahead as best I can. To think of repose is useless when great multitudes ask for bread and there is none to break it to them. The worst of it is that so many English priests are dying of the plague. Nine have died in Liverpool alone up to the present." Two months later he wrote that Father Gaudentius in his own community was down with typhus, and people said that the plague might continue for years. In February he was writing again that " here in England not a week passes without the death of some priests stricken down with the plague." No Passionist had died so far, but " I very much fear the year will not pass without someone being sacrificed. There are so few priests in England now! If we go on this way, there will soon be none left. And what then will become of our hopes for the conversion of England ? . . . If only you could send me a few more good subjects from Italy. They would not find pleasure, ease, comfort here, but a vast field of labour for the divine glory ; and at the end death, it may be, amid suffering and pain."

George Spencer contracted typhus during the summer, and was on the point of death, but recovered after receiving the last sacraments. Father Gaudentius likewise recovered. But all through the Midlands and the North its ravages continued. The most conspicuous victim among the English clergy was Dr. Riddell, who

[1] *Dominic Barberi in England,* p. 177.

succeeded Dr. Mostyn as Vicar-Apostolic of the Northern District in August, and died at the beginning of November after contracting " famine fever " among the Irish refugees in Newcastle. The approach of winter brought some alleviation, but on January 1, 1848, Barberi was writing that " although we are in the depth of winter there are eight or ten Irish people still ill with the plague at Stone. Imagine what it will be in the summer. Father Augustine has no lack of courage to assist these cases, but I do not know if the others have strength sufficient to resist the infection that is everywhere." He went among the sick constantly himself, and his health had been so undermined with fatigue and hardships that his escape was almost miraculous. At the end of March 1848 he wrote from Aston, after the death of one of his postulants : " My sorrows of late have sapped even my physical strength, and at times I am so prostrated as scarcely to be able to stand. I am ill from the crown of my head to the soles of my feet—and yet with God's help I am constantly on foot to assist those who are worse even than I. How will my own life end ? I know not. *Deus providebit*."

CHAPTER XII

PREPARATIONS FOR THE HIERARCHY

IN comparison with the flood of Irish immigrants, the influx of converts, even after Newman's conversion, was a minor problem for the English bishops. Wiseman was devoting himself constantly to their needs, and the principal seminaries and religious colleges were also giving assistance. Prior Park was, next to Oscott, the chief centre to which converts were going to be received. A few also went to St. Edmund's, and there W. G. Ward established himself in the immediate vicinity, having got Pugin to build a house for him at Old Hall. He had hopes that the College would find some use for his undoubted talents and learning, and being a genuinely humble man, he was prepared to undertake any sort of task that might be offered to him. But Bishop Griffiths told him [1] at once when he presented himself that though they were very glad to welcome him, " of course we have no work for you." Disappointed, but feeling that his previous impression of the lack of culture and learning among the old Catholics had been fully justified, Ward settled down to an almost monastic life at Old Hall for the next three years. Both Newman and Faber had, with several other leaders of the Movement, gone to Rome to undergo a course of preparation for the priesthood ; and the sudden stream of conversions which had followed theirs abated considerably during 1846 and 1847. But the growth of Catholic numbers had developed with such rapidity that the bishops were now convinced that steps must be taken quickly to establish more normal conditions in the administration of the Church. In Rome also it was felt that final decisions must be taken. The stream of converts had made a deep impression there, and the rapid growth of industrial cities with large populations was already recognised. Something like a deadlock had, however, arisen through the

[1] *W. G. Ward and the Catholic Revival,* by Wilfrid Ward, p. 8.

many misunderstandings which had hampered all relations between the Vicars-Apostolic and the Roman authorities. Cardinal Acton was the chief adviser in Rome on all matters concerning English affairs, and he felt, not without reason, that the English bishops were too conservative and too deeply rooted in the traditions of their former isolation. He believed that Rome must exert a stronger influence in insisting upon bold developments. There was no doubt that the older bishops were definitely antagonistic to the religious orders, on the ground that their coming only increased the existing confusion. They were always responsible to their own superiors, and the Vicars-Apostolic had so little effective authority already that it must be further weakened when new missions were created in which the bishops had to divide responsibility with the heads of religious orders. Yet it was obviously impossible to form new missions and to build new churches with secular clergy alone, on the scale which the pheno- menal increase in Catholic population demanded. Cardinal Acton believed that the situation would be met by the creation of more Vicars-Apostolic, who would still be directly subject to Propaganda in Rome. But the Vicars-Apostolic and the clergy generally believed that the time had come when a proper hierarchy should be restored, so that the ordinary Canon Law could be enforced. There would then be recognised means for settling disputes and dealing with all the problems of Church administra- tion as they arose. Rome, however, regarded the Vicars-Apostolic with such misgivings that this solution was solidly opposed.

Not the least difficulty was that Bishop Griffiths—whose ceaseless industry and constructive work were never appreciated properly in Rome, because of the disputes in which he had become involved —must naturally become the first archbishop in a restored hierarchy, as he was in charge of the London District. Bishop Baines had for long been regarded as the most troublesome of the English bishops from the Roman point of view, until he died in 1843. Relations improved when he was succeeded by Dr. Baggs, who had replaced Wiseman as Rector of the English College in Rome, and as agent for the English Vicars-Apostolic. But Dr. Baggs had died very soon afterwards, within a year of his return to England. Pope Gregory XIV had been unusually acquainted with English conditions, through his previous experience as Prefect of Propaganda, and during the sixteen years of his pontificate he had taken the closest interest in English affairs. He had relied largely upon the opinions of Wiseman, who had been his intimate friend before he was elected Pope. His long experience made him share the views of Cardinal Acton, that the time had not yet come when a full hierarchy could be established ; and they both were influenced considerably by their conviction that Bishop Griffiths would not be a suitable person to become the first archbishop in London and head of the reconstituted hierarchy.

As Bishop Griffiths was still in his early fifties, and Cardinal Acton was some ten years his junior, the prospect of any early solution to these difficulties seemed almost hopeless. But the Pope unexpectedly fell ill and died at the beginning of June 1846. The prospect of a thorough reorganisation in England was therefore directly affected when Cardinal Mastai Faretti was elected to succeed him as Pope Pius IX. Dr. Ullathorne had just been appointed to the Western District after the death of Dr. Baggs, and his influence and prestige in Rome was expected to assist matters very considerably. He had played a large part in negotiating the establishment of a hierarchy in Australia. His gifts were well known, and there had been disappointment that he had not been included among the four new Vicars-Apostolic six years before. But Ullathorne had no such ambitions. He had already succeeded in refusing several of the Australian sees, and he believed that he would escape nomination to a bishopric at home. He had been labouring with great success at Coventry, and had opened his new church there in the summer of 1844. He had hopes of opening a Benedictine priory there, and when he preached at the opening of the Church he boldly wore his full Benedictine dress and refused ever afterwards to preach without wearing it. On the death of Bishop Baggs he was nominated as his successor in the Western District, but he immediately declined the nomination. Cardinal Acton, however, had replied with a letter which he found it impossible to refuse. " If honour and riches had gathered round the mitre hanging over your Lordship's head," he wrote,[1] " then perhaps your virtue might have found out some motives to allege as a plea of excuse for resisting the offer. But in the present circumstances it is pain, trouble, and labour which is offered you, and therefore I trust that through love for Christ and His Church you will immediately accept the burden." Ullathorne took the letter with him into his chapel, and after reading it again decided that refusal would be ignoble.

On the election of the new Pope the Vicars-Apostolic decided to send a deputation to Rome, and they chose Wiseman and Bishop Sharples, who were coadjutors respectively to the Midland and Lancastrian Districts. It was symptomatic of the existing relations with the Holy See that none of the Vicars-Apostolic themselves went with the deputation, and that nearly a whole year elapsed before their deputies arrived in Rome. There had been negotiations on various matters by correspondence in the interval, and the result had been disquieting. Influences had been at work already to prejudice relations between the new Pope and the Vicars-Apostolic. Wiseman, with his long Roman experience, was obviously well equipped for dealing with the new situation, but he was returning to a new Rome in which the Pope who had been his friend for so many years was no longer there. His relations with Cardinal Acton were, however, most cordial. But while the two coadjutor bishops were on their journey to Rome, Cardinal Acton died unexpectedly at Naples at the early age of forty-four. From the point of view of the Vicars-Apostolic, his death undoubtedly eased matters considerably. He had been the chief adviser of the late Pope on English affairs in all the recent negotiations, and he had been openly opposed to their requests for a restoration of the hierarchy. Now both the Pope and Cardinal Acton had died within a year ; and the chief obstacle which remained was the conviction in Rome that Bishop Griffiths would be an impossible head of a new hierarchy. In July Wiseman wrote to report progress to Bishop Griffiths, and in August the substance of his

[1] *Life of Ullathorne*, I, p. 137.

letter [1] was reported by the Bishop to Ullathorne. Wiseman had found " that much sinister influence has been exerted at Rome against the present state of things in England, and consequently against the Bishops. From the remarks made by His Holiness and by others it would seem that the following are the principal subjects of complaint. 1. Want of sufficient means of religion, of churches, chapels, schools and priests, especially in large towns. This, of course, is attributed to want of proper exertion. 2. Want of zeal and activity, as though conversions could be increased indefinitely if proper efforts were made. 3. Arbitrary exercise of authority with regard to the clergy, and want of fixed rules for the suspension, removal, etc., of priests. 4. Administration of trusts to church property—the subject of rival bills this year."

Bishops Wiseman and Sharples had replied to these complaints by drawing up lists of the churches, chapels and religious houses opened in England during the past six years, and of the missions and retreats given. The Pope had been genuinely impressed, and had himself raised the question of making changes in the existing constitution of the Church in England ; while Wiseman reported that there had been talk of a further sub-division of the vicariates apostolic, which had been Cardinal Acton's plan. It had been agreed that they were to consult the English bishops and report further to the Pope. Bishop Griffiths, in writing to Ullathorne, had expressed his full agreement with Wiseman's letter. Cardinal Fransoni was still Prefect of Propaganda, but he was growing old and infirm, and a most important change had recently occurred, in the appointment of Mgr. Barnabó as secretary of Propaganda. The new secretary was rapidly acquiring a decisive voice in its affairs. Wiseman had quickly appreciated his force of character, and had succeeded in converting him to the Bishops' views. Mgr. Barnabó was now in favour of establishing a hierarchy in England, and he advised the two bishops to draw up a formal petition for its restoration. The obstacles were disappearing fast, and now yet another obstacle was to be removed. Bishop Griffiths had suddenly fallen ill, and his letter to Ullathorne was dictated by him to

[1] *Sequel to Catholic Emancipation,* II, p. 146.

Dr. Cox of St. Edmund's College. His strength had failed in a painful illness, and within a week he died. He had been Vicar-Apostolic in London for eleven years, and he was still only fifty-four. Wiseman was in Rome when his death was announced. The Bishop was buried on August 20, and nine days later the Pope nominated Wiseman to succeed him.

The haste with which Wiseman's appointment was made provoked much resentment in England, where the clergy had for years been agitating to obtain a voice in the nomination of new bishops. It was indeed one of the most important questions involved in the agitation for restoring a hierarchy. For years past it had been the practice for each Vicar-Apostolic to ask for the appointment of a coadjutor, after he had been in office for some time, and the choice of the coadjutor rested entirely with himself. The London clergy had particular reason to feel sore on the matter, because Bishop Griffiths himself had been made coadjutor without any sort of previous consultation. When old Bishop Bramston had desired a coadjutor, he had made what appeared to be a very reasonable choice by applying for Dr. Gradwell, the first Rector of the restored English College in Rome. Dr. Gradwell had been duly appointed, and had been replaced in Rome by Wiseman at a remarkably early age. But Dr. Gradwell's health failed soon after his return to England from Italy, and he died in the early spring of 1833. Dr. Bramston obviously required a coadjutor more than ever, as he was now five years older than when he had first applied for one. He chose Dr. Griffiths, who had been closely associated with him as President of St. Edmund's College, and who might have been his first choice instead of Dr. Gradwell if he had been old enough at the time. His appointment was in one way specially appropriate, because he thus became the first English bishop in modern times who had been entirely educated in England. But the fact that he had spent his whole life within the precincts of a seminary made him appear to the clergy as a man with insufficient training for his new duties. Moreover, he was known to be a man of inflexible obstinacy whenever he had to exercise responsibility. The clergy had felt for some time that they should have a voice in the selection of their future bishops, and in view of Bishop Bramston's age it was clear that the coadjutor would very soon succeed him as Vicar-Apostolic in London.

One of the principal clergy in London, Mr. Jones of Warwick Street, wrote a very candid letter [1] at the time to Dr. Lingard in Ushaw, which describes the extremely unsatisfactory way in which such appointments were made. "Bishop Bramston is an infirm man whose life at best is not worth six months' purchase, and he has nominated a successor who will, we conceive, be as ready to propagate the system of private nomination to the Apostolic Vicariate as he is to take it on that principle from Dr. Bramston. This day week, at St. Edmund's College, immediately after the removal of the dinner cloth, Dr. Griffiths was formally announced as Bishop of Olena. Bishop Bramston prefaced his announcement by assuring the company that it gave him more pleasure than he had ever heretofore enjoyed to inform them that his Holiness had graciously yielded to his request for his excellent friend at his left as his Coadjutor, that the bulls had arrived, and that nothing was wanting but consecration, which was to be performed as soon as possible, and that Dr. Griffiths was already Bishop inasmuch as he could not set aside the appointment. He therefore called upon the company (consisting of twelve priests, seven of whom were ordained on the previous Sunday, and five Professors and a Protestant relation of his, Mr. Yorke, who sat on his right) to drink the health of the new Bishop. Some tears of tenderness and congratulation were shed by the speaker, a partial applause followed the address, and the toast was drunk with three times three, with the subsequent intonation of *Ad multos annos*. The elect, much abashed and embarrassed, rose and returned thanks, and adroitly applying the words that had just been chanted, expressed a hope that his coadjutorship would last many years."

Dr. Lingard's reply to that cry of distress must be quoted, because the discontent of the clergy in regard to the appointment of new bishops had intensified notably during the intervening years of crowded activity and expansion. "The Bishops dispose

[1] *Sequel to Catholic Emancipation*, I, pp. 54-55.

of the succession as though they held their offices in fee simple, and had a right to leave them to whom they please," he replied [1] from Ushaw. "But while I admit the abuse, I know not where to discover a remedy which may not prove a worse evil. . . . To the prevailing method of appointment in general I would object, did I know to whom to transfer it. . . . I have sometimes thought that the only possible expedient for raising the clergy from their present degraded state would be the erection of a Chapter, say of twelve members in each vicariate, which Chapter should exercise jurisdiction *vacante episcopatu*, and have the right of presenting three names to the choice of the Pope whenever a Bishop or Coadjutor is to be appointed. This would be a first step of importance, as it would not only produce the benefit for which it would be ostensibly established, but also give existence to an acknowledged authority which on proper occasions might check the irresponsible and unlimited authority of the Bishop."

Although the expansion in the London District certainly required the assistance of a coadjutor, Bishop Griffiths had, in fact, never applied for one, because he was still a relatively young man at the time of his unexpected death. The clergy had been canvassing the subject for some time, and Wiseman was not one of the three names that they would have proposed. But now Rome had directly appointed Wiseman to the London District within a shorter time than had ever been thought sufficient before. The situation was, however, most abnormal, because the new Pope was already preparing to reconstitute the hierarchy. And as a token that the whole position was in a state of flux, Wiseman was nominated only as pro-Vicar-Apostolic for the time being. He returned to England in September, and took up his residence in Golden Square. There was no doubt that many of the clergy regarded him with hostility, but there was so much work before him that he had little time to consider such personal matters. For seven years he had been only a coadjutor bishop in the Midlands, and now he had the most important District in England under his personal jurisdiction. The chief complaints against Bishop

[1] *Sequel to Catholic Emancipation*, I, 55.

Griffiths in Rome had been that he had failed to encourage the converts from the Church of England, and that he had neglected the opportunity to extend religious development by discouraging the introduction of religious orders. Wiseman could at least hope that, by his personal connection with the convert clergyman, he would obtain a very substantial increase in the number of clergy ; and it was he also who had done most to promote the importation of religious missionaries from the Continent.

Newman had now been in Rome for more than a year, and after long deliberation he had come to the conclusion that Wiseman's earliest suggestion would be the most useful and congenial work that he could undertake as a Catholic priest. In January 1847 he had written [1] to Wiseman from Rome : " It is curious and very pleasant that, after all the thought we can give the matter, we must come to your Lordship's original idea, and feel we cannot do better than be Oratorians. . . . What we should want would be to hire a large room at Birmingham and, if it succeeded, then to build. The Superior of the Franciscans, Father Benigno, in the Trastevere, wishes us out of his own head to engage in an English Authorised Translation of the Bible. He is a learned man, and on the Congregation of the Index. What he wished was that we should take the Protestant translation, correct it by the Vulgate . . . and get sanctioned here. This might be our first work if your Lordship approved of it." In another letter [2] he wrote : " I have all along said to myself (as you may suppose) I can do nothing without Rome on my side. There is so much discord, so much jealousy in England, that I cannot get on without this support to carry me on. It is this which carries your Lordship on. I see here that no one scarcely is thought to be doing anything in England but those who are connected with you."

Newman had deliberately acquired the Roman outlook, partly because he knew well that he could never acquire that of the hereditary Catholics in England, but also because he was aware of the suspicions which he would meet when he returned to England, if he could not count upon absolute backing from Rome. His

---

[1] *Life of Wiseman,* I, p. 453.   [2] *Ibid.,* p. 456.

plans for the Oratory envisaged a gradual extension of its activities. Maryvale would, he hoped,[1] be "a sort of mother house, where novices might be trained, supposing the Institution spread into other towns besides Birmingham; where retreats might be held; where the Oratorian brothers might live (say) four months out of the year, as a time of recruiting after the work of the town, of reading and writing, also a sort of summer holiday place on St. Philip's plan. . . . As to the Oratory itself its structure must be different from anything ecclesiastical hitherto built in England; it is not a church or chapel. Ought it to be something like a chapter house? Your Lordship recollects the Oratory here. It must be a building for preaching and music; not an open roof, certainly no screen. I am afraid I shall shock Pugin."

He did indeed shock Pugin, even more violently than Wiseman shocked him by attempting to abolish the rood screen in St. Chad's Cathedral. Newman and his companions were duly ordained in Rome in October 1848, and returned to England at the end of the year. Before their return Newman had received an unexpected accession of strength through Father Faber's decision to close down the society of St. Wilfrid, which he had established at Cotton Hall, and join forces with Newman's new Institute of the Oratory. Wiseman, newly installed as Vicar-Apostolic in London, gave his cordial approval, subject to Newman's consent, and the fusion of forces provided a most remarkable group of convert clergymen established in a new Institute with Newman as their head. Faber had no illusions as to the difficulties that might arise from the amalgamation. "I shrink from the prospect before me very, very much," he wrote [2] frankly to Newman; "to fall from founder and superior to novice, and a novice who must naturally be an object of extreme jealousy from his influence over the rest of the brothers; to meet the ludibrium of all our old Catholic enemies; to stand the evil opinion of those who, as A. B. does, think all this from Satan, will require no little grace. It is possible to face it well in meditation, with the dignity of the sacrifice to support us, but the daily irritating detail, then will be the trial."

[1] *Life of Wiseman*, I, p. 459.   [2] *Life of Newman*, I, p. 197.

In February 1848, the English Oratory was formally erected at Birmingham. Wiseman's transference to London had deprived them of his immediate supervision, but it was too late to alter the arrangements. While Bishop Griffiths had lived Newman could look for no scope in the London District, and they had decided on Birmingham for that reason. " He was the *only* Bishop," Newman wrote [1] in confidence to Henry Wilberforce, " who did not cordially welcome me. He was a good, upright careful man, but timid. He was really kind to me personally, but he feared me ; so I felt myself cut out of London. He died just after the brief was finished."

All that Ambrose Phillipps and Pugin had hoped for during those earlier years seemed, indeed, to have come true at last. Wiseman was in England, and now in charge of the most important of the English vicariates. The " Oxford Men " had not only become Catholics, but were already ordained and preparing to commence their work for the conversion of England. Pugin himself had left his mark far and wide during the years since he became a Catholic. He had designed St. Chad's in Birmingham, the first Catholic cathedral to be opened since the Reformation. His work was to be seen at Oscott, at St. Edmund's, and in new churches, large or small, throughout the length of England. He had been entrusted with a still more important work in London, where he had been commissioned to design the new St. George's Cathedral in Southwark, to be erected on the very site of the worst riots against the Catholics led by Lord George Gordon within living memory. His first designs for it were intended to allow for future expansion in the course of generations. But they were overruled because resources were so inadequate that his plans seemed impossibly ambitious. He put them aside and began on a more modest scale, and the foundation had been begun in September 1840, when Wiseman was returning to England as a newly consecrated bishop. Delays of various kinds had protracted the work for eight years until Wiseman had become Vicar-Apostolic in London. But by the summer of 1848 the fine Gothic cathedral was ready for formal opening. Wiseman threw himself into the

[1] *Life of Newman*, I, p. 197.

preparations, and used all his influence abroad to assemble an attendance such as had never been seen in any Catholic church since the Reformation. As the cathedral was built on the site of the old Belgian Embassy Church, he invited all the Belgian bishops to assist, and the Bishops of Tournai and Liege accepted his invitation. The Bishops of Treves and Luxembourg accepted as well. Several French bishops also had promised to come, but the revolution in Paris made it impossible at the last moment for them to travel. Archbishop Affre was shot on the barricades in Paris while attempting to negotiate a truce only four days before the ceremonies, and Wiseman read out a letter from him, written a few days before his death, regretting his inability to leave the city. Thirteen bishops in all took part in the solemn ritual, and 240 priests, besides representatives of seven religious orders.

It was the climax of Pugin's work for the revival of Church architecture. After the appointment of Wiseman to the London District and the foundation of Newman's Oratory at Birmingham, he could no longer exercise the same ascendancy as before in all matters pertaining to religious art. Both Newman and Father Faber were determined that their Oratory should be modelled upon its Roman pattern, and they declined to be overborne by Pugin's tempestuous protests. Pugin and Ambrose Phillipps still maintained that all classical art was pagan, and that Gothic art alone was Christian ; but Faber was no less determined to create enthusiasm for Roman ways in England, than they were to revive the pre-Reformation traditions. A heated controversy soon arose, and strong language was used on both sides. It was solemnly reported to Newman, who was now Faber's superior in religion, that Phillipps and Pugin had " cursed the Oratory," and Newman felt that the matter could not be allowed to rest. The conflict had provoked widespread comment, and Newman exchanged a series of letters with Ambrose Phillipps during June 1848, which showed that the " Oxford Men " could no longer be reckoned as champions of all that Pugin and Phillipps had expected them to advocate. Newman wrote [1] to expostulate against the repetition of the strong

---

[1] *Life of Ambrose Phillipps,* II, pp. 204-206.

language which had been used against Father Faber. "If Mr. Pugin persists, as I cannot hope he will not, in loading with bad names the admirers of Italian architecture, he is going the very way to increase their number. Man will not be put down without authority which is infallible. And, if we go to authority, I suppose Popes have given greater sanction to Italian than to Gothic." Phillipps sent a reasoned reply which compelled Newman to write more fully. The actual words which Phillipps had used to Father Faber had been reported to him as being " Father Faber, God for your pride destroyed and brought to nought your first effort ; he will curse and destroy your order and it will perish if you go on thus." Phillipps was still persisting in his contention that Grecian and Italian art were all pagan, and Newman regarded the word pagan as being obviously a " term of reproach." " If it be pagan, it is Popish too," he answered, " for I suppose the Pope has given quite as much sanction to it as he has to Gregorian music, which by the by seems to be pagan in the same sense that Italian architecture is." He accused Phillipps, with gentle firmness, of " treating ritual opinions as doctrinal errors."

At the same time he informed Phillipps that there was now a prospect of another Oratory being established in London. They had been offered " a beautiful piece of ground, and a populous neighbourhood of rich and poor is rising around the spot." But Phillipps was still impenitent and Newman had to write yet again, protesting that " I will not let you say that we are ' preaching a Crusade ' against you or are throwing in what ' weight,' as you kindly say we have, against Mr. Pugin. It really is no such thing ; but the case stands thus. Mr. Pugin is a man of genius ; I have the greatest admiration of his talents, and willingly acknowledge that Catholics owe him a great debt for what he has done in the revival of Gothic architecture amongst us. His zeal, his innate diligence, his resources, his invention, his imagination, his sagacity in research, are all of the highest order. It is impossible that any one, not scientifically qualified to judge of his merits, can feel a profounder reverence than I do for the gift with which it has pleased the Author of all Truth and Beauty to endow him. But he has the great fault of a man of genius, as well as the merit. He is intolerant, and if I might use a stronger word, a bigot. He sees nothing good in any school of Christian art except that of which he is himself so great an ornament. The canons of Gothic architecture are to him points of faith, and every one is a heretic who would venture to question them." The dispute was a serious matter for the Oratorians, because Phillipps had become one of the recognised leaders of the Catholic laity and his influence with Lord Shrewsbury, the most munificent of Church benefactors in these years, might hamper their prospects very considerably when funds had to be raised. Phillipps did, in fact, refuse to subscribe towards the funds for the Brompton Oratory, and in a letter to Lord Shrewsbury he explained [1] that "I hear they are doing wonders : there is only one thing I regret about them, their strange and unaccountable enmity to Christian art and Gothick architecture. I hear that the new Oratory is to be built, not in the old ecclesiastical architecture but in the *classical style !* "

Pugin's feelings were still more vehement, and in a letter to Phillipps he wrote [2] bitterly : " The Oxford men, with some few exceptions, have turned out the most disappointing people in the world. They were three times as Catholic in their ideas before they were reconciled to the Church. It is really quite lamentable. They have got the most disgusting place possible for the Oratory [3] in London and fitted up in a horrible manner with a sort of Anglo-Roman altar. Those things are very sad and the mischief they do is inconceivable. What a glorious man Formby is. He is about the only man who has stuck to the true thing and never bowed the knee to Baal. A man may be judged by his feeling on Plaint Chaunt. If he likes Mozart he is no chancel and screen man. By their music you shall know them, and I lost all faith in the Oratorians when I found they were opposed to the old song." The hardest blow to him was when Faber opened the London Oratory in old Assembly Rooms. Pugin wrote [4] to Lord Shrewsbury in

---

[1] *Life of Ambrose Phillipps*, II, p. 216.   [2] *Ibid.*, p. 216.
[3] This refers to the first Oratory in King William Street.
[4] Ferrey's *Recollections of Pugin*, p. 127.

despair : "Has your Lordship heard that the Oratorians have opened the Lowther rooms as a Chapel ! ! ! A place for the vilest debauchery, masquerades, etc. One night a masked ball, next Benediction. This appears to me perfectly monstrous, and I give the whole order up for ever. What a degradation for religion ! Why, it is worse than the Socialists. What a place to celebrate the mysteries of religion in ! I cannot conceive how it is allowed. It cannot even be licensed or protected by the law since they only have it for a time. It is the greatest blow we have had for a long time ; no men have been so disappointing as these. Conceive the poet Faber come down to the Lowther rooms ! The man who wrote ' Thoughts and Sights in Foreign Churches ' ! ! ! hiring the Lowther rooms ! Well may they cry out against screens or anything else. I always said they wanted rooms, not churches, and now they have got them. Sad times. I cannot imagine what the world will come to if it goes on much longer."

The dispute was, in fact, much more than a conflict of personal opinions. But Pugin's eccentricity had increased with the years, and his mind was beginning to give way under the strain of incessant overwork. He was only thirty-seven when, in 1849, darkness descended upon that amazingly active brain, and he had to be taken to an asylum where he remained for some months. After a brief recovery he died in 1852. Nothing could have been more painful to Newman than this open quarrel with men who had seemed to him ten years before as the noblest exponents of religious revival in the Catholic body. But the whole future of his work as a Catholic was involved in the discussion. He had stated the case quite plainly in his letter [1] to Ambrose Phillipps in defence of Father Faber. "We know that the Church, while one and the same in doctrine ever, is ever modifying, adapting, varying her discipline and ritual, according to the times. In these respects the Middle Ages was not what the First Centuries were—nor is the Age Present the Middle Age. In order then that any style of Architecture should exactly suit the living ritual of the 19th century, it should be the living architecture of the 19th century—it should

[1] *Life of Ambrose Phillipps,* II, p. 206.

never have died—else, while the ritual has changed, the architecture has not kept pace with it. This defect is actually found in the case of Gothic. Gothic is now like an old dress, which fitted a man well 20 years back, but must be altered to fit him now. . . . Now for Oratorians, the birth of the 16th century, to assume the architecture simply and unconditionally of the 13th, would be as absurd as their putting on them the cowl of the Dominicans or adopting the tonsure of the Carthusians. We do not want a cloister or chapter room, but an Oratory. I, for one, believe that Gothic can be adapted, developed to the requisitions of an Oratory. Mr. Pugin does not : he implied, in conversation with me at Rome, that he would as soon build a Mechanical Institute as an Oratory. I begged him to see the Oratory at the Chiese Nueva, he gave me no hope he would do [so. Now is it wonderful that I prefer St. Philip to Mr. Pugin ? "

CHAPTER XIII

THE NEW ERA EMERGES

A NEW era had opened with Wiseman's appointment to the London District, while the death of Bishop Griffiths had symbolically closed the era of the Vicars-Apostolic. The change had coincided with Newman's return to England after his ordination in Rome, and Newman in his first clash with Pugin and Phillipps had declared himself openly on the side of the innovators. The intensive preparations of previous years were already fructifying when Wiseman left Birmingham for London. With the new cathedral in Southwark, there was now in London a religious centre adequate to the great development of Catholic life which was rapidly maturing. Wiseman's connection with the Midland District had focussed there the chief forces upon which he had counted hitherto, but he determined to extend their activities to London to assist him in his wide field of work. The establishment of Newman's Institute of the Oratory had been formally approved in Rome, and its headquarters had been fixed in Birmingham. It was impossible to alter that now, but Father Faber was free to make a second foundation in London. Dominic Barberi also had become anchored in the Midlands, but Wiseman lost no time in making arrangements for him to open another house in the London District. Father Dominic was still obliged to give part of his attention to the Passionist foundation which he had made in Belgium. He was there [1] in August 1847, while Wiseman was in Rome, at the time that Bishop Griffiths died, and he had read a report in a Belgian paper that Father Spencer had died of typhus ; but later reports showed that he was recovering. He heard that all the other Passionist priests were ill with typhus, and that Father Augustine had been sent for to " help in the work among the unfortunate Irish. I heard that more than fifty English priests have

[1] *Dominic Barberi in England*, p. 182.

died this year. If they all die what will we do in England?" But Wiseman's arrival as the new Vicar-Apostolic in London gave him new hope, and Wiseman was already looking for a house near London which might suit the Passionists.

By April [1] Wiseman had found them a house "about two miles from London, near a village called Hampstead, and fairly solitary. It is a fine building, and quite large enough, with ten bedrooms, eight of which could hold three or even four beds. There is of course no church, but there is a fine room on the ground floor fully able to hold a hundred people. This could easily be turned into a chapel. There is no parish attached, but one might easily be formed with possible converts. The Bishop, however, desires that this should be a house without parish work, so that the Religious may be left free to go here and there on mission work as occasion demands." By May all was ready, and Wiseman had secured the house himself to make sure of matters, while Father Dominic was trying to persuade his Order to send more priests from Italy. He was worn out himself with the fatigue of the past years. "I am sorry to tell you again," he wrote [2] to his General, "that my maladies seem ever worse and I am weighed down with infirmities of every kind. I seem almost decrepit, and aged beyond words. Yesterday someone told me that I looked more like a man of eighty than one not yet sixty! Were the truth known, it is anxiety and worry of every kind that have brought me to this extremity, rather than fatigue of body." Meanwhile he had to complete the new church at Aston, and build a house at Northfield, where Mr. Leigh had found that he could do no more than build the church. At Stone new cases of typhus were still occurring. But he had got the new house at Highgate ready, and when the four promised priests arrived he hoped that they would find "four or five straw mattresses to sleep on." There would be no parochial obligations and no income, so that they would have to "live on Divine Providence alone." The house, in fact, belonged to Wiseman's friend, Mr. Bagshawe, Q.C., and he was by no means ready to vacate it. He even told Barberi to go away when he

---

[1] *Dominic Barberi in England*, p. 191.   [2] *Ibid.*, p. 192.

arrived unexpectedly, but they both occupied the house for some weeks until Bagshawe was able to move. In the meantime they both assisted at the opening of St. George's Cathedral, where Barberi and Father Spencer walked together in the procession in full robes.

Wiseman's position and authority were still restricted by the fact that he had been nominated only as pro-Vicar-Apostolic, in view of the impending constitution of the regular hierarchy. It was fully possible that he might have to leave London when the new regime was introduced. The principle of restoring the hierarchy had been accepted by the new Pope before Wiseman returned to England, and Dr. Sharples came back some months later with instructions that the English bishops were to draw up the details of a scheme, which was to create twelve new dioceses out of the eight existing apostolic districts. In November 1847, the bishops met at Wiseman's episcopal residence in Golden Square, and the main points outstanding for decision were quite clear. Besides the actual delimitation of the twelve new sees, and the choice of titles for them, technical arrangements were required to assure continuity between the old regime and the new, especially in order to safeguard the tenure of ecclesiastical property and trusts. A further problem was to reach agreement on the person of the future Archbishop, who would be head of the hierarchy. With regard to the boundaries of the new sees, the only details which gave rise to any serious disagreement were the question whether London should be divided into two sees, north and south of the Thames, or treated as one diocese ; and whether Lancashire also should be divided, in view of the growth of industrial cities around Manchester. The question of titles for the new sees presented a curious problem, involving a conflict between practical and senti-mental considerations. It was obviously undesirable to revive the titles of such ancient sees as were now associated with the Estab-lished Church ; but there were a number of ancient titles no longer used, such as Hexham, or Dorchester in Oxfordshire, which could have been adopted. On the other hand, the chief centres or Catholic population were now in the modern cities, which were still without bishops, either Catholic or Protestant. And in the upshot, while reviving several of the old forgotten sees such as Beverley and Menevia, it was decided to establish most of the new sees with the titles of modern cities such as Liverpool, Birmingham, Newcastle, Nottingham, Northampton and Plymouth.

The problem of choosing the first Archbishop of the new hierarchy had been complicated rather than simplified by Wiseman's nomination to the London District. He was regarded with considerable distrust by some of the Vicars-Apostolic, and there was a general feeling that the bishops senior to him should not be passed over in his favour. Both Bishop Walsh in the Midlands and Bishop Briggs in the North had strong claims, and there were now two vacancies since the death of Bishop Riddell and through Wiseman's transference to London. After much consideration the bishops decided to leave the matter simply to the judgment of the Pope, and in the meantime considerable influences were brought to bear against Wiseman in Rome. Mgr. Barnabó's diplomacy found an ingenious solution, by proposing that old Bishop Walsh should be transferred from the Midlands to London as the first Archbishop, in recognition of his seniority and of his remarkable achievements, and that Wiseman should remain in London as his coadjutor, with right of succession to the Archbishopric. But Dr. Walsh felt himself to be too old for such arduous duties, and he begged to be left where he was. The Pope accepted his plea, and in November 1847, the full scheme was prepared in Rome for transmission to the bishops in England to obtain their final concurrence.[1] Dr. Walsh was to remain in the Midlands, and Wiseman was to become the first Archbishop of the new see in London, for which the bishops believed that the most suitable title would be Westminster.

This Roman scheme, however, was not forwarded to England, and a series of difficulties arose which were to postpone any further development for several years. The new Pope, Pius IX, had been elected when political discontent was assuming an acute form in the Papal States and when the movement for a united Italy was gathering momentum. For some years there had been a consider-

[1] *Sequel to Catholic Emancipation*, II, p. 208.

able party in Italy which believed that the unity of Italy could be accomplished by a federation of the Italian States with the Pope at its head, and among the chief advocates of this daring scheme had been Rosmini, the founder of the Institute of Charity. The proposal gained wider support when the new Pope showed himself to be determined to introduce a much more liberal regime than that of his predecessor, who had repressed political unrest by every possible means. Within a few months of his election, Pius IX declared an amnesty for all political prisoners, introduced a large number of reforms, and announced that a regular constitution would be established in the Papal States. Austria viewed these measures with grave suspicion, and invoked the rights granted under the Treaty of Vienna to send a garrison to occupy Ferrara. Resentment against Austria in Italy was immediately inflamed, and Pius IX turned towards the various States to obtain diplomatic support in resisting further encroachments. The British Government's concern in the matter had been clearly stated by Lord Palmerston after his appointment as Foreign Secretary in the new Liberal Ministry, and he had openly threatened that if need be, a British fleet would be sent to Trieste. English diplomatic support might yet be of important assistance to the new Pope, and there was a genuine desire in London to establish friendly relations with the new and liberal regime which had just been established in Rome. Lord Minto, the father-in-law of Lord John Russell, had been sent to Italy on a general mission of investigation, and Pius IX readily took the opportunity to seek the establishment of diplomatic relations between London and the Holy See.

These diplomatic negotiations had become so urgent that Wiseman had been sent back to London in August 1847, to establish direct contact with the British Government before even the brief of his nomination as the successor to Bishop Griffiths had been made out. The negotiations developed quickly, and in February a Bill was introduced by Lord Lansdowne to overcome any existing difficulties in the way of establishing diplomatic relations with the Vatican. In spite of the embarrassment which the Bill caused, it was passed with a large majority in the House of Lords after two amendments had been inserted. One, proposed by the Duke of Wellington, altered the designation of the Pope in the Bill from the " Sovereign Pontiff" to the " Sovereign of the Roman States." The other, which was nearly defeated by Lord Shrewsbury's opposition, insisted that any Nuncio appointed by the Pope must be a layman. An interval of six months followed before the Bill came before the House of Commons, and during that time unexpected opposition had been organised from the Catholic side. The Irish bishops saw in it possibilities of political interference through the exercise of diplomatic pressure in Rome, and they took active measures to defeat it. They sent a petition to the Pope, asking him to refuse the diplomatic relations which were offered by the Bill ; and they canvassed the English Vicars-Apostolic so effectively that Bishop Briggs of the Northern District joined forces with them and proceeded to Rome in company with Archbishop MacHale. Wiseman was personally identified with the proposed arrangement, and he had thus encountered the active opposition of the Irish bishops, as well as that of several of the ablest Vicars-Apostolic in England, on a matter of supreme concern to the future of the Church. A large meeting of Catholics in London was held which denounced the proposal in strong terms, and Wiseman's authority was thus challenged in his own district. He met the position with courage by publishing a pamphlet entitled *Words of Peace and Justice Addressed to the Catholic Clergy and Laity of the London District*, in which he argued powerfully on behalf of the Bill, and protested against the recent demonstrations as showing real disrespect to the Pope. Incidentally he protested against the display of hostility which had been shown at the meeting towards the Catholic aristocracy, which was a direct outcome of a conflict that had arisen between Lord Shrewsbury and Archbishop MacHale concerning political unrest in Ireland during the famine years.

Wiseman's pamphlet enhanced his prestige among the Vicars-Apostolic and most of the clergy ; but he had aroused against himself the direct opposition of important elements in England, and particularly of the Catholics in Ireland. They were now active in Rome, where Archbishop MacHale and Bishop Briggs had gone to lay their views before the Pope; and before long Wiseman received a letter [1] from a friend there which showed plainly that confidence in him was being seriously undermined. The main charges against him were that he was too much under the influence of the aristocracy; that he had incurred debts recklessly in the Midland District by building and by opening new Missions while he was coadjutor to Bishop Walsh; and that he had aroused jealousies and dissensions between the converts and the old Catholics. When the bishops held their annual meeting in Low Week, they were still without news from Rome of how matters were proceeding with regard to the creation of a hierarchy. They decided to send Bishop Ullathorne without delay to state their position and clear up the many matters which were causing them anxiety. In the meantime Parliament was in recess and the Diplomatic Relations Bill did not come up for consideration until August. It was then carried by a majority of three to one, and received the royal assent at the end of the month.

No steps, however, were taken for giving effect to the Act, which would, in fact, have resulted almost certainly in Government opposition to the restoration of a hierarchy in England. Gladstone, among others, had opposed the Bill, and had asked openly whether it was true that the Pope was contemplating the restoration of bishops with regular sees in England. Lord John Russell replied [2] that he did not know " that the Pope has authorised in any way, by any authority that he may have, the creation of Archbishops and Bishops with dioceses in England; but certainly I have not given my consent, nor should I give my consent if I were asked to do so, to any such formation of dioceses." The spiritual authority of the Pope, he insisted, must be left " quite unfettered. You cannot bind the Pope's spiritual influence unless you have such agreement." The Diplomatic Relations Act in itself would not have given any such power of control; but it was evident that strong opposition from the British Government to the restoration of a hierarchy, immediately after the establishment of diplomatic relations, would have compelled the Pope to delay any such

[1] *Sequel to Catholic Emancipation*, II, p. 209.
[2] Hansard, Vol. 101, col. 220.

decision. But even while the Bill was being considered in the House of Commons, it became apparent that its provisions would have to be left in abeyance for some time. A crisis had arisen in Rome which made it impossible to proceed with the establishment of diplomatic relations until normal conditions in the Roman States has been restored. Ullathorne had left England during May, and while he travelled across the Continent revolutions were already in eruption. In Paris the Commune had seized control. There had been a revolution in Vienna, resulting in the overthrow of Metternich, almost on the same day that the new constitution of the Papal States was proclaimed. In March Venice and Milan had both risen in revolt against Austria, and the Pope had been reluctantly compelled to call for volunteers to put his own army in a state of defence. The new Chamber of Deputies for the Papal States assembled in Rome on June 5, and the Minister for the Interior openly proclaimed his opposition to the Temporal Power. Ullathorne had arrived in Rome some ten days before the Chamber met, and he was in Rome for nine weeks during which unrest and anxiety rapidly increased. The new Ministry of the Papal States was determined upon war in spite of the Pope's known wishes, and the situation grew more menacing from day to day. The climax came in November, when Count Rossi was murdered on the steps of the Chamber. A riot ensued, and shots were fired into the Papal palace. On November 22 the Pope was obliged to leave Rome in disguise and take refuge at Gaeta under the protection of the King of Naples.

Ullathorne's mission in connection with the hierarchy had to proceed in an atmosphere of uncertainty and stress during the months before that crisis broke. But he found the Roman authorities anxious to expedite a final decision, and pleased that he had been sent to bring matters to a conclusion. The selection of the first Archbishop was still the main difficulty to be overcome. Ullathorne wrote [1] to Wiseman, stating that he had urged that Wiseman could not now be removed from London without an implied censure, and he had otherwise strongly supported his nomination. "I think I can assure your Lordship," he wrote,

[1] *Sequel to Catholic Emancipation*, II, p. 213.

" that you will not be removed, although some arrangement seems to be contemplated to soften, ' adolcire,' the feelings of some bishops and others. . . . I think it will be well for your Lordship to wait with tranquillity the issue, and to rely on Dr. Grant and myself to do our best for your Lordships' and the Districts' interests under all the circumstances of the case." By July 4 Ullathorne had placed copies of his detailed scheme in the hands of the Cardinals, and they met on July 17. Bishop Walsh had by this time sent another earnest appeal to be left in peace in the Midlands, and asking for the immediate appointment of a coadjutor to replace Wiseman. But the Cardinals were determined that he must become the first head of the new hierarchy, even after Ullathorne had supported the old Bishop's appeal to the extent of asserting that in his infirm state of health it would be " a farce " to appoint him.[1] But they fully appreciated the importance of the Midland District, not least because it included both Oxford and Oscott, and they now informed Ullathorne that he must himself go there from the Western District. As on the previous occasions, he resisted the promotion to the utmost, but his objections were overruled.

In the first week of August 1848, Ullathorne arrived back in England in time to attend the meeting of the bishops in Manchester. It had been timed to coincide with the opening of another imposing new church, St. John's, which was to be for Manchester what St. Chad's was to Birmingham and St. George's to London. All the Vicars-Apostolic were present, with the single exception of Bishop Walsh, whose infirmity made travelling impossible. Ullathorne had to report in full on the instructions he had received in Rome, which included the transference of Bishop Walsh to London. With exemplary obedience the old Bishop undertook the move, and he published his first pastoral as Vicar-Apostolic for the London District within a week. It stated clearly, however, that his work would consist in supporting Wiseman as his co-adjutor, whose zeal and energy they knew well. By the end of August Ullathorne himself had taken formal possession of St. Chad's Cathedral in Birmingham. Only a few details remained

[1] *Sequel to Catholic Emancipation*, II, p. 215.

to be settled before the hierarchy could be fully constituted. The names had to be given to the twelve new sees, and there was still dispute as to whether London should be one see or should be divided by the Thames. But while correspondence on these matters was still continuing, and Irish influences in Rome were being strongly exercised against Wiseman's nomination as head of the new hierarchy, the murder of Count Rossi and the enforced flight of the Pope to Gaeta brought all further progress to a standstill.

In Birmingham Ullathorne was now confronted with the complicated situation that had been created by Wiseman's energy and enthusiasm during the previous eight years. Newman was established at his new Oratory at Edgbaston, and the relations between converts and old Catholics were marked by an inevitable sense of uneasiness on both sides. The difficulties were increased by the activity of the Passionists and Rosminians and Redemptorists whom Wiseman had brought to England from Italy. "We had some converts," Ullathorne wrote [1] afterwards, in describing the conditions as he found them, "as well as some branches of the old Catholic stock, and a section of the newly arrived clergy from abroad who gave to their undisciplined zeal a new channel. They took to wondering why the external development of religion in England was not at that moment exactly like that of Italy or Belgium, and why England was not being very fast converted. Ignorant of the circumstances out of which we were emerging, and especially ignorant of the nature of the difficulties with which we were contending with all our strength, it became the fashion to talk these fancies aloud in even the Eternal City. And loudly were both prelates and clergy blamed as men lost to the true sense of their position. With these gentlemen the old clergy, the old orders, the old bishops, everything old in Catholic England, was wrong, nay dead ; only things new or freshly imparted were living or aright. The Holy See, with its usual wisdom and perspicacity soon discerned the true state of things. It was a grain or two of truth that had got confounded in a bushel of injustice. But at that moment these matters were fermenting and causing some trouble."

[1] *Life of Fr. Gentili*, p. 332.

Ullathorne himself, being of Yorkshire stock which had remained staunchly Catholic through all the penal times, resented as strongly as anyone this attitude of condescension and reproach on the part of both converts and foreign missionaries. He was in all respects a blunt and downright Englishman ; and his English character was only emphasised by the fact that he dropped his aitches, having gone to sea as a boy and thus escaped the conventional education at home. But he had profound admiration for the spirit of the Italian missionaries. He approved entirely of their insistence upon wearing the ecclesiastical costume of their orders, and he was the first to insist upon wearing the Benedictine habit himself. He shared also their desire to introduce public devotions of a kind which the old Catholics almost dreaded, as being likely to provoke ridicule or hostility. In Australia he had learned from personal experience the immense opportunities of missionary work in the open, and he promoted public missions when he assumed his first duties in England on going to Coventry. Not having time to undertake such missionary work himself in his large parish, he brought Father Gentili to conduct a mission there, as a public protest against the indecency of the Lady Godiva processions. Father Gentili was quite fearless, from long practice ; and he announced that the congregation would hold a procession in honour of Our Lady in expiation. With the help of Sister Margaret Hallahan preparations were made on an ambitious scale, and on three evenings the statue of Our Lady was carried before a great procession round the church. Crowds of sightseers came to look on, and were shepherded through the church by Dr. Gentili in the wake of the religious procession. When Ullathorne left Coventry to become Vicar-Apostolic of the Western District he repeated the invitation to Gentili, and highly successful missions were given there in 1847 and 1848. The second mission lasted a whole month, and Gentili was by this time worn out by his ardent exertions in England. He died soon afterwards, and Ullathorne regarded his death as a very great loss to the Church in England. In the weeks before his death Gentili and Ullathorne had many long conversations, and in a letter to Newman afterwards Ullathorne wrote [1] that " his view of the facts of our position and of the nature of our contest had become wonderfully changed in the course of his missions. . . . He had become much more moderate in his mode of instruction, though he lamented its necessity. He saw that many things in the clergy which he had formerly attributed to sluggishness were to be ascribed to prudence. . . . The foreign missioners, he conceived, had for a time fallen into the same mistake. He longed himself to go to Rome to give in person this corrected view of things, as his more intimate experience had found to be the case."

Gentili's vivid personality and ardent zeal had contributed greatly to the growth of a more enterprising spirit in the younger generation, of which Wiseman and Ullathorne were the outstanding leaders. A born orator, with a strikingly handsome presence and unbounded natural courage, he had carried the Catholic faith into the streets of the new industrial cities as well as into the villages of the Midlands and the West. Newman had been deeply impressed by him during the years of his gradual conversion. He had worn himself out with passionate exertions, and he was only fifty when he died. Dominic Barberi had never possessed his natural advantages as a popular preacher, and he had reported to Rome only a few years before [2] that " at the moment the Rosminians are doing much more than we are, and we must praise God for it." Bishop Griffiths had invited Gentili to preach in London after he had refused to permit a mission by the Passionists. " We are doing what we can in small places," Father Dominic wrote. " God keeps us humble for our own good. Besides, for some time now I have been troubled with a constant pain in the head. This, added to my other maladies, makes me little suited for great fatigue. As long as the breath is in my body I will do what I can." The overwhelming strain of ministration among the Irish victims of typhus had worn him to a shadow, but he was still busy with his new foundations both in Belgium and in England, while being constantly in demand for giving retreats to the English clergy.

[1] *Sequel to Catholic Emancipation*, I, p. 139.
[2] *Dominic Barberi in England*, p. 160.

In September 1848 he reported that Mr. Leigh had now given a fine organ to the church at Northfield. " I fear he wants to make us too rich," he wrote [1] to a friend. " The land assigned to us at first was more than sufficient *pro domestico usu*. To have more may, I fear, have evil consequences—the renting of a portion for example—and thus lead to having fixed rents coming in, a thing fatal to our profession of poverty." He was relying much on Father Spencer, and in the autumn of 1848 he sent Spencer to Ireland to give a retreat to the clergy, and Spencer collected money for his work in England while he was there. At the end of the year Father Dominic was arranging for another new foundation, in Lancashire. He had now made his headquarters in London at the house near Hampstead, which was afterwards given up for the present St. Joseph's at Highgate. There he was in constant touch with Wiseman, and able to keep in communication with the various houses he had founded. On August 27 he was to travel to Woodchester for the opening of the new church which had been built by Mr. Leigh's generosity. He had grown so feeble that he now talked frequently of approaching death, and it was evident that he could not last much longer. He set out with one of his priests from Paddington by train, and during the journey the pain in his head became so acute that he had to be helped out when the train stopped at Pangbourne. A doctor was summoned, who said that he must be taken immediately to hospital in Reading, and as the pain made it impossible for him to sit, straw was laid on the platform for him to lie on until the train arrived. The Pangbourne doctor went with them, and at Reading they carried him to the old railway hotel, where he died within an hour. As he lay dying he instructed his companion to send for Father Spencer immediately he was dead, and tell him to assume charge of the English province until further orders came from Rome. Father Dominic's body was taken back next day to Aston, where he was buried amid scenes of extraordinary popular grief, crowds gathering from all the surrounding district to follow his coffin to the grave.

[1] *Dominic Barberi in England*, p. 205.

CHAPTER XIV

THE POPE IN EXILE

WHEN the Pope had to flee from Rome to Gaeta at the end of November 1848, all prospect of a restoration of the English hierarchy seemed to have receded into a remote future, while conditions in Rome itself became increasingly menacing. Ullathorne, who took every opportunity of observing events at first hand, had himself witnessed many scenes of growing revolt in Rome while he was there in June and July. In Paris, on his outward journey at the end of May,[1] he had been in the streets while revolutionary riots were in progress, which gave him a clear idea of what might happen in Rome if matters got out of hand. When he heard the drums beating the reveille all over Paris he had dismissed his carriage in the Place de la Concorde so that he could mingle with the crowd and see what was happening. Later in the day he had watched extraordinary conflicts from a window in the Rue de Rivoli, and he had stayed the night with friends while it was feared that the city would be set on fire. In Rome, while he was engaged in the hierarchy negotiations during June and July, he had found the situation going from bad to worse.[2] His friend, the Bishop of Natchez, had been " attacked by a band of ruffians " almost immediately after arriving in Rome, and had " with difficulty escaped into a shop in the Corso." Conditions grew much more tense after Ullathorne had returned to England, and in November, when the Pope's palace was attacked, one of the prelates most closely connected with English affairs, Mgr. Palma, was killed by a shot which entered his window.

Not only in Protestant countries, but in Rome itself there was a widespread belief that the Pope's rule in Rome would never survive his exile, and that the Papacy itself had reached its end. The Republicans in Rome rapidly gained the upper hand, after the

[1] *Autobiography*, pp. 254–256.   [2] *Ibid.*, p. 266.

first shock of the Pope's departure from the Vatican. The formation of a Constituent Assembly was announced, and the Pope's decree, forbidding Catholics to vote in the elections, could not prevent the proclamation of the Roman Republic in February 1849. In the previous summer Ullathorne had already urged Dr. Grant at the English College to remove the students to their country house. The safety of the College itself was now endangered, and in London Wiseman waited upon Lord Palmerston to ask his protection for the old College at which he had been one of the first students when it was re-opened thirty years before. In March Garibaldi entered the city, and Church property was confiscated and priests were put to death. The intervention of France soon afterwards brought the Republican regime to an end, when the French troops occupied Rome in July. But the Pope did not return to Rome until the following April. In the interval of some eighteen months the ordinary administration of the Church was largely in abeyance, and few meetings of the Congregation could be held. Ullathorne records[1] that during the Republic Mgr. Barnabó, who had been the chief agent in the English hierarchy negotiations, was "living with the Armenian Fathers under protection of the Turkish flag."

In the meantime, however, one principal problem concerning the English hierarchy had been solved by the death of old Bishop Walsh in February 1849, ten days after the declaration of the Roman Republic. Mgr. Barnabó's ingenious compromise, which had transferred him from Birmingham to London with Wiseman as his coadjutor, had produced the desired result. Wiseman now succeeded him as Vicar-Apostolic for the London District, in right of succession, and his status as the leading figure among the English bishops was thus firmly established. His wide experience of diplomatic affairs both in Rome and as agent for the English bishops in dealing with the British Government was invaluable in the extremely delicate situation which had arisen. The Diplomatic Relations Act, in connection with which he had been closely consulted, was by this time already in abeyance, and there could be

[1] *Autobiography*, p. 292.

no question of the British Government appointing a Minister to the Holy See until the Pope had returned to Rome and normal conditions there had been fully restored. That unexpected difficulty had, in fact, opened the way to a resumption of the hierarchy plans without requiring any direct consultation with the Government. In England generally it was believed that the Pope's power had been irretrievably broken by his exile, and enthusiasm for Garibaldi and the leaders of Young Italy was already rising fast.

But the Pope's flight to Gaeta had not affected all observers even in England with the same conviction of helplessness and defeat. Newman had returned to England, and was in charge of his new Oratory at Edgbaston during those critical months, and his impressions were to be written not long afterwards in his *Lectures on Anglican Difficulties*,[1] in one of the most memorable passages of all his writing :

"How different is the bearing of the temporal power upon the spiritual! Its promptitude, decisiveness, keenness, and force are well represented in the military host which is its instrument. Punctual in its movements, precise in its operations, imposing in its equipments, with its spirits high and its step firm, with its haughty clarions and its black artillery, behold, the mighty world is gone forth to war, with what? With an unknown something, which it feels but cannot see, which flits around it, which flaps against its cheek, with the air, with the wind. It charges and it slashes, and it fires its volleys, and it bayonets, and it is mocked by a foe who dwells in another sphere, and is far beyond the force of its analysis, or the capacities of its calculus. The air gives way, and it returns again ; it exerts a gentle but constant pressure on every side ; moreover, it is of vital necessity to the very power which it is attacking. Whom have you gone out against ? A few old men, with red hats and stockings, or a hundred pale students with eyes on the ground, and beads in their girdle ; they are as stubble ; destroy them :—then there will be other old men and other pale students instead of them.

[1] Vol. I, p. 156.

But we will direct our rage against one ; he flees : what is to be done with him ? Cast him out upon the wide world ! but nothing can go on without him. Then bring him back ! but he will give us no guarantee for the future. Then leave him alone ; his power is gone, he is at an end, or he will take a new course of himself ; he will take part with the State or the people. Meanwhile, the multitude of interests in active operation all over the great Catholic body rise up, as it were, all around, and encircle the combat, and hide the fortunes of the day from the eyes of the world : and unreal judgments are hazarded, and rash predictions, till the mists clear away, and then the old man is found in his own place, as before, saying Mass over the tomb of the Apostles."

Newman and the recent converts were not alone in believing that the Pope's defiance of civil usurpation had strengthened, rather than lessened, his influence and authority throughout Christendom in a materialistic age. Archdeacon Manning of Chichester, who had become the principal champion of the High Church movement since Newman's surrender, had been in Rome, on one of many such journeys of pilgrimage, during the summer before the Pope's Prime Minister was assassinated and the Pope was obliged to leave the city. He was on terms of intimate friendship with Gladstone, and they had exchanged letters constantly over many years ; and together they had steeled themselves against further advance towards Rome when the Oxford Movement was disrupted in 1845. To Gladstone Manning had written [1] from Rome, a few weeks before his first private audience, as an Anglican, with Pio Nono : " It is wonderful to see the Catholic Church in America, France and Italy distinctly of the progress and popular party—indeed in many ways at the head of it. It falls in with an old belief of mine in which I think you share, I mean that the Church of the last ages will be as the Church of the first, isolated and separate from the Civil Powers of the World."

In a sermon in his later years Manning was to describe his own impression of the Pope's attitude at this time when he had become

[1] Leslie's *Life of Manning,* p. 83.

an object of scorn in Protestant countries : " I know no more majestic, more royal, more pontifical sight in the history of the Pontiffs, than the Holy Father on the Rock of Gaeta issuing in the moment of his weakness and exile his three great appeals to the Christian world : one, the excommunication of the spoilers of the patrimony of the Church, another, a protest to all Christian princes against the wrong that had been done, a third, to all his sons, the episcopate throughout the world. And these three decrees have all wrought their work with power. Supernatural virtue went out with them. The first wrought the downfall of the spoilers who had invaded the Church of God. The second called together the princes of Christendom to do homage to the Vicar of Christ. The third evoked such a response from the hearts of all the bishops of Catholic unity that in all the annals of the Church there is not to be found anything to compare with the acts of filial love and devotion which the episcopate of the Catholic world laid at his sacred feet."

Manning returned to England from a long tour in Italy, recovering from a severe illness, more attached than ever to his memories of its sacred shrines, but still firmly convinced that the English Church was part of the Catholic Church. Even the installation of Hampden as Bishop of Hereford did not shake his conviction, though it jarred more than ever, as a sign that religious orthodoxy was not required of the Anglican episcopate. But in April 1849 a new crisis arose, when the Bishop of Exeter refused to accept the nomination of Mr. Gorham to a living in his diocese, on the ground that he repudiated belief in baptism. Gladstone shared Manning's dismay, while the Bishop's refusal was being referred to a judicial decision by the civil courts. " If Mr. Gorham be carried through and that upon the merits," he wrote [1] to Manning, " I say not only is there no doctrine of baptismal regeneration in the Church of England as State interpreted, but there is no doctrine at all ! " Manning recognised that a test had been applied from which there could be no flinching. After a long year's suspense the Gorham Judgment was given against their convictions, and the Bishop of Exeter was legally required to institute Mr. Gorham in the parish.

[1] Leslie's *Life of Manning*, p. 89.

Manning had mobilised all the leading figures whom he could collect at Gladstone's house to sign a resolution before the judgment was given ; and while Gladstone issued his own protest separately, Manning felt that there could be no turning back.

In a letter during the following month, while he was facing the necessity to resign his position as Archdeacon, he wrote : [1] " A Theology of 300 years is in conflict with a Faith of 1800 years. I was born in the 300. My mature thoughts transplant me into the 1800. This is the real balance, but people will not so look at it. I believe a man might hold what he likes in the English Church if he would be quiet and uphold the Church. The dishonesty is to be honest." In June he wrote,[2] in reply to an anxious letter from Gladstone, " I dare not say that my conscience will not submit itself to the Church which has its circuits throughout the world and its centre by accident in Rome."

The Gorham Judgment had produced a new religious crisis in the Church of England comparable only to the events which had hastened Newman's submission in 1845. A new accession of converts was beginning to flow in. But Wiseman was now too deeply immersed in his complicated tasks as Vicar-Apostolic in London to follow the controversy with the former breathless concentration of his years at Oscott. He had been in charge of the London District since August 1847, first as pro-Vicar-Apostolic, then as coadjutor to old Bishop Walsh, and since February 1849 as Vicar-Apostolic with full status and authority. Death had recently deprived him of the assistance of both Father Dominic Barberi and Dr. Gentili, but George Spencer had now replaced Father Dominic as head of the Passionists in England. Newman was anchored in Birmingham, but Father Faber had been able to establish a second branch of the Oratory in London, which Wiseman opened in May 1849. Two months later, after a protracted dispute with Bishop Walsh over the division of responsibilities—which was settled by a compromise that greatly reduced their possibilities of usefulness under existing conditions—the Jesuits also had opened their church in Farm Street.

[1] *Op. cit.*, p. 91. [2] *Ibid.*, p. 92.

Wiseman was giving his fullest encouragement to the religious orders, though he found in practice after a time that each Order in turn became absorbed in its own special tasks, and that he was as far as ever from obtaining the assistance which he desired for organising new missions and a general extension of Catholic activity. His problems and difficulties were subsequently described in a long letter [1] in October 1852, in which he told Faber of all his troubles. "When I first came to London," he wrote, "I saw that the neglected part was the poor, and to that I resolved to give immediate attention. After having consulted some zealous priests I concluded on the plan of local missions in the midst of them." One priest, Mr. Hodgson, gave up "the best mission in the district" to undertake such work, and his efforts resulted in the formation of three permanent and flourishing new missions. But his achievement was almost unique, and Wiseman had soon realised the necessity of introducing missionary orders for general purposes. He brought about the introduction of five important Congregations, including the Oratorians, but within a few years every one of them had disappointed him bitterly, because their rules prevented them from carrying out the work he desired. Thus the Jesuits, with a full community at Farm Street, were unable to do work elsewhere, so that they had "only a church, which by its splendour attracts and absorbs the wealth of two parishes, but maintains no schools and contributes nothing to the education of the poor at its very door." The Redemptorists, whom he had cordially welcomed as a missionary order, had similarly become "as far as London is concerned a parochial body, taking excellent care of Clapham," but "they have exerted no local influence." The Passionists, since Father Dominic's death, had disappointed him still more, having dug themselves into their local quarters at St. John's Wood and "have never done me a stroke of work among the poor." The Marists he had brought in for a purely local purpose, which they were performing well, but Wiseman "dared not ask them about general work." As a devout respecter of religious rules and discipline, Wiseman made no actual complaint of the recurring

[1] Purcell's *Life of Manning*, II, pp. 2-9.

difficulty which he found in every case, that the rules of the religious order concerned would not permit whatever he asked. But to Father Faber he appealed passionately to ask whether some relaxation of the rules of the new Oratorian Institute could not be obtained in order to help him.

This apparent paralysing of his efforts was less surprising in the case of the Oratorians, because Newman had recognised at the outset that he must fortify himself with a cast iron constitution approved in Rome, in order to overcome the inevitable suspicions with which his community of convert clergymen would be regarded. He had started work cautiously in Edgbaston just before Wiseman's translation to London, and he had as yet no sure confidence in the future friendliness of Ullathorne as his new bishop. In his anxiety to have his status defined beyond all ambiguity, he came into collision with Ullathorne within the first few months of their association. Ullathorne, like Wiseman in London, had had painful experience of the deadlocks that could arise when the Bishop and the head of a religious order exercised a competing jurisdiction over their clergy. Soon after his arrival in Birmingham he desired to get this question clarified in the case of the Oratorians, who had just taken over work in a parish. When Ullathorne wrote [1] formally to ask Newman whether he claimed exemption from episcopal jurisdiction and, if so, to produce his proofs, Newman replied guardedly that " when any question arises between your Lordship and ourselves on any particular point, we shall be ready to produce our proofs. Before such an event, in itself not very likely, your Lordship will agree with us that it is a waste of precious time to employ your Lordship and ourselves on abstract or contingent questions." Newman's reply was not intended to be evasive, but Ullathorne was the last man to accept an indefinite answer to a straight question. He replied, kindly but firmly, explaining that he had no objection on principle to the Oratory being exempt, but that he must know clearly how matters stood. " Do not, my dear sir," he wrote, " suppose that there is anything either abstract or contingent in the question of exemption,

[1] *Life of Ullathorne,* I, p. 161.

which is a question upon which both your own acts and mine depend."

Newman's record as an Anglican was certainly not calculated to reassure any bishop who found him established in his diocese as the head of an extremely influential religious community. Ullathorne was fully conscious of the possibility of future conflicts, and it was vastly to the credit of both men that they established relations of absolute confidence and friendship as soon as the initial doubts on both sides had been overcome. Newman's Anglican experiences had made him unusually adept in asserting his own views and rights within the limits of strict obedience to episcopal authority. But greater danger of conflict lay in the fact that Newman had for years been the leader of a devoted following, and had acquired the habit of shielding his followers if any of them were attacked. An instance of such conflict arose almost at once after Ullathorne became his bishop in Birmingham.

Faber, who was now one of Newman's community in the Oratory, had desired to continue the series of popular *Lives of the Saints* which Newman and his disciples had first published in their Tractarian days. With his usual caution, Newman consulted Ullathorne on the proposal, and Ullathorne took the opinion of other bishops and experts. He found the general opinion that Faber's zeal had outrun discretion, and that his preface to the *Life of St. Rose of Lima* particularly conveyed the impression that an unbounded belief in miracles and an attitude of exaggerated piety were expected of every Catholic. He reported to Newman [1] that the general opinion of the bishops and of Catholic superiors was that " the spirit of the Lives as given in these translations is not adapted to the state of this country. Religious persons and nuns do not find in them a wisdom according to sobriety." It was unfortunate that Faber's writing had just been attacked with immoderate denunciation in a Catholic magazine, by a priest whose review virtually charged Faber with idolatry. On receiving Ullathorne's letter Newman decided to discontinue the series, but he announced his decision in a circular [2] letter which defended Faber warmly.

[1] *Life of Ullathorne*, I, p. 155.   [2] *Life of Wiseman*, II, p. 223.

Ullathorne read Newman's circular with apprehension, and decided to write to him with utmost frankness. Extracts from the letter have been published in the official Lives of Wiseman and Ullathorne, but the personal passages [1] quoted by Abbot Butler are particularly revealing. " Under the impression that the ' Lives ' had been stopped by authority," wrote Ullathorne, " the circular was thought to betray pugnacity and sensitiveness. The former impression is now removed, but still the sensitiveness of the circular, regarding as it does the lives of the meek and honourable servants of God, has widely left a painful impression." Newman, in his circular, had stated that " to this feeling we consider it a duty, for the sake of peace, to defer." But he had also said : " You know well how absolutely I identify myself with you in this matter," and that he had " no sympathy at all with the feeling to which I have alluded." He had concluded by assuring Faber that " in particular, no one can assail your name without striking at mine." It was these sentences which made Ullathorne write his earnest and confidential protest. " It is the manifestation," he wrote to Newman, " of sensitiveness in holy religious men, personal sensitiveness, the ' blow struck at *me*,' for example, in a matter concerning the edification of the world by the lives of those who perfected themselves, in patience by long suffering, in many trials, and whose obedience, so secret, so tranquil, so humble, knew no touch of bitterness. My dear Mr. Newman, I can with difficulty refrain from tears whilst I write. I love you so much, and yet I feel so anxious for the spirit recently, I think, indicated a little, to say the least. I know that your lives have been lives of warfare and contest, and that you have had painfully to controvert the authorities under which you were brought up. We have not had that fierce trial. . . . See what faith I have in your humility." That letter unquestionably was the beginning of a friendship between the two men which grew to closest intimacy, through many years of suffering and discouragement.

Wiseman at no time gained the absolute confidence of Newman as Ullathorne gained it in Birmingham. But Wiseman's life's

[1] *Life of Ullathorne*, I, p. 156.

work was now broadened on a scale which left little scope for the personal attachments of his earlier years. In London he was absorbed in ceaseless activity, between attempting to organise new missions, particularly in the poorest districts where Catholic labourers were swarming in appalling conditions, and the increasing diplomatic responsibilities of his position. While the Pope was in exile at Gaeta many matters were thrown upon the bishops which would normally be referred to Rome. A letter [1] to his old friend, Dr. Newsham, at Ushaw in July 1849, says that " during the last six weeks (what is called the London Season) I have not been allowed one moment's leisure. If at home, there are calls from morning till night ; and if I am out, it is to attend public dinners, meetings, sermons, openings, etc., so that at last I was quite wearied in body and mind." To the same friend in January 1850, he gave a fuller report [2] of what he had been able to accomplish. Within less than two years he had established seven new communities of nuns and three of men, had opened two orphanages, set up a grammar school, besides opening " four new missions in the heart of the poor population, and at least seven others in different parts." A real religious revival was also in progress, with a " vast increase of communions, numbers of admirable conversions, the spread of devotional and charitable associations, the increased piety of the faithful in every class." He could claim that " in a year or little more 15,000 persons have been reclaimed by the Retreats given in convents and abbeys, etc. In one place, the very worst street in London, we boldly planted a mission among thieves and prosti- tutes." The change was " so visible that a Protestant policeman asked if it would not go on again, and observed that the Government ' ought to support it.'"

Such were his chief preoccupations at the beginning of 1850, when on March 8 the Privy Council delivered its judgment on the Gorham case and spread consternation among the survivors of the Tractarian movement who had so far refused to follow Newman in his submission to Rome. Wiseman was deeply stirred, and on March 17 he preached in St. George's Cathedral, a sermon dealing

[1] *Life of Wiseman*, I, p. 510. [2] *Ibid.*, p. 516.

with the whole dispute ; and asking would the Church of England now " dare to appeal to the Universal Church in which so many of her writers declare, lies the ultimate appeal in matters of faith ? " Hopes of a new tide of conversions rose high and gave him a new eagerness to continue the heavy work that he had begun so well. But in May there came to him from Rome a letter which threw him into utter despondency for a time.

The Pope had returned to Rome from Gaeta on April 12, and almost immediately he decided that he required the assistance of Wiseman as an English Cardinal permanently resident at the Vatican. Cardinal Antonelli, the Secretary of State, sent the formal communication, which announced that he was to be made a Cardinal. It was the highest tribute to his devoted work and his great talents, but it meant a complete cessation of the activities which seemed to be on the point of achieving their greatest triumphs under his personal guidance. Preparations for restoring the English hierarchy had been completed during the period of the Pope's absence from Rome, and the whole matter was now ready for decision. The Pope's message to Wiseman had arrived early in May, and by June the rumour had spread so widely that Wiseman felt free to write in confidence to a few intimate friends. " To those who speak to me I am obliged to content myself with not denying it," he wrote to Ullathorne.[1] " I have been in a state of unnatural constraint from not being able to write to my brethren on a matter in which naturally I should have wished to consult with them." " I have written to Rome as much as one may write for himself, but in vain ; " the letter continued, " and I fear my total separation from England in about a month is decided. What I have felt and what I feel is known to God alone. I dare not act in any way that were to oppose His holy will, but to leave the work that is going on now here is to me the heaviest trial that has ever befallen me."

To his friend Dr. Russell in Maynooth he had written some days previously in early July,[2] " The truth is that I leave England (for ever) next month. In September the Consistory is to be held

---

[1] *Autobiography*, p. 293.   [2] *Life of Wiseman*, I, p. 521.

which binds me in golden fetters for life, and cuts off all my hopes, all my aspirations, all my life's wish to labour for England's conversion in England, in the midst of the strife with heresy, and the triumphs of the Church. I have written as plainly and as strongly as one can about oneself, but a peremptory answer has come that I am wanted in Rome, and that a successor will be provided. It was only in February '49 that, by the death of good Bishop Walsh, I first became properly a free agent, acting on my own responsibility, and in May 1850 I am again thrown back into a vague and indefinite position. This, however, consoles me : the event depresses me, crushes me, nay, *buries* me for ever in this life ; and so it *must* be good for me. . . . While, therefore, I bow to the mandate, and in it to the Divine Will, I cannot but feel in it a reproof that my work has been badly done, and must be taken from me and given to others."

On August 9 he left England, having previously visited Ullathorne in Birmingham to tell him that for certain reasons he believed that Ullathorne would be his successor in London and the first head of the hierarchy. But Ullathorne was not only anxious to avoid all such honours, but deeply convinced that Wiseman's presence in England was necessary. Other bishops shared his view and wrote strongly to that effect to Rome, so that Mgr. Barnabó requested Ullathorne to draw up a memorandum to lay before the Cardinals. Further support was also forthcoming from an influential Canadian Sulpician, the Abbé Quiblier, and his statement impressed the Pope particularly. By the time Wiseman reached Rome, the decision had already been re-considered, and he found that his return to England as head of the restored hierarchy was almost certain. But at the time of his departure he was fully convinced that he was leaving England for ever, and it was a most unfortunate factor in subsequent misunderstandings that he informed the Prime Minister, Lord John Russell, that this would be the case, when he called upon him before leaving London.

CHAPTER XV

THE PAPAL AGGRESSION

WISEMAN had reached Rome on September 5, resigned to the prospect of leading a life of honourable retirement from active work, and even with plans to build or buy a villa [1] near Monte Porzio, where he could escape for short spells of comparative freedom. He had a private audience with the Pope on the day of his arrival, but it was not until his formal audience a week later that he learned definitely that the Pope had altered his intentions and now proposed to make him a Cardinal Archbishop in England. On the 13th he wrote [2] to his friend Bagshawe that it was now "more than probable" that the hierarchy would be proclaimed before the Consistory at which he was to be made a Cardinal ; and that "in the spring I shall return to London, where we shall hold the first Synod (Provincial) since the Reformation." On his arrival in Rome, he explained, he had "found the Pope, all the Cardinals, and Propaganda of the same mind, that if possible, and if compatible with the Cardinalitial dignity, I ought to return." Another audience with the Pope followed on September 24, and six days later, when the Consistory was held, Wiseman was nominated a Cardinal. The Papal Brief which re-established the English hierarchy was dated for the day before, September 29. Its promulgation was announced by Wiseman himself in his first pastoral letter as Cardinal Archbishop of Westminster, which was dated October 7, but did not reach his Vicar-General in London, Dr. Whitty, until ten days later.

Wiseman's emotional temperament had been aroused to exultation by the swift revival of his hopes after the dejection and disappointment of the previous months. The plans for the hierarchy had been virtually complete for two years, and he knew that everything was now ready for putting them into operation. Before

---

[1] *Life of Wiseman,* I, p. 524.   [2] *Ibid.,* p. 526.

leaving Rome he brought a large deputation to offer their thanks to the Pope, including Dr. Grant, his successor as Rector of the English College, with all its students and a number of British residents in Rome. The Pope addressed them [1] in a speech which told them that he had intended to keep the new Cardinal in Rome but had later decided to send him to England as head of the new hierarchy. "I do not think there will be anything to apprehend in consequence," he said. "I spoke of it at the time to Lord Minto and I understood that the English Government would not oppose the execution of my design. I send back therefore to England the eminent Cardinal, and I invite you all to pray unceasingly, that the Lord will remove all difficulties and that He will lead into the Church a million—three millions—of your fellow countrymen still separated from us, to the end that He may cause them all to enter, even to the last man." Wiseman replied in an address which declared his own conviction also that there would be no difficulty with the English Government.

The Consistory, and Wiseman's appointment as a Cardinal, had indeed been reported already in remarkably friendly terms by the *Times*. It had noted particularly [2] that ten of the fourteen new Cardinals had been " chosen from foreign States, only four of them being Italians ". " It has long been admitted in theory," it wrote, " that the Papacy is not merely an Italian but a European or, to speak more properly, a universal, power. Its Italian character, however, has generally so far preponderated as to make the superficial observer overlook its now extended relations. . . . Its recent disasters have produced for it one advantage—they have shown that its importance is not to be measured by the few square miles of its territory or by the small numbers of its population. All the Powers of the Old and New World have felt, spoken and acted towards it in a way which would be ridiculous if they regarded only its size or its physical resources, and for the first time in history

[1] *Sequel*, II, p. 284. A report of the Pope's speech was published in the *Ami de la Religion*, and was afterwards repeated in the *Times*. See *Life of Wiseman*, I, p. 545.

[2] *Ibid.*, p. 538.

the combined action of some of the principal nations in Europe has replaced the Pope on the oldest throne in the World. Thus has been effected what in some sense may be called the ' rehabilitation of the Papacy as more than an Italian State,' and Pius IX, following out the idea, has looked beyond Italy for counsellors and called to the honour of the purple a greater proportion of foreign Cardinals than former precedents in the last three hundred years would have authorised."

When the *Times* could regard the Pope's actions, and particularly the creation of a new English Cardinal, in such a friendly manner, it is scarcely surprising that Wiseman's own announcement of the news in his first pastoral should have been expressed in enthusiastic language. He even took the precaution of conveying the information to the *Times* in a letter from Rome intended for publication before the official documents were yet available ; and he then started for home in a journey which assumed the character of a triumphal procession. At Florence, Siena, Bologna and Venice, he was accorded public honours, and in Vienna he dined with the Emperor on November 1. Meanwhile his pastoral had reached London, where his Vicar-General, Dr. Whitty, realised at once that its exuberant language would almost certainly provoke a storm of protest. The Brief of the hierarchy had already reached Paris, where it was published in Louis Veuillot's *Univers,* so that the details of the new episcopal sees and their titles had become known in England several weeks before the official promulgation in Wiseman's pastoral arrived.

Ullathorne states positively[1] that the *Times* had received Wiseman's communication from Rome three days before it was published, when " its managers decided as to what course they should adopt. They finally resolved to raise the country, and it must be remembered that the letter arrived at the most vacant time of the year in politics." He had informed them that the hierarchy was to be restored, with titular sees, and when the full details became available through the *Univers,* the *Times* developed its attack into a grand offensive. Before Wiseman's pastoral had yet

[1] *Autobiography,* p. 295.

reached his Vicar-General, the *Times* published his letter with an editorial which said of his elevation as a Cardinal : " It is no concern of ours whether Dr. Wiseman chooses in Rome to be ranked with the Monsignori of the capital. He is simply at Rome in the position of an English subject, who has thought fit to enter the service of a foreign Power and accept its spurious dignities." But the official gazette of Rome had disclosed that " the Pope having recently been pleased to erect the city of Westminster into an archbishopric and to appoint Dr. Wiseman to that see, it is on this new fangled Archbishop of Westminster, so appointed, that the rank of Cardinal is so conferred. . . . If this appointment be not intended as a clumsy joke, we confess that we can only regard it as one of the grossest acts of folly and impertinence which the Court of Rome has ventured to commit since the Crown and people of England threw off its yoke."

This outburst, and much more to the same effect, had already appeared in the *Times*, when Dr. Whitty was confronted with the new Cardinal's pastoral [1] letter which he had rashly dated " from the Flaminian Gate of Rome." It bore every trace of the excitement that had stirred Wiseman when the decree had been made in Rome. " By a Brief dated the same day," he wrote, " his Holiness was further pleased to appoint us, though most unworthy, to the Archiepiscopal See of Westminster, established by the above-mentioned Letters Apostolic, giving us at the same time the administration of the Episcopal See of Southwark. So that at present, and till such time as the Holy See shall think fit otherwise to provide, we govern and shall continue to govern, the counties of Middlesex, Hertford and Essex, as Ordinary thereof, and those of Surrey, Sussex, Kent, Berkshire, and Hampshire, with the islands annexed, as Administrator with Ordinary jurisdiction." He announced that he had been made " a Cardinal Priest of the Holy Roman Church," and that " in that same Consistory we were enabled ourselves to ask for the archiepiscopal Pallium for our new see of Westminster, and this day we have been invested, by the hands of the Supreme Pastor and Pontiff himself, with this badge of metropolitan jurisdiction."

[1] The full text is given in *Sequel*, II, pp. 305-308.

"The great work, then, is complete," he continued : "what you have long desired and prayed for is granted. Your beloved country has received a place among the fair Churches which, normally constituted, form the splendid aggregate of the Catholic Communion ; Catholic England has been restored to its orbit in the ecclesiastical firmament, from which its light had long vanished, and begins now anew its course of regularly adjusted action round the centre of unity, the source of jurisdiction, of light and vigour. How wonderfully all this has been brought about, how clearly the hand of God has been shown in every state, we have not now leisure to relate, but we may hope soon to recount to you by word of mouth. . . .

"Then truly is this day to us a day of joy and exaltation of spirit, the crowning day of long hopes, and the opening day of bright prospects. How must the Saints of our country, whether Roman or British, Saxon or Norman, look down from their seats of bliss, with beaming glance, upon this new evidence of the faith and Church which led them to glory, sympathising with those who have faithfully adhered to them through centuries of ill repute for the truth's sake, and now reap the fruit of their patience and long-suffering. And all those blessed martyrs of these latter ages, who have fought the battles of the faith under such discouragement, who mourned, more than over their own fetters or their own pain, over the desolate ways of their own Sion, and the departure of England's religious glory ; oh ! how must they bless God, who hath again visited His people—now take part in our joy, as they see the lamp of the temple again enkindled and rebrightening, as they behold the silver links of that chain which has connected their country with the see of Peter in its vicarial government changed into burnished gold : not stronger, nor more closely knit, but more beautifully wrought and more brightly arrayed."

To publish this document while a storm of protest against the new hierarchy was already rising was obviously a serious risk, and Dr. Whitty as Vicar-General had grave misgivings when he read it. "Every day symptoms of the coming storm were speedily becoming more unmistakable," he wrote afterwards.[1] But there

[1] *Life of Wiseman*, I, p. 541.

was no possibility of consulting Wiseman, who had given no address at which he could be reached until he arrived in Bruges ; and the Catholic public was anxiously waiting for some official statement in view of the popular agitation against the Pope. Dr. Whitty felt that he " could not withhold it without a clear obligation of duty. Still less could I dare suppress or tamper with any of its expressions at my own discretion. On the other hand, not a few were beginning to apprehend a repetition of the Gordon riots, and no one could say what occasion might be seized upon. I was alone, and had no one whom I could consult, and the decision had to be come to at once. After a short prayer for light, I decided on publishing the Pastoral just as it was."

Ullathorne, always a severely practical man, would have counselled human rather than supernatural consultations, and he remonstrated bluntly with Dr. Whitty when he hurried to London [1] after the pastoral had been published and the public outcry was in full blast. " I asked him ' How could you publish that Pastoral ? You must have known that Cardinal Wiseman never contemplated the state of things amidst which it was destined to appear ; and that, had he known what was going on, he would not have written in that style ? ' He said, ' I am young and inexperienced, and in my perplexity did not know what to do, so I thought it best to obey the injunction within it, that it should be read in the churches on the Sunday following its arrival.' I asked him why, in an affair of such importance which involved our common interests, he had not taken the advice of some of the senior Bishops before doing so. He said he had not thought of that."

The storm broke with a vengeance when the pastoral was published at full length in the *Times*, which declared that " until we saw the whole scheme in black and white before us, we confess that we were still incredulous of the extent of its impudence and absurdity. . . . All this laid down with the authority and minuteness of an Act of Parliament by a Papal Bull certainly constitutes one of the strangest pieces of mummery we ever remember to have witnessed. . . . As it is, we can only receive it as an audacious and

[1] *Autobiography*, p. 296.

conspicuous display of pretensions to resume the absolute spiritual dominion of this island which Rome has never abandoned, but which, by the blessing of Providence and the will of the English people, she shall never accomplish. . . . The erection of a Hierarchy assuming the names of cities and provinces and distributing counties amongst their sees, is a step which the Pope could not have taken in any other civilised country in Europe, and it is hardly less preposterous than the Bull of one of his predecessors in the fifteenth century which assigned to the crown of Portugal the undiscovered limits of the New World."

No hint of hostility had reached Wiseman, while the press in London was raging over his pastoral, until he saw a copy of the *Times* in Vienna on November 3, with its insulting comments on his nomination as a Cardinal. He wrote at once [1] from Vienna to Lord John Russell, to assure him in the first place that when they had met just before his departure from England " I was most sincere when I spoke of my departure as final, with no idea that I should return. I am anxious that no impression should remain on your Lordship's mind that I had the slightest intention to deceive you." He explained also that the newspaper comment was entirely misleading, and that " I am invested with a purely ecclesiastical dignity ; that I have no secular or temporal delegation whatever ; that my duties will be what they have ever been, to promote the morality of those committed to my charge, especially the masses of the poor ; and to keep up those feelings of goodwill and friendly intercommunion which I flatter myself I have been the means of somewhat improving." As soon as he was back in England, he would " give any explanation that your Lordship may desire, in full confidence that it will be in my power to remove particularly the offensive interpretation put upon the late act of the Holy See— that it was suggested by political views or by any hostile feelings."

But long before this letter could reach the Prime Minister, Lord John had become thoroughly committed to the anti-Papal agitation. The Bishop of Durham had addressed to him a vehement protest against the Pope's " insolent and insidious " action ; and

[1] *Life of Wiseman*, I, p. 535.

Lord John replied with a public letter on November 4 which expressed his full agreement. "There is an assumption of power in all the documents which have come from Rome," he wrote, —"a pretension to supremacy over the realm of England, and a claim to sole and undivided sway, which is inconsistent with the Queen's supremacy, with the rights of our bishops and clergy, and with the spiritual independence of the nation, as asserted even in Roman Catholic times." But his "alarm was not equal to his indignation." What "alarmed him much more than any aggression of a foreign Sovereign" was "the danger within the gates from the unworthy sons of the Church of England herself"—who had been "the most forward in leading their flocks step by step to the very verge of the precipice. The honour paid to saints, the claim of infallibility for the Church, the superstitious use of the sign of the Cross, the muttering of the Liturgy so as to disguise its language in which it is written, the recommendation of auricular confession, and the administration of penance and absolution—all these things are pointed out by clergymen of the Church of England as worthy of adoption, and are now openly reprehended by the Bishop of London in his Charge to the clergy of his diocese."

Ullathorne, in his record of the time,[1] throws an interesting light on the surprising contrast between the previous friendliness of the Government and its sudden hostility after the hierarchy was established. The project had been openly discussed for years, and when Ullathorne came back from Rome early in 1847 it had even been reported publicly, without arousing any opposition, that the hierarchy was already established. He recalls that "when Bishop Wiseman was sent from Rome with a special mission to the English Government in 1846 he sent before him a letter addressed to the *Times* expounding the policy involved in his mission. The Pope was then extremely popular in England and the letter was well received. The result, however, of that mission was the sending of Lord Minto to Rome as a sort of non-official envoy from England. Intended to be a support to the Pope, he became an embarrassment, leaguing himself with the party of revolution."

[1] *Autobiography*, pp. 294-295.

Wiseman, on becoming a Cardinal, had expected a similar attitude of courtesy from the *Times* when he wrote to give them the information in advance. But the *Times* had seen possibilities of making " political capital " out of the announcement " at the most vacant time of the year in politics." " That the Queen got excited by the unguarded language of the Pastoral appears probable," he writes, " as was said at the time ; that the Cardinal wrote it never dreaming of the excited state of the country and of the use the *Times* was prepared to make of it is quite certain." Other factors had also contributed to the opposition which it aroused. Lord Clarendon, the Viceroy in Ireland, had written to the Pope about the Irish Colleges without receiving any reply. Mr. Romilly's Bill for settling Catholic property had been treated with discourtesy. " There were the troubles and controversies connected with Lord Minto's visit to Rome. He had been sent by Lord John Russell, who was his own son-in-law, and was sent on the Pope's invitation through Cardinal Wiseman. True, he had acted a disloyal part to the Pope, but Lord John had been badgered about it, and this did not sweeten his testy temper. Then Cardinal Wiseman, instead of coming direct to England, went direct to Vienna, was entertained by the young Emperor, and it was just after the affair of the brutal treatment of one of the Emperor's generals in a London brewery, which had caused irritation on the side of Austria. And the Cardinal wrote a letter with something of the tone of patronage to Lord John from Vienna, at least so the letter announcing his return as Cardinal to England was interpreted."

Some of these disquieting reflections must have been in Wiseman's mind as he hurried home from Vienna without any further thought of celebrations on the way. But he had no idea of what bitterness and anger had been aroused by his pastoral. The Anglican bishops began to fulminate in language of extraordinary insult against " foreign intruders " and " foreign bondage," and Wiseman's biographer afterwards was able to produce a remarkable collection [1] of the abusive epithets they chose. Eventually they sent a joint address to the Queen in protest against this " un-

[1] *Life of Wiseman*, I, pp. 549-560.

warrantable insult," in which they petitioned her "to discountenance by all constitutional means the claims and usurpations of the Church of Rome." These outbursts and protests continued for several months, but the climax of the agitation was reached on Guy Fawkes' Day, November 5, when effigies of the Pope and of Wiseman and the new hierarchy were burned in public in many places.[1]

There was real danger of anti-Catholic riots and violence in the Lord George Gordon tradition, and Wiseman's return to London was awaited with deep anxiety. Mobs had broken the windows of Catholic churches, and Catholic priests had been hooted and pelted in the streets. Dr. Whitty convened a meeting of leading Catholic laymen at Sir George Bowyer's rooms in the Temple to decide whether Wiseman should be urged to delay his return, as soon as they could meet him in Bruges. Some thought he should go back to Rome and consult the Pope, others that he should remain on the Continent until the excitement died down. But they agreed that he must decide for himself, and when Dr. Whitty's report reached him in Bruges, he did not hesitate. His own house was undergoing repairs, and he arrived at Mr. Bagshawe's house in London on November 11 before anyone knew that he was coming. Next day, with unflinching courage, he went publicly to St. George's Cathedral in Southwark, and there officiated at High Mass. A crowd gathered, but made no hostile demonstration, though stones were often thrown at his carriage elsewhere. His first step had been to get Sir George Bowyer to interview Ministers on his behalf, and Lord Lansdowne was soon convinced that an "enormous misunderstanding" had arisen. He said quite frankly that Lord John Russell had written his famous letter without consulting any of his colleagues. Some at least of them, however, shared his views, for the Lord Chancellor, Lyndhurst, had made a speech in the Mansion House on November 9 in which he caused wild applause by quoting the lines:

> Under our feet we'll stamp thy Cardinal's hat,
> In spite of Pope or dignitaries of Church.

[1] *Life of Wiseman*, I, pp. 551-552, gives some amusing descriptions of such scenes, particularly at Salisbury, Ware and Peckham.

Meanwhile Wiseman was working feverishly at a full reply to his critics, although many of his friends must have felt that his next pronouncement could only add to the provocation of his pastoral. He began writing his " Appeal to the People of England " on the first morning he was back in London, and within four days it was in the printer's hands. It was written practically without an erasure, which seemed to show that he had been preparing it during his journey home. But, in fact, it consisted very largely of material which had been prepared for him by Ullathorne [1] after the crisis had arisen. He and Canon Eastcourt had " got together the passages from Lord John Russell's former parliamentary speeches in which he had assumed the principles upon which the Hierarchy had been established," and the no less effective statements made by the Lord Chancellor on former occasions. On November 20 it appeared in full in five London newspapers, including the *Times*. As a pamphlet it had an immediate and enormous sale, and its effect was astonishing. It was a plain and straightforward appeal for fair play, written with a directness and force that his more florid writings would never have suggested. After describing the whirlwind agitation that had been aroused, he attacked Lord John Russell openly for his part in it. " The head of Her Majesty's Government," he wrote, " has astonished not this country alone, but all Europe, by a letter which leaves us little hope that any appeal to the high authority which rules over the Empire would be received, to say the least, with favour." After recalling the Lord Chancellor's outburst, he asked, " when the very highest judicial authority has prejudged and cut off all appeal from us, what recourse have we left ? What hope of justice ? One in which, after God's unfailing providence, we place unbounded confidence. There still remains the manly sense and honest heart of a generous people ; that love of honourable dealing and fair play which, in joke or in earnest, is equally the instinct of an Englishman ; that hatred of all mean advantage taken, of all base tricks and paltry claptrap and party cries employed to hunt down even a rival or a foe. To this open-fronted and warm-hearted tribunal I make my

[1] *Autobiography*, p. 297.

appeal, and claim, on behalf of myself and my fellow Catholics, a fair, free and impartial hearing. Fellow-subjects, Englishmen, be you at least just and equitable. You have been deceived—you have been misled, both as to facts and as to intentions."

Here certainly was no " foreign intruder," but an Englishman steeped in the tradition to which the English people could be expected to respond. The pamphlet proceeded with a detailed refutation of the charges that had been made, showing the glaring contradiction between the complaints of the Prime Minister and Lord Chancellor and others and their own previous statements or actions. But its most telling passage was the conclusion which dealt with his own position and duties as Archbishop of Westminster. " The Chapter of Westminster," he wrote, " has been the first to protest against the new Archiepiscopal title, as though some practical attempt at jurisdiction within the *Abbey* was intended. Then let me give them assurance on that point, and let us come to a fair division and a good understanding.

" The diocese, indeed, of Westminster embraces a large district ; but Westminster proper consists of two very different parts. One comprises the stately Abbey, with its adjacent palaces and its royal parks. To this portion the duties and occupation of the Dean and Chapter are mainly confined ; and they shall range there undisturbed. To the venerable old Church I may repair, as I have been wont to do. But perhaps the Dean and Chapter are not aware that, were I disposed to claim more than the right to tread the Catholic pavement of that noble building, and breathe its air of ancient consecration, another might step in with a prior claim. For successive generations there has existed ever, in the Benedictine Order, an Abbot of Westminster, the representative, in religious dignity, of those who erected, and beautified and governed that Church and cloister. Have they ever been disturbed by this ' titular ? ' Have they ever heard of any claim or protest on his part, touching their temporalities ? Then, let them fear no greater aggression now. Like him, I may visit, as I have said, the old Abbey, and say my prayer by the Shrine of good St. Edward, and meditate on the olden times, when the church filled without a coronation, and multitudes hourly worshipped without a service.

" But in their temporal rights, or their quiet possession of any dignity and title, they will not suffer. Whenever I go in, I will pay my entrance fee like other liege subjects, and resign myself to the guidance of the beadle, and listen, without rebuke, when he points out to my admiration, detestable monuments, or shows me a hole in the wall for a confessional.

" Yet this splendid monument, its treasures of art, and its fitting endowments, form not the part of Westminster which will concern me. For there is another part which stands in frightful contrast, though in immediate contact, with this magnificence. In ancient times, the existence of an abbey on any spot, with a large staff of clergy and ample revenues, would have sufficed to create around it a little paradise of comfort, cheerfulness and ease. This, however, is not now the case. Close under the Abbey of Westminster there lie concealed labyrinths of lanes and courts, and alleys and slums, nests of ignorance, vice, depravity, and crime, as well as of squalour, wretchedness and disease ; whose atmosphere is typhus, whose ventilation is cholera ; in which swarms a huge and almost countless population, in great measure, nominally at least, Catholic ; haunts of filth, which no sewage committee can reach—dark corners which no lighting-board can brighten.

" This is the part of Westminster which alone I covet, and which I shall be glad to claim and visit, as a blessed pasture in which sheep of holy Church are to be tended, in which a bishop's godly work has to be done, of consoling, converting and preserving. And if, as I humbly trust in God, it shall be seen that this special culture, arising from the establishment of our Hierarchy, bears fruit of order, peacefulness, decency, religion and virtue, it may be that the Holy See shall not be thought to have acted unwisely when it bound up the very soul and salvation of a chief pastor with those of a city, whereof the name indeed is glorious, but the purlieus infamous—in which the very grandeur of its public edifices is as a shadow to screen from the public eye sin and misery the most appalling. If the wealth of the Abbey be stagnant and not diffusive, if it in no way rescues the neighbouring population from the depths in which it is sunk, let there be no jealousy of anyone who, by whatever name, is ready to make the latter his care without interfering with the former."

Wiseman's "Appeal," and the bold courage with which he faced a most unexpected and formidable crisis, had revealed powers of leadership which had not been anticipated by his warmest admirers. He had become a national figure almost overnight, by sheer strength of character and an unbounded faith. Ullathorne, who had shouldered the full weight of the controversy in the interval before Wiseman's return, could scarcely be expected to feel that the pastoral had been anything but a "mistake." "The error was in the Vicar-General's giving publication under circumstances wholly different from those contemplated by its eminent author," he wrote [1] long afterwards; and again,[2] "if it could have been quietly promulgated amongst ourselves at that period, we should have settled down in peace." But Wiseman's triumphant handling of the crisis, and his emergence as a personality of the first order, far more than compensated for the anxieties and even the sufferings which the agitation produced. Only a very few of the Catholic laity revealed themselves as lacking the courage of their religious faith; but they included two of the leading Catholic peers. Lord Beaumont, before Wiseman's "Appeal" had yet appeared, wrote a letter [3] to the Earl of Zetland declaring that Lord John Russell's protest against the hierarchy was "that of a true friend of the British Constitution," and that the Pope's edict "cannot be received or accepted by English Roman Catholics without a violation of their duties as citizens." The Duke of Norfolk was unmoved even by Wiseman's "Appeal," and on November 28 he wrote to Lord Beaumont to express his support, saying:[4] "I should think that many must feel as we do, that ultramontane opinions are totally incompatible with allegiance to our Sovereign and with our Constitution." He gave further confirmation of this attitude by accepting the sacrament of the Church

[1] *Autobiography*, p. 295. [2] *Hierarchy*, p. 74.
[3] *Life of Wiseman*, II, p. 15. [4] *Ibid.*, p. 16.

of England, and for many years afterwards he remained in apostasy from the Catholic Church.

But the effect upon the Catholic body as a whole was immensely stimulating. The converts, who had welcomed the hierarchy particularly, because the former conditions had seemed so unsatisfactory in comparison with the Anglican organisation, were startled and encouraged by Wiseman's performance. Even Newman, who loathed public agitation and turmoil, wrote [1] to Sir George Bowyer that Wiseman " is made for this world and he rises with the occasion. Highly as I put his gifts, I was not prepared for such a display of vigour, power, judgment and sustained energy as the last two months has brought. I heard a dear friend of his say that the news of the opposition would kill him. How he has been out! It is the event of the time. In my own remembrance there has been nothing like it."

[1] *Life of Newman,* I, p. 534.

CHAPTER XVI

THE HIERARCHY RESTORED

A STRONG reaction against the No Popery agitation had set in even before Wiseman's " Appeal " was published ; and as it gathered momentum there resulted a new influx of distinguished converts to the Catholic Church. Lord John Russell's letter to the Bishop of Durham had been directed against the Catholicising influences in the Church of England even more than against Wiseman and the new hierarchy. " What then is the danger to be apprehended from a foreign prince of no great power," he had written, " compared to the danger within the gates from the unworthy sons of the Church of England herself ? I have little hope that the propounders and framers of these innovations will desist from their insidious course. But I rely with confidence on the people of England, and I will not bate a jot of heart or hope so long as the glorious principles and the immortal martyrs of the Reformation shall be held in reverence by the great mass of a nation which looks with contempt on the mummeries of superstition, and with scorn at the laborious endeavours which are now making to confine the intellect and enslave the soul."

This inflammatory language from the Prime Minister had been published just before the usual noisy demonstrations on Guy Fawkes' day. Accordingly they concentrated in many places against those Anglican churches which were known to have Catholic tendencies. The rector of the parish in which Lord John Russell lived had been one of the chief targets for rowdy behaviour, and on several Sundays his church was surrounded by hostile crowds, while copies of Lord John's letter to the Bishop of Durham were being openly distributed outside. It became necessary even to have a police guard round the church continuously for some days, until the indignant rector, Mr. Bennett, was compelled to address a letter to the Prime Minister himself. A force of one hundred constables, he protested, had been required " to keep the mob from overt acts of violence ; notwithstanding the exertions of the police much violence was committed and the leader of the rioters taken into custody." The Bishop of London had been mentioned with approval in Lord John's letter for having denounced the ritualists among his clergy, and he now reprimanded Mr. Bennett vigorously for this protest, and eventually compelled him to resign his living. But his action only deepened the distress of the surviving Tractarians, who had been gravely disturbed throughout the whole year by the Gorham Judgment, which had compelled the Bishop of Exeter to institute a clergyman who proclaimed his disbelief in baptism.

Among those who had been most distressed by the Gorham Judgment in March was Archdeacon Manning at Chichester. Many months had passed during which his friends and followers had waited anxiously for a reassuring statement from him, in view of the resolutions against the Judgment which had been published by him and his associates immediately afterwards. The truth was that Manning had virtually made up his mind that his withdrawal from the Church of England would soon be inevitable. A series of intimate letters written by him during those months to Robert Wilberforce and to Gladstone [1] show the growing conviction that his position had become untenable, his desire to go abroad for the whole winter, and his doubts as to whether he could honestly refrain from resigning at once. He was in these throes of indecision at the beginning of November when the No Popery agitation suddenly swept through the whole country and confronted him with a direct issue that could not be evaded.

By November 7 Manning had already received two requisitions to convene his clergy as Archdeacon to protest against the " Papal Aggression." To Robert Wilberforce he appealed earnestly for counsel as to whether he should resign at once or convene the meeting and then announce his disagreement. Events moved quickly, and after an interview with his Bishop he went [2] to the clergy meeting and opened it formally without any address. They

[1] Purcell's *Life of Manning*, I, chapter xxvi.
[2] *Ibid.*, II, p. 579.

then passed their resolutions against the Papal Aggression. Manning replied to a vote of thanks with a brief speech which announced his sorrow at leaving them, then parted from them for ever, with expressions of the deepest grief on both sides. " It was our last meeting," Manning recorded afterwards, " and the end of my work in the Church of England ; for after that I only preached once, or may be a second time, at Lavington : on 8th December, I think, I left it and never came back." In November he was already breaking the news to his brother and sister ; while Gladstone, who was travelling in Italy, and had scarcely yet heard of the No Popery agitation in any detail, continued to bombard him with letters which accused him of inconsistency. He felt bereft of all friends, but he had one staunch ally in the barrister, James Hope, Q.C., who had been actively concerned in promoting the joint protest against the Gorham Judgment in the previous spring. Hope agreed that they should act together in whatever their final decision might be ; but in the meantime they both required time for circumspection. Manning's formal resignation as Archdeacon was not yet announced, but he went into retirement in London and did not officiate as a clergyman, though he continued to attend Anglican services. Meanwhile some of his closest friends who had already become Catholics—Allies, Bellasis, Dodsworth, Henry Wilberforce and his former confessor Laprimaudaye—were writing to him letters of encouragement to take the final step. The winter passed while he was still wrestling with old difficulties and ties, and it was not until March that he resigned his office and benefice by legal process.

It was in the " little chapel off the Buckingham Palace Road," where he had gone in Gladstone's company, that the final decision was reached. Just before the Communion Service commenced [1] he turned to Gladstone and said, " I can no longer take the Communion in the Church of England. I rose up—' St. Paul is standing by his side '—and laying my hand on Mr. Gladstone's shoulder, said ' Come.' It was the parting of the ways. Mr. Gladstone remained ; and I went my way." James Hope followed him, and together they were received into the Church by the Jesuit Father

[1] *Purcell,* I, p. 617.

Brownhill on Passion Sunday, April 6. On Palm Sunday they were confirmed by Wiseman in his private chapel, and Wiseman gave Manning the tonsure on the same day, having expressed his intention of ordaining him to the priesthood at Whitsuntide. Such rapid advancement to the priesthood was without precedent, and it scandalised many of the older Catholics. But Wiseman's joy was so unbounded that he accepted entire responsibility, regardless of all former criticisms and discouragements. When he had confirmed Manning he said to him solemnly at once,[1] " I look upon you as one of the first fruits of the restoration of the Hierarchy by Our Holy Father Pius IX. Go forth, my son, and bring your brethren and fellow-countrymen by thousands and tens of thousands into the one true fold of Christ." Rome approved Wiseman's request for a special dispensation to hasten his ordination, and on June 16 Manning said his first Mass in the Jesuit church in Farm Street. It had been arranged that he was to go to Rome immediately afterwards to undergo the usual training, but his departure was delayed until the autumn to avoid the summer heat of Rome. When he left England there was an acid announcement in the *Tablet* that he was now leaving to " commence his ecclesiastical studies."

Newman during these months after the No Popery agitation had been living with his Oratorians in Edgbaston. The violence and vulgarity of the agitation had shocked him deeply, and he found evidence on all sides of the vindictive treatment of Catholics,[2] and particularly of converts who in many cases had become Catholics under his influence. He had disliked public controversy for years before he became a Catholic, but he felt under a strong moral obligation to play his part in refuting the common misrepresentations of the Catholic Church. Reluctantly in the previous year he had agreed to deliver a series of weekly lectures on " The Difficulties of Anglicans " at the King William Street Oratory in London. " I am writing them intellectually against the grain more

[1] *Purcell*, I, p. 617.

[2] See *Memorials of Sergeant Bellasis*, pp. 110-112, for typical instances of such treatment.

than I ever recollect doing anything," he had confided in Father
Faber at the time.[1]   But their success had been undeniable, and in
face of the outcry against the new hierarchy he felt that he must
enter the lists again.   He had been immensely impressed by
Wiseman's courage and resourcefulness in mastering the agitation,
but he had misgivings as to the future, when the tasks of the new
hierarchy had to be faced.   The Government had introduced an
Ecclesiastical Titles Bill, to prevent the new bishops from using
their episcopal titles, which was, in fact, passed into law, though it
obviously could not be enforced, and it became a dead letter from
the start.   To his friend Capes, who had undertaken a series of
public lectures in defence of the hierarchy, he wrote in February,[2]
" Preaching, confession, publishing, no Bill can touch, and these
are our proper weapons.   The Bill only touches Puginism and its
offshoots.   We are not ripe ourselves for a Hierarchy.   Now they
have one they can't fill up the Sees, positively *can't*.   Don't repeat
all this—but it really is a question whether one should not look on
it as a means of getting us out of a scrape that this Bill is passed.
We want Seminaries far more than Sees.   We want education,
view, combination, organisation."

    Mr. Capes was obliged to discontinue his lectures through
ill-health, and Newman had discussed them with him so fully that
he felt impelled to undertake a similar series himself.   At the end
of June, just after Manning had been ordained in London, he
delivered the first of his weekly " Lectures on Catholicism in
England " in the Corn Exchange in Birmingham.   It was the first
time that he had attempted popular lectures on a topical question,
and he wrote them with a freedom and vigour that he had never
before employed.   He told Dean Church afterwards that he
regarded them as " the best written " of all his works, and he
spared no pains in compiling them.   They were a trenchant attack
on the prejudice and ignorance with which the Catholic Church
was regarded in England, and he chose his instances with careful
preparation.   There was no lack of material, but one instance had
seemed to him so outrageous that he devoted a section of one

[1] *Life of Newman*, I, p. 231.   [2] *Ibid.*, p. 260.

lecture to it. Part of his general thesis had been that Protestant opposition to the Catholic Church was prepared to accept any evidence, no matter how ludicrous or how discredited. Even before the No Popery agitation broke out, the Protestant polemists had discovered a new champion in the apostate Italian priest, Father Achilli, who had been imprisoned in Rome but released through the influence of English friends. He came to England in 1850, and was received in person by Lord Palmerston as Foreign Secretary, accompanied by a deputation from the Evangelical Alliance.

By writings and lectures Achilli attained such celebrity in Protestant circles that Wiseman himself had thought it necessary to publish a full exposure of his criminal record in the *Dublin Review*. The article had given full details of his many crimes and convictions, and had even been republished as a pamphlet, without provoking any reply. Newman now decided to make full use of these facts as a conspicuous illustration of Protestant bigotry. He consulted Hope as to the possibility of incurring a libel action, but Hope thought that the risk was negligible, since no reply to Wiseman's charges had ever been attempted. Accordingly Newman introduced into his fifth lecture in Birmingham a full exposure of Achilli's record, using all his gifts of irony and invective without remorse. One passage from his lecture—which was withdrawn from the subsequent editions—demands quotation as showing both the recklessness with which the Protestant opposition were prepared to employ any witness against the Catholic Church, and the vigour with which Newman replied to the Church's critics :

" It is indeed our great confusion, that our Holy Mother could have had a priest like him. He feels the force of the argument, and he shows himself to the multitude that is gazing on him. ' Mothers of families,' he seems to say, ' gentle maidens, innocent children, look at me, for I am worth looking at. You do not see such a sight every day. Can any Church live over the reputation of such a product as I am ? I have been a Catholic and an infidel ; I have been a Roman priest and a hypocrite ; I have been a profligate under a cowl. I am that Father Achilli who, as early as

1826, was deprived of my faculty to lecture, for an offence which my superiors did their best to conceal, and who, in 1827, had already earned the reputation of a scandalous friar. I am that Achilli who, in the diocese of Viterbo in February 1831, robbed of her honour a young woman of eighteen; who in September 1833, was found guilty of a second such crime, in the case of a person of twenty-eight; and who perpetrated a third in July 1834, in the case of another aged twenty-four. I am he who afterwards was found guilty of sins, similar or worse, in the towns of the neighbourhood. I am that son of St. Dominic who is known to have repeated the offence at Capua, in 1834 and 1835; and at Naples again in 1840, in the case of a child of fifteen. I am he who chose the sacristy of the church for one of these crimes and Good Friday for another. Look on me, ye mothers of England, a confessor against Popery, for ye, "ne'er may look upon my like again." I am that veritable priest who, after all this, began to speak against not only the Catholic faith, but the moral law, and perverted others by my teaching. I am the Cavaliere Achilli who then went to Corfu, made the wife of a tailor faithless to her husband, and lived publicly and travelled about with the wife of a chorus singer. I am that professor in the Protestant College at Malta who, with two others, was dismissed from my post for offences which the authorities cannot get themselves to describe. And now, attend to me, such as I am, and you shall see what you shall see about the barbarity and the profligacy of the inquisitors of Rome.' "

Less than a month passed before Achilli instituted proceedings for criminal libel against Newman. Wiseman had all the relevant documents in his possession, but when Newman asked for them they had been mislaid. He now found that every separate accusation in his indictment must be proved in court, and that failure to prove even one charge among so many would mean a verdict against him. To collect witnesses, emissaries were sent urgently to Naples, Rome and Paris, but many of them could not be traced or would not come. After an immense expenditure of money and labour it was found impossible to establish every charge. Lord

Campbell, the judge before whom the case was tried, showed himself to be as prejudiced on the bench as he was known to be outside as a No Popery champion. When the trial took place late in June 1852, it lasted for three days, and resulted in a jury's verdict against Newman. The case had been conducted with such unfairness that even the *Times*, in a leading article, declared [1] that " a great blow has been given to the administration of justice in this country and that Roman Catholics will henceforth have only too good reason for asserting that there is no justice for them in cases tending to arouse the Protestant feelings of judges and juries." Judgment was deferred until November, while Newman resigned himself to the apparent certainty of a term of imprisonment, and found consolation in the extraordinary response from many countries to the appeal for funds to defray the heavy costs he had incurred, particularly in trying to collect his witnesses.

Wiseman's inability to give him adequate support in the trial was scarcely surprising, for his days had been overwhelmed with public activities of every kind since the hierarchy was announced. Organisation of the new conditions required constant and urgent attention, and there were many conflicts of view and of vested interests to reconcile. His former opponents among the clergy who distrusted both his Roman training and his eager encouragement of the converts, were more or less in occupation at St. Edmund's College, the seminary for his vast diocese, and strenuous efforts were being made to have its President, Dr. Cox, appointed as the first Bishop of Southwark. But Wiseman succeeded in removing Dr. Cox from the presidency of the College to take charge of the important mission in Southampton ; and he secured the appointment of his old friend, Dr. Grant, from the English College in Rome to the see of Southwark. Meanwhile he was working incessantly to improve conditions in the poor districts in London where Catholics were most numerous, and he took part himself in conducting open-air missions. " I found the place crammed from end to end," he reported [2] to Mgr. Talbot in Rome, after concluding one such mission near Spanish Place, " all round

---

[1] *Life of Newman,* I, p. 292.   [2] *Dublin Review,* Jan., 1919, p. 23.

and behind the platform. Every window was filled with tiers of faces, the whole line covered with legs dangling over the parapets— most with candles in their hands, and every window illuminated, while against the walls were illuminations with lamps, so that altogether on coming to the entrance and looking down, it had the appearance of a street Madonna festival in Rome. On alighting I went into the crowd, which made way, and our procession formed." He preached to them and announced that henceforward a priest would come every Saturday " to hear confessions, say prayers, preach and keep them in order," and that Mass would be said in a room. There was no possibility as yet of even building a church in this which was, as he told Talbot, " one of the very worst " districts in London. " The cheering as we went along to the carriage must have been heard for miles," he continued. " I never heard anything like it. Every one wanted to touch me, of course ; but there was no disorder or confusion, and everyone who witnessed the scene was amazed. Sergeant Bellasis was in the midst of the crowd, and said he was now satisfied that I might trust myself confidently to the people—he never knew before what the Church can do." Bellasis had become a Catholic just before the No Popery agitation, and he had written several vigorous pamphlets in defence of the hierarchy.

In his efforts to provide more missions and more priests, Wiseman was constantly inviting the help of religious orders, but their rules always prevented them from extending their activities.[1] In his well-known letter to Faber [2] appealing for greater help from the Oratorians in the autumn of 1852 he described his difficulties. " Having believed, having preached, having assured bishops and clergy, that in no great city could the salvation of multitudes be carried out by the limited parochial clergy, but that religious communities alone *can* and *will* undertake the huge work of con- verting and preserving the corrupted masses : I have acted on this conviction. I have introduced or greatly encouraged the estab- lishment of five religious congregations in my diocese ; and I am just (for the great work) where I first began ! Not one of them

[1] See Chapter XIV, p. 208.   [2] *Purcell,* II, pp. 2-9.

can (for it cannot be want of will) undertake it. It comes within the purpose of none of them to try." He was convinced already that some special community organised for this express purpose must be established ; and he had discerned in Manning the ruture organiser of the work he had in view—preaching among the poor, and laying the foundations of permanent missions in poor districts ; the continued care of young people after they left school ; the direction of converts and charitable institutions ; retreats to the clergy ; special courses of sermons in Lent and other seasons ; and periodical missions everywhere. " Mr. Manning, I think," he told Faber, " understands my wishes and feelings and is ready to assist me ; several will I hope join him, and I hope also some old and good priests. We shall be able to work together ; because there will be no exceptions from episcopal direction, and none of the jealousy on one side, and the delicacy on the other, of interference or suggestion. I do not see how the multifarious missionary work I have proposed can be carried on without frequent communication with the bishop." He had judged rightly indeed in choosing Manning as the organiser of the mobile force. But his days were still occupied with wider tasks than those of the diocese itself ; and even his hastening of Manning's ordination could not dispense with the necessity for him to undergo a course of theological study in Rome.

Preparations for the first Synod had taken much more time than Wiseman had imagined when the hierarchy was announced, and it did not actually meet until July 1852. Oscott, where Wiseman had assisted Bishop Walsh in completing new buildings some twelve years before, provided an admirable setting where all the bishops could assemble, with representatives from each of the newly erected Chapters and also of the various religious orders. The Synod opened on Wednesday, July 7, when Wiseman himself preached the inaugural sermon besides celebrating Mass. On Sunday Ullathorne officiated, and Manning, who had been a Catholic for little more than a year, but was already returned from Rome, delivered one of his first sermons as a Catholic priest. He had already acquired the authentic accent of the Catholic ministry.

" The Church in England in Synod," he said,[1] " takes up its work again after a silence of three hundred years. It reopens its proceedings with a familiarity as prompt, and a readiness as calm, as if it resumed to-day the deliberations of last night. Though centuries of time have rolled away since it sat in council, the last Synod in England is but as the session of yesterday to the session of to-morrow." But it was Newman's sermon at the opening of the second session on the following Tuesday, when Dr. Briggs as the senior Bishop officiated, that expressed most vividly the feelings of all present, in one of the most memorable discourses ever written. That the two principal sermons, besides Wiseman's, should be preached by converts of such eminence, was a symbol of the Church's triumphant revival in the previous years. Newman's presence commanded all the more sympathy because it was only a few weeks since he had undergone the trial for criminal libel against Father Achilli. He could have received no clearer sign of the support and gratitude of the whole Catholic community.

The inauguration of the hierarchy had never made the same appeal to Newman, as a public manifestation of the Catholic revival, that it made to less critical observers. But its spiritual significance had stirred him profoundly. In an earlier chapter [2] some passages of his sermon have been quoted, describing the " utter contempt into which Catholicism had fallen by the time that we were born." It had been " a great change," he went on, " an awful contrast, between the time-honoured church of St. Augustine and St. Thomas, and the poor remnant of their children in the beginning of the nineteenth century. It was a miracle, I might say, to have pulled down that lordly power, but there was a greater and a truer one in store. No one could have prophesied its fall, but still less would any one have ventured to prophesy its rise again. . . . I must speak cautiously and according to my knowledge ; but I recollect no parallel to it. . . . Who then could have dared to hope that, out of so sacrilegious a nation as this is, a people would have been formed again into their Saviour ? What signs did it show that it was to be singled out from among the nations ? Had it

[1] *Pastoral Office*, p. 221.   [2] See Chapter I.

been prophesied some fifty years ago, would not the very notion have seemed preposterous and wild ? " The eloquence and music of his style rose superbly as he described the ending of that winter and the return of spring. " A second temple rises on the ruins of the old. Canterbury has gone its way, and York is gone, and Durham is gone, and Winchester is gone. It was sore to part with them. We clung to the vision of past greatness, and would not believe that it could come to nought ; but the Church in England has died, and the Church lives again. Westminster and Nottingham, Beverley and Hexham, Northampton and Shrewsbury, if the world lasts, shall be names as musical to the ear, as stirring to the heart, as the glories we have lost ; and Saints shall arise out of them, if God so will, and Doctors once again shall give the law to Israel, and Preachers call to penance and to justice, as at the beginning.

" Yes, my Fathers and Brothers, and if it be God's blessed will, not Saints alone, not Doctors only, not Preachers only, shall be ours—but Martyrs, too, shall re-consecrate the soil to God. We know not what is before us, ere we win our own ; we are engaged in a great, a joyful work, but in proportion to God's grace is the fury of His enemies. . . . And as that suffering of the Martyrs is not yet recompensed, so, perchance, it is not yet exhausted. Something, for what we know, remains to be undergone, to complete the necessary sacrifice. May God forbid it, for this poor nation's sake ! But still could we be surprised, my Fathers and my Brothers, if the winter even now should not yet be quite over ? Have we any right to take it strange if, in this English land, the spring time of the Church should turn out to be an English spring, an uncertain, anxious time of hope and fear, of joy and suffering—of bright promise and budding hopes, yet withal of keen blasts, and cold showers, and sudden storms ? One thing alone I know—that according to our need, so will be our strength. One thing I am sure of, that the more the enemy rages against us, so much more will the Saints in heaven plead for us : the more fearful are our trials from the world, the more present to us will be our Mother Mary, and our good Patrons, and Angel Guardians ; the more malicious are the devices of men against us, the louder cry of supplication will ascend from the bosom of the whole Church to God for us."

Newman's talents were never exercised with more complete effect in the official service of the Church. Almost all his life as a Catholic was to be frustrated in one attempt after another which he undertook at the invitation of his superiors. Many of the tasks which were put to him were distasteful to his sensitive and retiring nature, or even plainly incongruous with his character. Ullathorne records,[1] for instance, how it had even been suggested by Dr. Briggs, as the senior Bishop, that Newman ought to write an immediate reply to Lord John Russell while Wiseman's return to England was awaited after his pastoral announcing the restoration of the hierarchy. Ullathorne " as in duty bound " had shown the Bishop's letter to Newman, " who could only give a silent shrug, as I expected." But for once the invitation to preach at the Synod at Oscott provided the fullest scope for his unrivalled powers. Not since his farewell sermon as an Anglican at St. Mary's in Oxford had he felt so deeply in his preaching, and the effect upon his hearers was overwhelming. One of the Canons present described afterwards [2] how, before he had finished, " all were weeping, most of us silently, but some audibly : as to the big-hearted Cardinal, he fairly gave up the effort at dignity and self-control, and sobbed like a child." Newman himself was so exhausted and overcome by emotional strain that Manning, who was present, had to assist him to his room.

But if the ceremonies showed the deeply emotional character of Wiseman, the Synod itself revealed his unsuspected powers of organisation to an extent comparable only to the revelation of his gifts of leadership during the agitation against the new hierarchy. " The conducting of the first Provincial Synod," writes Ullathorne,[3] who was certainly no hero-worshipper, " was the masterpiece of Cardinal Wiseman. He it was who drew up the decrees, all except the Constitutions for the Cathedral Chapters, which was committed

[1] *Autobiography*, p. 296.   [2] *Life of Bishop Grant*, p. 103.
[3] *Autobiography*, p. 299.

to Bishop Grant and myself, although their main substance is the work of Bishop Grant. The unity and harmony which pervaded that Chapter is one of the most delightful reminiscences of my episcopal life. Certainly no one but Cardinal Wiseman, who concentrated his whole capacious mind upon it in one of his happiest periods could have brought it to so successful an issue ; and have given to it so great an amount of ecclesiastical splendour. And there the rule and precedent was established for the conducting of our future Synods." The story would be incomplete without paying tribute to the unassuming but indispensable work of Bishop Grant who had for years, as Rector of the English College in Rome, been conducting the delicate negotiations concerning the hierarchy. Ullathorne had special knowledge of his services during those years, and he has stated his definite opinion [1] that he was " the ablest, most judicious and influential agent that the English bishops ever had in Rome. He kept them well informed at all times on whatever concerned their interests, whilst he overlooked nothing in Rome in which he could serve them. To him, more than to anyone, so far as English action was concerned, from the beginning to the end of those negotiations, the success was mainly due." His appointment to one of the new sees in England was inevitable, and Wiseman soon brought him to his own aid as the first Bishop of Southwark. Yet his services in Rome had been such that Cardinal Barnabó told Wiseman at the time that " you would gain more by having him in Rome. You will never have his like as agent again. He has never misled us in a single case. His documents were so complete and so accurate that we depended on them, and it was never requisite to draw them up anew. When the Pope or Propaganda sees Dr. Grant's handwriting, they know it is all right."

Grant had been installed as Bishop of Southwark in the summer of 1851, and Wiseman had been relieved of more than half the immense territorial district for which he had been responsible at first, with jurisdiction over what is now divided into the four dioceses of Westminster, Brentwood, Southwark and Portsmouth.

[1] *Life of Bishop Grant,* p. 79.

Grant's long experience of ecclesiastical procedure and negotiations was now available to assist him, while so much of Wiseman's time was occupied by public functions and by his apostolic work among the poorest districts of London. But the combination which should have worked admirably was doomed to failure almost from the start, when technical conflicts arose between them over the partition of the London District. Wiseman's failing health gradually weakened his grasp, and dissensions, deepening with extraordinary rapidity, arose between him and even those who had loved and served him most devotedly in the previous years. The subsequent history makes sad reading, with its record of misunderstandings and frustrations and embittered controversies. But with the conversion of Newman and so many of his followers, and the constantly broadening stream of converts to the Catholic Church, the restoration of the hierarchy and the first Synod which laid the foundations on which the later expansion and strengthening of the Church in England has since developed, Wiseman's main work was already done before he had yet completed his fiftieth year. Abbot Butler, in the concluding chapter of his *Life of Ullathorne*,[1] sums up his personality with a tribute which few students of the period will challenge. " After reading again and again, and maturely pondering over the materials collected for the Lives of the four great churchmen, Wiseman, Manning, Newman, Ullathorne, the impression finally and clearly graven on my mind is that, taken all in all, Wiseman stands out as the greatest. He was not the deep acute thinker that Newman was ; nor the masterful resourceful man of affairs that Manning was ; nor had he the sound practical grip of men and things that Ullathorne had : but in the combination of richly endowed nature, and attractive lovable personality, and well-balanced, all-round character, and many-sided intellectual attainments, and successful achievement of a great lifework—in short, as a complete man, he surpassed them all."

[1] *Life of Ullathorne*, II, p. 299.

INDEX